SUPERCULTURE
American Popular Culture and Europe

SUPERCULTURE

American Popular Culture and Europe

Edited by C.W.E. Bigsby

Bowling Green University Popular Press
Bowling Green, Ohio 43403

For Malcolm and Elizabeth Bradbury

Library of Congress Catalogue Card Number: 74-84638
ISBN: 0-87972-070-0

Printed in Great Britain

CONTENTS

ILLUSTRATIONS
Between pages 130 and 131

New York in 1924 from Brooklyn Bridge
Redesign of Mobil filling stations by Eliot Noyes
The Las Vegas Strip in 1970
The Original Dixieland Jazz Band, *c*. 1919 *N.V. Philips*
Ken Colyer's Jazzmen, early years *Paul Oliver*
The Beatles at London Airport, August 1966 *Central Press Photos Ltd*
Bardney (Lincolnshire) Pop Festival, May 1972 *Central Press Photos Ltd*
Eddie Constantine in *Alphaville*, 1965
Sami Frey and Claude Brasseur in *Bande A Part*, 1964 *Gala Film Distributors Ltd*
Jean Paul Belmondo and Jean Seberg in *A Bout de Souffle*, 1959
Jack Palance, Brigitte Bardot and Michel Piccoli in *Le Mépris*, 1963 *Contemporary Films Ltd*
Jean-Pierre Léaud in *Made in USA*, 1966
Anna Karina and Jean Paul Belmondo in *Pierrot Le Fou*, 1965

vii

NOTES ON CONTRIBUTORS

REYNER BANHAM, Professor of the History of Architecture at University College, London, is the author of numerous books including *Theory and Design in the First Machine Age; Guide to Modern Architecture; The New Brutalism; The Architecture of the Well-Tempered Environment;* and *Los Angeles: The Architecture of Four Ecologies.*

JENS PETER BECKER is a Lecturer in English at Kiel University. Besides several articles on Poe and Chandler he published a book on the English detective novel in 1973 with Paul G. Buchloh, *Der Detektivroman. Studien zur Geschichte und Form der englischen und amerikanischen Detektivliteratur.* In the same year his study of English spy fiction (*Der englische Spionageroman*) appeared. He is now working on another book on detective fiction (*Sherlock Holmes & Co.*) which deals with Wallace, Allingham, Innes, Himes *et al.*

C.W.E. BIGSBY, Senior Lecturer in American Literature at the University of East Anglia, is the author of *Confrontation and Commitment: A Study of Contemporary American Drama; Albee; Dada and Surrealism; Edward Albee;* and editor of *The Black American Writer.*

GÉRARD CORDESSE, a Lecturer at the University of Toulouse, is currently engaged in research into the themes and motifs of American science fiction. He is also working on the contemporary American novel.

DAVID CRYSTAL, Reader in Linguistics at the University of Reading, is the author of many books including *Language and Religion; Prosodic Systems and Intonation in English Linguistics; What is Linguistics?* and *The English Language.* He is advisory editor in Linguistics to Penguin Books, and has travelled widely as a British Council Lecturer.

THOMAS ELSASSER, Lecturer in Comparative Literature at the University of East Anglia, is editor of *Monogram*, a cinema magazine. He has published stylistic studies of Hollywood directors and articles on the musical, film and the novel of consciousness in *Brighton Film Review, Monogram, Screen* and *Twentieth Century Studies.*

MARTIN ESSLIN, Head of Drama for BBC Radio, is the author of *Brecht: The Man and His Work; The Theatre of the Absurd; Reflections* and *The Peopled Wound: The Plays of Harold Pinter.* He is a former faculty member of the Salzburg Seminar and has lectured widely around the world.

LESLIE FIEDLER, Samuel L. Clemens Professor at the State University of New York at Buffalo, is a novelist, a short-story writer and a critic. Among his critical works are *An End to Innocence; Love and Death in the American Novel; No! In Thunder* and *The Return of the Vanishing American.* He is presently completing a science fiction novel and preparing an anthology of science fiction for use in American universities.

ROGER LEWIS, a graduate of the University of Bristol, is the author of an unpublished thesis on the effects of opiate addiction in nineteenth and twentieth century literature. He has also published a study of the underground press in America entitled *Outlaws of America.* He is currently working on a study of William Burroughs.

MARSHALL McLUHAN, Professor at St Michael's College, University of Toronto, is the author of numerous books including *The Mechanical Bride: Folklore of Industrial Man; The Gutenberg Galaxy: The Making of Typographic Man; Understanding Media; The Medium is the Massage; War and Peace in the Global Village* and *From Cliche to Archetype.* Marshall McLuhan is a Fellow of the Royal Society of Canada and a Companion of the Order of Canada.

PETER MASSON has worked for S.H. Benson Advertising, for INTAM, as consultant to UNESCO and in 1968 he formed his own company specialising in European advertising planning and research.

He is a regular contributor to journals and conferences and has twice won the Prix Marcel Dassault.

PAUL OLIVER, Principal of Dartington College of Art, is the author of numerous books on the blues including *Bessie Smith; Blues Fell This Morning; Conversation With The Blues; Screening the Blues; The Story of the Blues* and *The Meaning of the Blues*. One of the few white men whose work is respected by black musicians, he has concerned himself not only with music criticism but also with assembling an impressive body of field recordings.

MAGNUS PYKE, Secretary and Chairman of the Council of the British Association for the Advancement of Science, has worked for many years on various aspects of food science. During World War Two he served in the Scientific Adviser's Division of the British Ministry of Food and was subsequently nutrition adviser to the Allied Commission for Austria. Among his more important books are *Manual of Nutrition; Industrial Nutrition; Food and Society; Man and Food* and *Synthetic Food*. He is a Fellow of the Royal Society of Edinburgh.

ANDREW THORBURN has a B.Sc. in International Business from the University of Washington, D.C. and an MBA in Marketing from the University of Michigan at Ann Arbor. He is now a European media/marketing consultant with Peter Masson and Partners.

MICHAEL WATTS is the assistant editor of *Melody Maker*. A regular broadcaster, he recently spent a year in North America researching the origins of popular music, and has written extensively on the subject for magazines in America, Europe and Australia.

BRYAN WILSON, Reader in Sociology and Fellow of All Souls College, Oxford, is the author of a number of books, including *Sects and Society; Religion in Secular Society; The Youth Culture and the Universities* and *Religious Sects*. He is also author of the forthcoming *Magic and Millennial Movements*. He is a former Harkness and ACLS Fellow.

PREFACE

The function of a preface is conventionally the subtle transmutation of vices into virtues, as critics are forestalled either by a breathtaking confession of inadequacy or elaborate demonstrations of integrity of purpose. This is not such a preface but it is intended to draw attention to some of the peculiar problems of a book of this kind.

It must, for example, be admitted that Europe is a great deal more heterogeneous than current political enthusiasms would allow. As an article in a European newspaper supplement, published by *Le Monde, La Stampa, The Times* and *Die Welt*, recently pointed out:

'West Germany has 60 million inhabitants yet Luxemburg has only 400,000, fewer than in Bristol or Leeds. France has an area twice that of the United Kingdom or West Germany. In Holland there are 30 times more people to the square kilometre than in Norway. Average family earnings in Portugal are only one sixth of those in Switzerland. In Portugal a third of the population are still working on the land; but in Sweden only 10 per cent do so, and in Britain only 3 per cent.

In France 63 per cent of all households have a bank account but in Switzerland, surprisingly, only 26 per cent have one. . . . Within a fairly short distance the staple diet changes from spaghetti to potato chips,* or from salami to sausage. Belgians eat three times as many potatoes as Italians do; the Italians five times as much rice as the Belgians. The French consume as much butter as the British,

---

* The choice of 'potato chips' rather than 'potato crisps' is itself evidence of American influence, at least on the author of the article.

but much less margarine, and they eat more meat than even the Americans.

In Switzerland 95 per cent of households own a washing machine, in Portugal 75 per cent of housewives do their own washing by hand and a further 19 per cent employ a washer-woman. . . . The Danes do not laugh at the same jokes as people in the South of France.'[1]

In other words, the Europe of which we speak so confidently is, in fact, a series of disparate peoples with differing habits, lifestyles, conventions, prejudices, and aspirations. It follows that an attempt to trace the impact of American popular culture on Europe as a whole, within each individual essay, would result in an impossible series of tendentious generalizations and provisos of little value. Besides which, certain countries are more susceptible to such influence while others tend to act as mediators, absorbing American modes and attitudes and re-exporting them to their European neighbours. Principal among these, for obvious linguistic reasons, is the United Kingdom, though the important role which England has played with regard to popular music, first enthusiastically responding to American forms and then refining and deriving its own distinctive style, admittedly owed little to linguistic convenience. But it follows from this that several of the essays which follow consider the impact of American popular culture on individual European countries. Thus, Hollywood is discussed in relation to the French cinema, on which it had its most creative and important European impact, rather than in terms of the many other national cinema industries which were affected to a lesser degree.

The effect of such an approach is necessarily to place considerable emphasis on the Anglo-American connection. This is unavoidable given the realities of European-American relations and, one might add, a certain academic hermeticism which is only now being broken down for the first time. Nonetheless, I believe that the total picture presented in the ensuing pages offers a useful and perceptive insight into the process of cultural interaction. And if the comparative approach adopted in one or two of the essays indicates that there have been limits to this process and reminds us of the obvious truth that influence is a two-way phenomenon, this is perhaps a necessary corrective to what would otherwise seem simply a catalogue of cultural intrusions. Indeed, this book is by no means intended as an attack on 'cultural imperialism'. Far from being a lament over conflicting values, it is presented as an examination of the nature and extent of cultural vitality in an area too often ignored as a subject for serious study.

It should also be noted that although American popular culture necessarily carries the imprint of the society which produced it, its movement beyond the confines of America changes both meaning and structure. It becomes plastic, a superculture, detached from its roots, and widely available for adaptation, absorption and mediation. As Marshall McLuhan points out, later in this book, the 'meaning' of Coca Cola depends on those who drink it as well as on those who created its formula. And it is precisely that process which is the special concern of this book.

One central difficulty, of course, is the whole question of definition of 'popular culture' and this issue is discussed, at some length, in the first two chapters. But it will be obvious from the table of contents that, for the purposes of this study, I have accepted a broad definition which permits an examination of those forces, such as language, religious beliefs, dietary habits and the consumer environment, which help to shape the immediate world which we inhabit and which mediate our response to our surroundings. Professor Fiedler actually argues for the abandonment of distinctions, which he sees as essentially rooted in social prejudice. Whether or not the reader accepts this contention, however, I trust that he or she will accept another of this book's implicit propositions, namely the need for a serious examination of phenomena which form such a substantial part of the daily realities, myths, images and dreams which delineate the nature of our fears and hopes, which create, in other words, some part of that doubtful universe which we inhabit.

C.W.E. Bigsby

Europe, America and the Cultural Debate

C.W.E. BIGSBY

Writing of the Americans who travelled to Europe in the 1920s, F. Scott Fitzgerald described them as 'fantastic neanderthals', empty creatures carrying their wealth and philistinism to a devastated Europe. The First World War had left the stark power of American money as one of the central realities of economic and political existence in a world which struggled to sustain the old verities. The vast industrial and logistical system of world supply seemed suddenly geared only to meet the frivolous demands of heedless Americans, such as the heroine of *Tender is the Night*, Nicole Diver, who slowly but inevitably defined the texture of existence for a post-war international society which existed only as a backdrop to their own anarchic psychodramas.

> 'Nicole' [Fitzgerald tells us] 'was the product of much ingenuity and toil. For her sake trains began their run in Chicago and traversed the round belly of the continent to California; chicle factories fumed and link belts grew link by link in factories; men mixed toothpaste in vats and drew mouthwash out of copper hogsheads; girls canned tomatoes quickly in August or worked rudely at the Five-and-Tens on Christmas Eve; half-breed Indians toiled on Brazilian coffee plantations and dreamers were muscled out of patent rights in new tractors — these were some of the people who gave a tythe to Nicole, as the whole system swayed and thundered onward.'[1]

For Fitzgerald the appropriate image for a world whose social and cultural life was determined by a dominant America was that of a

train, rushing blindly forwards. Nearly forty years later both image
and tone had changed as Eldridge Cleaver asserted that:

> 'it is not an overstatement to say that the destiny of the entire
> human race depends on the outcome of what is going on in
> America today. This is a staggering reality to the rest of the world:
> they must feel like passengers in a supersonic jet liner who are
> forced to watch helplessly while a passle of drunks, hypes, freaks
> and madmen fight for the controls and the pilot's seat.'[2]

At its most obvious this power resides in American nuclear
capability and in a commercial enterprise and dominance which
potentially threatens national autonomy. Less tangibly, but an
inevitable consequence of this power, American values, ideals, myths
and ideas penetrate the consciousness of a world for whom the
modern experience is coeval with the American experience.

And this power is expressed in many ways, not least in the
influence exerted by the millions of Americans who choose to visit
Europe every year as tourists, not only carrying their own culture
with them but recreating a familiar world in the societies which they
visit.

Thomas Cook's excursions, which started in 1840, merely
heralded a movement of people which today has reached proportions
which more than rival in sheer numbers the peak year for
immigration into the United States. In 1907 there were 1,285,349
immigrants to the United States, mostly from Europe.[3] In 1970
2,898,000 Americans visited Europe, 1,567,000 going to the United
Kingdom alone (whose population was then approximately half that
of America in 1907).[4] In 1972 nearly four million Americans arrived
in Europe. Almost certainly, more Americans will visit Europe
between the years 1974 and 1980 than Europeans emigrated to the
United States in the one hundred and fifty years between 1820 and
1970.

Since the first American Express traveller's cheque was copyrighted in 1891 the impact of American tourism (a word which was
itself a nineteenth century invention) has been considerable, as
coffee shops, hamburger bars and pancake houses cater for the visitor
en route in his Avis rented, General Motors manufactured car from
his Sheraton Hotel to see an import from Broadway or Hollywood
and then dine at the local Playboy Club. In a sense Max Frisch was
right in suggesting that travel has become 'atavistic' for it scarcely
needs Conrad Hilton's frank admission that he intended to create 'a
little America' wherever his hotels were sited to recognise the impact
of these cultural outposts on the immediate environment. A recent

advertisement for Sheraton Hotels, which appeared in the American
news magazine, *Newsweek* (which itself is of course widely available
in Europe) proudly and chillingly announced that there were 'now
more than three hundred Sheraton Hotels and Motor Inns around the
world.* The new Sheraton in Lisbon,' it added, 'is the tallest building
in Portugal, in the heart of the city only fifteen minutes from the
airport,' while 'the handsome new Brussels-Sheraton is a dynamic
part of the growing Manhattan Centre, located in the Place Rogier.'
The physical dominance of these hotels, invariably situated in central
locations, provides a useful image of what has frequently and
revealingly been called the 'penetration' of Europe.

Clearly economics cannot be divorced from the whole question of
cultural influence. As Jean-Jacques Servan-Schreiber has pointed out:

> 'There is no way of leaving the "economic area" to the Americans
> so that we can get on with political, social, and cultural areas in
> our own way. . . . Naturally there will not be any "American
> committee" to administer Europe, as Paul Valéry imagined.
> Citizens would continue to vote, trade unions to strike, and
> parliaments to deliberate. But it would all take place in a vacuum.
> With our growth rate, our investment priorities, and the distri-
> bution of our national income determined by the United States, it
> is not even necessary to imagine secret meetings between Wall
> Street bankers and European cabinet ministers to understand that
> the areas that really count would lie outside the democratic
> process. The European elite would be trained at Harvard,
> Stanford, or Berkeley, continuing a precedent that has already
> begun. This élite would no doubt worm itself into a kind of
> Atlantic oligarchy, and even gain some influence over its
> decisions. . . . A few leading firms, subsidiaries of American
> Corporations, would decide how much European workers would
> earn and how they would live — work methods, human relations
> on the job, standards for wages and promotion, and job
> security. . . . American capital and American management will not
> stop short at the gates of our society. No taboo of the sacred will
> keep these managers from crossing the threshold of the European
> sanctuary. They will take a majority interest in, and then control,
> the firms that dominate the market in publishing, the press,
> phonographic recording, and television production. The formulas,

* Hilton International, a subsidiary of Trans World Airlines, has twenty hotels in
Europe, and Sheraton Hotels, owned by ITT, owns eight. Holiday Inns has
established forty-five hotels in four years while Intercontinental, owned by Pan
American Airways, has 21 European hotels. The Loews group contributes a
further seven.

if not all the details, of our cultural "messages" would be imported. Our system of education — in the large sense of channels of communication by which customs are transmitted and ways of life and thought formulated — would be controlled from the outside.'[5]

By 1980, it has been estimated, between 20 and 25 per cent of manufacturing output in the United Kingdom may be in the hands of American-controlled concerns. Whatever the economic impact of this, it is clear that a year which may also see three million American tourists visit the country will also witness considerably greater exposure to those cultural messages which slowly modify the nature of cultural reality. And the greatest influence will undoubtedly be in the area of popular culture, as American corporations shape the physical and mental environment, influence eating habits, define leisure pursuits, produce television programmes and movies;* devise, in other words, the fact and fantasy of the late twentieth century.

And though these cultural messages are likely to be as hetero- geneous as the America which they reflect, and to be mediated in turn by the diverse experiences of their recipients, they may not be entirely detached from the values of the corporations which produce and disseminate them.† The heroes celebrated by the media express the values which their producers are prepared to validate and which their domestic market will accept, and these are the values projected by hundreds of hours of television programmes exported to Europe by American companies.

Thus, for example, the tension between individualism and con- formity, identified by foreign observers from de Tocqueville to Denis

* As Thomas H. Guback points out ('Film as International Business,' *Journal of Communication*, Winter 1974), not only do American movies now occupy more than 50 per cent of world screen time but, since American companies have a virtual monopoly of international distribution networks and play a dominant role in financing European films (in the period 1962-72 two out of three 'British' features exhibited on the country's two main circuits were partially or entirely financed by American subsidiaries), they exert considerable influence on the kinds of films produced. 'American involvement in the financing and distributing of European films', he insists, 'has wide political, social, and economic consequences' in that 'preference is given to those kinds of pictures whose international marketing possibilities seem most satisfactory,' with the effect that indigenous cultural characteristics defer to international values. Reflecting Servan-Schreiber's more general point, he asserts that 'Europeans cannot lose control of the economic end of film-making and expect to retain autonomy in the cultural or social spheres.'

† Under the Informational Media Guaranty Program American film companies actually received $16 million between 1948 and 1966 for exporting material which reflected the best elements of American life. (Guback, p. 94.)

Brogan and by native writers from Cooper to Melville, Whitman to Albee as the heart of the American experience and the essence of liberalism, is retained in a simplified form by the electronic media. But the conflict between citizen and corporation, individual and mass is seen merely as a prelude to a seemingly logical embrace of consensus. The Western and private eye movies, which used to propound the simple moral virtues of the individual, private man, now resurface as television series in which the hero is little more than a representative of the forces of authority. In the case of the Western he has been transformed into a wealthy rancher or the uncomplaining agent of such a rancher. Where, in the movies of the 1930s, 40s, and 50s, the hero would oppose the avarice of such men with raw courage and Emersonian self-reliance he now endorses the essentially capitalist corporation values for which he stands (*Bonanza, The Virginian, The High Chaparral, Lancer*). The values endorsed now become those of the family and the family business. In the case of crime films, the hero is no longer the poor and solitary private eye. He is now either a faithful servant of established law (*McCloud, Columbo, Madigan, Ironside, Kojak, MacMillan and Wife*), or wealthy executive with large financial backing and all the resources of a corporation executive (*Cannon, Banacek, A Cool Million*). In its most extreme form these servants of the system become little more than barely human extrusions of high technology (*Mission Impossible, Search Control, Star Trek*) serving the chillingly messianic ends of private corporation and State until the two become indistinguishable from one another. The long-running and successful *FBI* series is a perfect example of this presumed symbiosis. For not only does the programme have the support of the FBI but the Bureau approves all scripts and maintains a representative on the set whose job it is to see that the attitudes and values presented are those approved by the Bureau. In the world created by such television programmes the individual may justifiably fret at petty restrictions, may even exercise his initiative in such a way as to circumvent unnecessary red-tape and arrive at intuitive or deductive perceptions more quickly than the slow-moving bureaucracy for which he works, but there is never any doubt as to the rightness of that institution or the desirability of working within its protective framework. The individual tolerates the organisation; the corporation. tolerates its employee.

It has been argued that it is precisely the provision of such adjustment patterns which explains the essence of popular culture. And when we consider the fact that an American child born today will spend approximately nine years of its life watching television (and a European child not much less), the importance of these manufactured dreams can be gauged.

Yet the potential for social subversion which popular culture also clearly possesses (as in the comic book, pornography, the lyrics of acid-rock), explains the difficulty in defining a phenomenon which has been seen both as the cause and effect of social dislocation and the embodiment of a liberated democratic spirit.

But fear of a growing mass culture, and of the forces which it expressed, was by no means a phenomenon of the latter half of the present century. Post-literate popular culture is very much a product of the machine age, of the period of rapid urbanisation and industrialisation with which it is justifiably linked but with which it is frequently confused. Indeed, opposition to popular culture and complaints about Americanisation have often amounted to little more than laments over a changing world — sparked by the distresses of living in a new era dominated by the realities of city life and a technologically-defined environment. That these tensions were felt most acutely in the United States, a country widely regarded as lacking in the redeeming structure of tradition, led to a natural identification of America as the source of the problem rather than as the place where that problem first surfaced on a considerable scale. Each generation feels the ground slipping beneath its feet and fears the approach of barbarism, which it invariably associates with the forces of change. Americanisation frequently means little more than the incidence of change, and hence the new modes are afforded the usual respect paid to novelty: they are characterised as brash, crude, unsubtle, mindless and, as Matthew Arnold insisted, destructive of taste and tradition. The debate over popular culture has thus from the very beginning been intimately connected with a concern for the material realities it was taken to express, while the United States has inevitably been invoked as the paradigm of a society lacking the necessary spiritual and national qualities required to resist what has all too often been regarded as the onset of moral and aesthetic decay.

The assumptions which had provided the foundation for Matthew Arnold's definition of culture (the existence of unquestioned moral and aesthetic standards, liberal ideas of personal accountability and human progress) had come under pressure at precisely the moment when he chose to articulate his commitment to them. Indeed culture was to be defined in opposition to the anarchy which he saw as threatening his generation, and which was most clearly manifested in the twin evils of urbanisation and mechanisation. He attacked what he regarded as the increasing bondage to machinery and prescribed conscription as the antidote to a liberated working class. Not for him the enthusiasm with which Walt Whitman greeted the transatlantic cable and the popular press as the unifiers of mankind, annihilating time and space to bring people together for a brief epiphany of shared experience. Indeed, in identifying America as in many ways the symbol of the anarchy which he feared, he described it with customary coldness as 'that chosen home of newspapers and politics . . . without general intelligence' and asserted that 'in the things of the mind, and in culture and totality, America, instead of surpassing us all, falls short.'[6] America thus became the symbol of a particularly virulent brutalism for two main reasons. Firstly, it was a society whose cultural identity was forged in an industrial age and, secondly, lacking any established tradition and evidencing none of the structures necessary to the validation of such a tradition, it had no resources with which to counter what he saw as a pernicious democratic mediocrity. Indeed, he went so far as to endorse the sentiment of a French observer, M. Renan, for whom 'countries which, like the United States, have created a considerable popular instruction without any serious higher instruction, will long have to expiate this fault by their intellectual mediocrity, their vulgarity of manners, their superficial spirit, their lack of general intelligence.'[7]

To an extent this was simply the peevishness of a cosmopolitan towards the provincialism of an upstart, an expression of the kind of intolerance which Mrs Trollope (from a vastly different perspective) had perpetrated in a fit of pique in her book, *Domestic Manners of the Americans* (1832). But Arnold was by no means alone in his analysis. Some eighty years later Oswald Spengler pushed his apocalyptic imagery even further, for he identified urbanisation and mechanisation as terminal stages in a development which had taken human history from Spring to Winter, from Nature to the Megalopolis and from Culture to formless, inorganic mass, able only to proliferate distraction and observe unheedingly the decay of meaning and purpose. Like Arnold he identified the press as the public symbol of a changing relationship between the individual and his society, for this was a product of mass literate society and in its power to forge opinion and propound ideology was both a child and an expression of the age. As he explained in *The Decline of the West*:

'English-American politics have created *through the press* a force-field of world-wide intellectual and financial tensions in which every individual unconsciously takes up the place allotted to him, so that he must think, will, and act as a ruling personality somewhere or other in the distance he thinks fit. This is dynamics against statics, Faustian against Apollonian world-feeling. . . . Man does not speak to man; the press and its associate, the electrical news-service, keep the waking-consciousness of whole peoples and continents under a deafening drum-fire of theses, catchwords,

standpoints, scenes, feelings, day by day and year by year, so that
every Ego becomes a mere function of a monstrous intellectual
Something. Money does not pass, politically, from one hand to the
other. It does not turn itself into cards and wine. It is turned into
force, and its quantity determines the intensity of its working
influence.'[8]

Thus are established the central images of America in relation to
the debate over culture. It stands as a country with no tradition, with
a tendency to flaccid thinking and mediocre intelligence, dominated
by media which in turn are manipulated by the money forces. For
Spengler America was the new Carthage and he a new Cato. And
what he saw there was not the boundless open territory, the
existential world of possibility celebrated by its native authors, nor
even the heroic potential for man in conflict with nature celebrated
by Goethe and Byron. What he saw was money and technology and
the offspring of this union — the city, the megalopolis, or city-as-
world, which he regarded as 'the centre in which the course of a
world history ends by winding itself up'.[9] For such cities divide the
world into provincials and cosmopolitans and the new cosmopolis
severs all links with the countryside which gave it birth and hence
with the temporal continuity which is the essence of national
identity and culture alike. Instead of a people rooted in a particular
geographical and spiritual place, cosmopolis creates a 'mass of
tenants and bed-occupiers'[10] whose commitment is to nothing
beyond themselves.

And the result of this process is outlined by Spengler in a
prognosis which would have won the support not only of Matthew
Arnold, and, for that matter, Walt Whitman, but also the Marxist
critics who subsequently indicted the frivolous irrelevance of the
distractions created by capitalist society. For he saw the resulting
tensions of urban, technological life as producing no longer a genuine
sense of *joie de vivre* and relaxation but a need to seek the relief of
'intellectual tension by the bodily tension of sport, of bodily tension
by the sensual straining after "pleasure" and the spiritual straining
after the "excitements" of betting and competitions, of the pure
logic of the day's work by a consciously enjoyed mysticism — all
this' he claimed, 'is common to the world-cities of all the
Civilizations. Cinema, Expressionism, Theosophy, boxing contests,
nigger dances, poker, and racing — one can find it all in Rome.'[11] In
other words Spengler was propounding the thesis that popular
culture is not merely a chance phenomenon of modern existence but
a necessary product of urban, technological life.

Like Arnold, Spengler saw the decline of the book as a logical consequence of the invasion by the press of an area of experience formerly reserved for the insight of the creative writer. The manipulation of thought and imagination by the privately-owned and politically aligned newspaper defined what he regarded as the style of the twentieth century. And despite his own uncertain taste in art and literature, which led him to dismiss as decadent some of the more important developments of modernist thought, and side with the forces of a technology which he had identified as itself the final phase of an historical cycle, he perceived clearly enough the political and technological developments of his age.

To Spengler 'culture' is a descriptive term for an organic community — a living force characterised by what he chooses to call 'soul'. To this concept he opposed 'civilisation', a closed and dead phenomenon which is an expression of 'intellect'. The contrast is essentially that between Greece and Rome — between the imaginative and the vital on the one hand, and the utilitarian, non-metaphysical on the other. And this transition in the modern Western world he saw as occurring in the nineteenth century.

'In place of a type-true people, born of and grown on the soil, there is a new sort of nomad, cohering unstably in fluid masses, the parasitical city-dweller, traditionless, utterly matter-of-fact, religionless, clever, unfruitful. . . . This is a very great stride towards the inorganic, towards the end. . . . After Syracuse, Athens and Alexandria comes Rome. After Madrid, Paris, London come Berlin and New York.'[1][2]

And to this 'world-city belongs not a folk but a mass. Its uncomprehending hostility to all the traditions representative of the Culture (nobility, church, privileges, dynasties, convention in art and limits of knowledge in science), the keen and cold intelligence that confounds the wisdom of the peasant, the new-fashioned naturalism that in relation to all matters of sex and society goes back far beyond Rousseau and Socrates to quite primitive instincts and conditions, the re-appearance of the *panem et circenses* in the form of wage-disputes and football-grounds — all these things betoken the definite closing-down of the Culture and the opening of a quite new phase of human existence.'[1][3]

Spengler's basically rural point of reference gives him an atavistic air but this should not be allowed to cloud his importance for a generation which was to draw so directly on his observations and imagery. And the generation which followed his own was indeed intensely aware of the significance of the social and cultural changes occurring around them. Within the space of two years four central texts were published. In 1930 F.R. Leavis published *Mass Civilisation and Minority Culture*, and Ortega y Gasset, *The Revolt of the Masses*; in 1931 Karl Jaspers' *Man in the Modern Age* appeared and Dover Wilson finished editing Arnold's *Culture and Anarchy* which was published the following year, its first appearance for fifty seven years.

To F.R. Leavis, the natural heir of Matthew Arnold and one who shared his predecessor's conviction that 'a wave ... of more than American vulgarity, moral, intellectual and social' was 'preparing to break over'[14] his generation, Spengler's distinctions were real enough. As he said in 1930, though using the terms in a rather different sense from his predecessor, ' "Civilisation" and "culture" are coming to be antithetical terms'.[15] He was not, however, prepared to grant any inevitability to this process and while identifying a state of crisis, sought, as Arnold had before him, not only to sustain the integrity of cultural life (using the term in Arnold's sense) but to propose it as the central bulwark against a new barbarism which he, once again, associated with technology, a thoughtless democratisation, the emergence of a powerful and philistine press and, finally, the increasing dominance of the United States. This theme has echoed through his work to the present day. In 1930 he wrote:

'It is a commonplace that we are being Americanised, but again a commonplace that seems, as a rule, to carry little understanding with it. . . . For those who are most defiant of America do not propose to reverse the processes consequent upon the machine. . . . When we consider, for instance, the processes of mass-production and standardisation in the form represented by the Press, it becomes obviously of sinister significance that they should be accompanied by a process of levelling-down.'[16]

By 1972 the tone had become more shrill as he denounced what he called 'American conditions' in strictly Spenglerian terms, for he identified those conditions as 'the rootlessness, the vacuity, the inhuman scale, the failure of organic cultural life, the anti-human reductivism that favours the American neo-imperialism of the computer.'[17] Like Arnold and Spengler, he saw in the United States a vision of the imminent fate of the Western world in which, as in Huxley's dystopia, *Brave New World*, technological advance was united with spiritual sterility (indeed for Huxley and Spengler quite literal sterility), 'the energy, the triumphant technology, the productivity, the high standard of living and the life-impoverishment — the human emptiness; emptiness and boredom craving alcohol — of one kind or another'.[18] And one brand of alcohol, as identified by Leavis in his earlier book, was precisely those mass arts which Spengler had seen as a necessary consequence of the final stage of the historical cycle — a time in which culture has been detached from the power, authority and tradition seen by Arnold as its essential underpinning.

Writer after writer reiterated the same points. Karl Jaspers, like Spengler, drew on Imperial Rome for his paradigm of a society intent on distracting itself with sport and trivial entertainment. While rejecting the apocalyptic mood of the decade, he shared Leavis's fear of a decline in the quality of life, a collapse of values which evidences itself in a decay of spiritual identity and cultural purpose. And once again the newspaper becomes the image of a trivialisation of existence.

> 'In the life of the mass-order, the culture of the generality tends to conform to the demands of the average human being. Spirituality decays through being diffused among the masses when knowledge is impoverished in every possible way by rationalisation until it becomes accessible to the crude understanding of all. As a result of the levelling-down process characteristic of the mass-order, there is a tendency towards the disappearance of that stratum of cultured persons who have come into being thanks to a continuous disciplining of their thoughts and feelings so that they have been rendered capable of mental creation. The mass-man has very little spare time, does not live a life that appertains to a whole, does not want to exert himself except for some concrete aim which can be expressed in terms of utility; he will not wait patiently while things ripen; everything for him must provide some immediate gratification; and even his mental life must minister to his fleeting pleasures. That is why the essay has become the customary form of literature, why newspapers are taking the place of books and why desultory reading has been substituted for the perusal of works that can serve as an accompaniment to life.'[19]

And when he proceeded to identify an increasing homogenisation in life he drew not only on Spengler's image of reified intellectualism but, in his emphasis on the increasing power of technological civilisations, granted also Spengler's thesis of the megalopolis, of which New York had formed the main example.

> 'With the unification of our planet, [he observed] there has begun a process of levelling-down which people contemplate with horror. That which has today become general to our species is always the most superficial, the most trivial, and the most indifferent of human possibilities. Yet men strive to effect the levelling-down as

if, in that way, the unification of mankind could be brought about. On tropical plantations and in the fishing villages of the Far North, the films of the great capitals are thrown on the screen. People dress alike. The conventionalities of daily intercourse are cosmopolitan; the same dances, the same types of thought, and the same catchwords... are making their way all over the world.'[20]

The striking similarity in the language employed by such critics, from different countries and disciplines, underlines not merely a shared apprehension of the changes wrought by technology and its resultant social dislocation, but also the cultural impact of so fundamental an alteration in the relationship between the individual and his environment.

But if there were those who feared the new realities of the modern era there were others who regarded such changes as long overdue and who responded enthusiastically to the new machine age. Whether it be Harriet Monroe, standing entranced at the Centennial Exhibition in Philadelphia in front of the Corliss Steam Engine, or Henry Adams seizing on the Dynamo as the image of his age, sheer exultance in technological proficiency typified a whole generation. The Crystal Palace, at the Great Exhibition in London, the Eiffel Tower at the 1889 Paris Exposition, both attested to an era not only of the machine but of mass man. And if these were evidence of precisely that fascination with the vast and the technically proficient which Spengler, Jaspers and Ortega y Gasset had seen as a natural product of the modern mentality, they were also symbols of a mechanical power which could, at least in theory, liberate human energy for the business of living. As the expressionists were to indicate, such revolutions may carry their own form of servitude but this perception did not blunt the excitement of those for whom the machine offered an aesthetic and ethical liberation from the dominance of a class-centred culture and morality.

Most brash in their welcome of the machine age, of course, were the Futurists whose outrageous embrace of the new was a gesture of defiance aimed at formal conceptions of art. They discovered beauty in the new products of the machine and as such were the harbingers of a popular culture which could find its image of aesthetic achievement in the sleek lines of a racing car 'with its bonnet draped with exhaust-pipes like fire-breathing serpents — a roaring racing car rattling along like a machine-gun.'[21] This, which for Leavis had been one of the basic images of a fragmenting society, the futurists considered 'more beautiful than the winged experience of Samothrace'. Le Corbusier was later to design a house called Citrohan, which expressed in his mind something of the spirit of the car whose name it parodied. In Germany the Werkbund and the Bauhaus sought to combine craft with industrial techniques, turning out the objects which have helped to define the modern environment and hence popular culture in the broader sense. Mart Stam's tubular steel chair has become the commonplace of every school and village hall in Europe. Meanwhile the *de Stijl* group in Holland aided in defining the machine aesthetic of the twenties. As Oud remarked at the time:

> 'automobiles, steamers, yachts, men's wear, sports clothes, electrical and sanitary equipment, table-ware and so forth possess within themselves, as the purest expression of their time, the elements of a new language of aesthetic form, and can be considered as the point of departure for a new art, though their restrained form is largely due to their new, mechanical methods of production.'[22]

The Futurists of course were very different from those who followed them. Theirs was a romantic flourish which flirted with apocalypse. The machine was anarchic and their enthusiasm for it contained an element of anti-humanist relish which made them in some ways fit converts to Fascism. Those who urged a machine-aesthetic in the twenties, however, were entirely serious in their advocacy of utilitarian form and though this was consciously developed in Europe, its advocates constantly turned, as had the Futurists before them, to the United States for the essence of what they pursued. Just as the Futurists had seen in New York a functioning example of their own visions, so the architects and designers who worked in *de Stijl* and the Bauhaus discovered a pattern for their own aspirations in the simple lines of American grain elevators or the monumental grandeur of American railroad stations. Nor was the machine simply regarded as an agent for social and aesthetic liberation. It was seen by some as possessing a spiritual dimension, resonant in the hum of the dynamo and the space-conquering essence of mechanical speed and electrical energy. It was thus that Whitman welcomed it and despite the international implications which he chose to stress, it was clear that in a machine age the United States was bound to be of central significance. For this was the first nation whose institutions and cultural identity had been forged almost wholly in a technological era. It was here that massive urbanisation became a basic fact of life for people drawn to the country as much for the wealth which that technology could generate as for the political system which seemed to guarantee a new freedom. For millions of people a move to the United States was precisely the exchange of a rural for an industrial system and the life-style and cultural ethos which they developed there was necessarily a response to that situation. And if writers from Mark Twain (*A Connecticut Yankee at the Court of King Arthur*) to Saul Bellow (*Henderson the Rain King*) have seen pride in technological superiority as inseparable from a form of moral weakness, it remains true that, as Leavis had suggested, America's present is Europe's future and the consequences of industrial society immediately observable in the configurations of American life.

Yet Ortega y Gasset reminds us that technology was a European and not an American invention and in rejecting what he regarded as naive complaints about the Americanisation of Europe, he advanced the idea that the 'levelling-down', which he saw as afflicting Europe was simply an inevitable movement by European society towards a position which had long been a 'constitutional fact' in the United States. However, inevitably for a man who regarded the emergence and dominance of the masses (by which he meant the average man rather than the working class) as a major crisis and who confessed to regarding human society as inherently aristocratic, he deplored this process as profoundly as any of his contemporaries who, like Leavis, were bemoaning the emergence of a standardised civilisation or, like T.S. Eliot, lamenting over the hollow men distracted from distraction by distraction. And, despite his protestations to the contrary, his uncritical repetition of the cliché that 'to be different' in the United States, 'is to be indecent'[23] revealed his conviction that what Europe must be saved from was essentially the American experience, which, in its rootlessness and in its contempt for the continuities offered by established tradition, was offering a paradigm of modern existence.

Tocqueville's observation that 'since the past has ceased to throw its light upon the future, the mind of man wanders in obscurity'[24] has indeed become the essential insight of an age. The move from *gemeinschaft* to *gesellschaft*, from what, in a different sense, Reisman has called an 'inner directed' to 'other directed' social system, has not only left man alienated from himself and his own past but also has posed a central challenge to a whole culture whose identity derives from its own history. This was a challenge first met in the arts by the modernist movement, which appeared to offer a discrete world of its own, narcissistic in some respects, but representing an alternative system of order to that subscribed to by the eighteenth century. But the modernists did not sunder themselves so completely from the past. Art has always contained its own history, even in the moment of revolt — indeed especially in the moment of revolt. It sustains an historical sense and contains meaning precisely by reference to its predecessors. And it is the paradox of the modernist movement that it was simultaneously a product of the break in temporal continuity and implicitly a denial of it. Popular culture, on the other hand, is avowedly ahistorical. It makes a virtue of its own ephemerality and hardly survives the moment of its own creation without devolving into absurdity. It celebrates its own birth, making no appeal to tradition and seeking no sanction beyond its immediate acceptability. It concedes no future, except in so far as this is domesticated — a projection of an everlasting present merely advanced a few stages along the techno-logical curve. No doubts obtrude, for popular culture is indeed a consumer product; it must be fully consumable with no area of undigested mystery. The commonplaces of Hollywood, Broadway, the cartoon, the comic book, the Western, the detective story, are all concerned with offering assurance that things are under control, that ambiguity will be resolved, that violence is assimilable, that disorder will resolve into order, that sexuality is not anarchic, that death is not real, that injustice is a temporary state, that rebellion is a predictable phase which will be subsumed eventually in a necessary corporate stability.

Art and literature, on the other hand are rooted in a fundamental dissonance between appearance and reality, indeed express a basic conviction that reality is indefinable. Marx's observation that science would be superfluous if the appearance and essence of things coincided could be applied with equal validity to culture. All information is imperfect — the writer, the artist and the musician know this as clearly as the physicist. But popular culture deals in certainties. From the hard rationality of the detective story to the hermetic moralism of the Western, from the closely structured and self-justifying pop song to the necessarily self-defining contour of the cartoon, popular culture presents a model not merely of balance and completion but also of confident assurance — an assurance contained in the product itself and therefore projected on to those exposed to it. And this, indeed, is the basis of Marcuse's attack on popular culture for, to his mind, it serves to deny the reality of genuine social conflict, to satisfy 'false' aspirations and to blunt our awareness of transcendent needs by invading the 'private space' of the imagination and personal conscience. Since the needs thus satisfied bear no relation to the fundamental requirements of personal and social life, any apparent sense of a community of interests and values arising from shared possession of a popular culture generated by public media simply testifies to the effectiveness with which our conscious-ness has been subverted, and the degree to which ideals of justice and true equality have been deflected into a spurious materialism. For this in turn leads to a 'flattening out of the contrast (or conflict) between the given and the possible, between the satisfied and the unsatisfied needs. Here, the so-called equalization of class distinctions reveals its ideological function. If the worker and his boss enjoy the same television programme and visit the same resort places, if the typist is as attractively made-up as the daughter of her employer, if the Negro owns a Cadillac, if they all read the same newspaper, then this assimilation indicates not the disappearance of classes, but the extent to which the needs and satisfactions that serve the preservation of the Establishment are shared by the underlying population. Indeed, in the most highly developed areas of contemporary society, the transplantation of social into individual needs is so effective that the difference between them seems to be purely theoretical. Can one really distinguish between the mass media as instruments of information and entertainment, and as agents of manipulation and indoctrination?'[25]

It is no wonder that the totalitarian mind should be so distrustful of the ambiguities of culture nor that it should reveal a marked tendency to transform high culture into popular culture (as the Third Reich did with Wagner) and popular culture into high culture (as the Soviet Union did with Socialist Realism). As Walter Benjamin has suggested, 'the logical result of Fascism is the introduction of aesthetics into political life'[26] and, one might add, vice versa.

Perhaps though some of the animus directed against popular culture derives not so much from what the French are prone to call the 'spectacular society', the enervating materialism of modern society, as from a conviction that we are living through a lean time in the arts — a period of experimentation but not a period of real achievement — and that the all-pervasive nature of popular culture may hold some responsibility for this. The gap which was assumed to exist between culture and popular culture seems to be narrowing and the humane values which had formed the central justification and the distinguishing feature of 'high' art are no longer so apparent in work which increasingly reflects the reified world which produces it. The cosmic confidence, evidenced in the figure of the nineteenth century omniscient narrator, can no longer sustain our credibility. Even the bleak but comprehensive vision of the naturalistic novel has given way to the value-free perspective of the *nouveau roman* which owes more to the cinema camera than to the humane vision of the artistic sensibility. From the confident expression of liberal values which one finds in Ibsen we have moved to the desolate vision of the absurdist. The angular stage settings of the Expressionists implied an awareness of the diminishing autonomy of the individual but maintained the possibility of change; the desolate *mise en scène* found in Beckett is an expression of an irrevocable devastation which has reached to the very core of existence. The appearance of spring, the flicker of a smile, become searing ironies rather than images of spiritual commitment. The failure of nerve, if that is indeed what it is, is reflected in a conscious surrender of control, in a refusal to perpetuate even the notion of artistic order. Humanistic assumptions are surrendered and that autonomy which, in Western art, has always been the distinguishing characteristic of the artist and the basis for the distinction between culture and popular culture, abandoned. This is by no means a general movement but it is precisely the fact that the avant-garde are drawn to this stance which suggests the importance of such a development. Musicians like John Cage and LaMont Young deliberately set out to devise compositions which will evade their mediation as far as possible. William Burroughs and others create novels which readers may re-arrange at will. Dramatists, like Jean-Claude van Itallie, willingly surrender the role of playwright to actors, directors and the pressure of performance. Peter Brook and his company of actors devise a play in a totally new language so as to escape the tyranny of traditional meaning, latent content and implied values which, for Arnold and Leavis, were the very essence of cultural meaning. To Marcuse this was an inevitable movement for 'the higher culture of the West — whose moral, aesthetic, and intellectual values industrial society still professes — was a pre-technological culture in a functional as well as chronological sense. Its validity was derived from the experience of a world which no longer exists and which cannot be recaptured because it is in a strict sense invalidated by technological society.'[27]

The related fear that contemporary reality might be outstripping the ability of the creative mind to sustain itself, that imagination might itself be a victim of the age, has perhaps hastened the contemporary movement from fiction to reportage which Spengler had predicted and which George Steiner has identified in his book *Language and Silence*. To Steiner, the novel is essentially a conveyor of factual information, of the solid realities of its day, and is thus naturally undermined by a technology which can accomplish the same task with greater speed, precision and compelling vividness. It is an interpretation of the novel with which one can legitimately argue, the more so since he draws attention, by way of proof, to the 'vast and explicit load of fact'[28] in *Moby Dick* while seemingly oblivious to the nature of a book committed to revealing the inadequacy and, indeed, the danger of a mind which seeks to reduce the metaphysical to a spurious facticity. Yet many writers have in fact confessed to a feeling of inadequacy in the face of contemporary reality, Brecht asserting that it could only be portrayed in the conviction that change was possible, and Adorno insisting that poetry is no longer possible after Auschwitz. Even Norman Mailer has implicitly recognised the problem in countering a dehumanising deluge of factual information and technological reification with a neutralising explosion of language in *Fire on the Moon*. Nor is this simply a case of the artist being overwhelmed by the sheer extent of contemporary reality. Both Brecht and Adorno were implying a far more radical crisis than this. They identified a social culpability which neutralised the values which were presumed to be reflected in Western art. For, as Marcuse has suggested, it is arguable that

> 'the achievements and the failures of this society invalidate its higher culture. The celebration of the autonomous personality, of humanism, of tragic and romantic love appears to be the ideal of a backward stage of the development. What is happening now is not the deterioration of higher culture into mass culture but the refutation of this culture by reality. The reality surpasses its culture. . . . [It] has betrayed the hope and destroyed the truth which were preserved in the sublimations of higher culture. . . . Today's novel feature is the flattening out of the antagonism between culture and social reality through the obliteration of the oppositional, alien and transcendent elements in the higher culture by virtue of which it constituted *another dimension* of reality.'[2][9]

It is true, nonetheless, that in many respects the artist has begun to turn towards popular culture for images, styles and forms which, as products of a technological society, seem particularly capable of expressing the forces at work within it. Hence the painter utilises images created by the advertising agency, the novelist assumes the style and typographical layout of the newspaper. The dramatist turns to the caricature of the cartoon-strip and even the press headline, with its direct and familiar impact. Yet, it is asserted, there remains a crucial self-consciousness, a critical distance which distinguishes the work which employs the images of popular culture from the thing itself, which maintains the integrity of individual insight and action. And this is a vital distinction if it can be sustained. Writing in 1947, Robert Warshow asked an important question: 'how shall we regain the use of our experience in the world of mass culture' for, in his view, popular culture by definition not only usurped the imagination, it also relieved 'one of the necessity of experiencing one's life directly'. While conceding that 'serious art, too, is separated from reality, for it permits one to contemplate experience without being personally involved,' he insisted that this 'is not an evasion' since, 'by its very detachment, it opens up new possibilities of understanding and pleasure derivable from reality, and it thus becomes an enrichment of experience.' But the problem is that mass culture is 'the screen through which we see reality and the mirror in which we see ourselves', while its 'ultimate tendency is to supersede reality'. And this, as Warshow recognises, creates a problem for the artist who must both perceive reality and have access to a language which has not itself been subverted. He sees the problem as having been solved in modern poetry by just that self-consciousness described above, that is by the use of irony, 'by employing the vocabulary of mass culture in a more serious context, the poet expresses both his rejection of mass culture and the difficulty he faces in trying to transcend it.'[30]

But irony of course presupposes the existence of autonomous values existing outside the terms defined by mass culture and it is precisely the reality of such a supposition in the contemporary world which is being questioned, for the artist is the product of his times, employing the technology of his own era and necessarily himself absorbing something of his knowledge of the world through the mediation of those communications systems which he purports to judge. Certainly there are many critics today who doubt the possibility and the value of such an objectivity. For in so far as the individual protects himself from the media to that extent also he fails to share the experience of his fellows and one implication of such a stance is a complacent élitism. Certainly distinctions between high and popular culture scarcely existed in the late eighteenth century or, indeed, throughout most of the nineteenth. Cooper, Scott, Twain and Dickens, were hardly concerned with locating themselves in terms of a debate which had little meaning until Arnold sought to give it substance. In 1889 Mark Twain insisted that 'I have never tried in even one simple instance . . . to help cultivate the cultivated classes. I was not equipped for it, either by native gifts or training. And I never had any ambition in that direction, but always hunted for bigger game — the masses',[31] while Scott had earlier asserted: 'I care not who knows it — I write for general amusement.'[32] But the spread of literacy suddenly seemed to threaten to undermine the cultural hegemony of a class bred to regard itself as the natural inheritors of a past encoded, for the most part, in the written word. Universal literacy meant the breaking of the cipher and the creation of a popular literature which seemed merely a symbol of that wilful licence which Arnold regarded as threatening the State. Since literature itself no longer distinguished ruler from ruled, cultured from Philistine, a new standard had to be invoked to redress the balance threatened by an unrepentant democratic spirit. Hence, to

critics such as Leslie Fiedler, the need to distinguish between high
and low art, like the absurd proliferation of phrases to distinguish
fanciful class distinctions, derived less from a genuine difference than
from a social imperative mistakenly repeated thereafter by those who
confused Arnold's liberal educational ideals with his aristocratic
convictions.

Other critics, like Susan Sontag, have attacked a critical tradition
which attempts to distinguish values by identifying enfolding levels
of meaning, to be unravelled by the full panoply of critical apparatus
honed to a sharp edge in order to dissect ambiguity from confusion,
irony from bathos. In doing so, and in asserting that 'transparence is
the highest, most liberating value in art'[33] she too implicitly destroys
the distinction between culture and a popular culture whose essential
element is likewise transparency. And here she is reflecting a whole
movement in the contemporary arts led in many respects by
America, which insists on the authenticity of immediate response, on
the validity of sensory experience, and which defends an aesthetic of
the ephemeral. As Susan Sontag has suggested, 'in place of a
hermaneutics we need an erotics of art.'[34] Indeed, in an essay on
'One Culture and the New Sensibility' she specifically rejects the
Arnoldian distinctions and asserts that 'the distinction between
"high" and "low" culture seems less and less meaningful' because it
'does not make sense for a creative community of artists and
scientists engaged in programming sensations, uninterested in art as a
species of moral journalism.'[35] The weakness of such distinctions,
forged in a literary age, becomes exposed as soon as the dominant
form becomes visual. And the failure, for more than fifty years, to
accommodate the products of the cinema or even to formulate a
satisfactory language in which to discuss the film or, now, television,
reveals the expediency of a debate which was in truth a disguised
dialogue on the state of society rather than art, an historical
footnote, more interesting for what it revealed about Arnold and
Victorian sensibility than for truths about the nature of art. Indeed it
is precisely this kind of criticism which, rooted in the belief that
literature should be concerned with propounding moral ideas, finds
itself helpless before the work of Alain Robbe-Grillet, of Edward
Bond or Joe Orton and which can only come to terms with Samuel
Beckett by discovering a 'rich vein of humanism' in his bleak
re-enactments of human absurdity. It is a criticism which fails to
penetrate the happening or the work of Roy Lichtenstein or Andy
Warhol.

Perhaps what we have witnessed in recent art and literature,
therefore, is a genuine decline not only in the critical spirit but also
in the autonomy of which it is an expression. For since, as Roland

Barthes has suggested, 'language is never innocent',[36] the writer or artist is bound to reflect the values of an age in which he lives. Just as the eighteenth century novelist could conceive of works constructed entirely of interminable letters, because the temporal sense of the writer was fundamentally different from that of the nineteenth century novelist who released his works in easily and quickly digested serial form, so the reified vision and style of Ishmael Reed, Richard Brautigan and Donald Barthelme reflect a contemporary vision which in turn is profoundly different from that pertaining at the turn of the century. Since narration implies faith in orderly progress and patterned existence, belief in the process of communication, confident possession of past experience and an assured movement towards a predictable future, the modernist sought for some basis to undermine the very implications of his own stance. In doing so he invoked the anarchic force of the sub-conscious and invested his work with a degree of self-conscious artifice which could serve to signal the limitations to the autonomous world there created — thereby suggesting the path which art would take in the twentieth century.

The surrender of control by the surrealists and later by other experimental writers and artists across a wide spectrum was merely an inevitable consequence of this and a revolt against the unquestioning assurance which had typified Arnold and those writers whom he presumed to be exemplars of a timelessness endemic to art but which was in fact contingent on conditions which even then were disappearing. Control, essential to Arnold in literature as in life is now surrendered, as the only means of gaining possession of a real world which has long since ceased to offer evidence of the coherence suggested by the eighteenth century writer. When Antonin Artaud, the French theatre theoretician, calls for 'No more masterpieces' he is deliberately rejecting the idea of tradition and insisting, no matter how unrealistically (since even revolt is shaped by the forces it would displace), on the need for the artist to serve the moment, unshackled by past forms and formulations. As Roland Barthes has pointed out:

'a modern masterpiece is impossible, since the writer is forced by his writing into a cleft stick: either the object of the work is naively attuned to the conventions of its form, Literature remaining deaf to our present History, and not going beyond the literary myth; or else the writer acknowledges the vast novelty of the present world, but finds that in order to express it he has at his disposal only a language which is splendid but lifeless. In front of the virgin sheet of paper, at the moment of choosing the words which must frankly signify his place in History, and testify that he assumes its data, he observes a tragic disparity between what he does and what he sees. Before his eyes, the world of society now exists as a veritable Nature, and this Nature speaks, elaborating living languages from which the writer is excluded: on the contrary, History puts in his hands a decorative and compromising instrument, a writing inherited from a previous and different History, for which he is not responsible and yet which is the only one he can use. Thus is born a tragic element in writing, since the conscious writer must henceforth fight against ancestral and all-powerful signs which, from the depths of a past foreign to him, impose Literature on him like some ritual, not like a recon-ciliation.'[37]

Contemporary writers and artists have made use of the popular arts as a way of neutralising this weight of the past, invoking a confessedly ephemeral form as an antidote to the tradition which they can no longer regard as embodying moral or aesthetic values to which they can subscribe. In the very act of doing so, however, they have helped to dismantle the assumptions on which Arnold and Leavis had based their opposition to the spread of a mass culture and hence to cast in doubt distinctions based on outmoded versions both of the individual and of his society.

What then does popular culture imply? Having been alternately roundly denounced and, in one form or another, enthusiastically embraced for over a hundred years, does it now suggest an upward cultural mobility or a consumer durable aesthetic; the public expression of values and fears, or a society serviced by culture industries quoted on the stock market and responding to a public taste cynically manipulated by commercial concerns? Dwight Macdonald, writing in 1953, was in no doubt: popular culture, which he preferred to call mass culture, was, in his view, 'at best a vulgarised reflection of High Culture' and as such was unavoidably engaged in a battle for survival with the values and products of high art. 'There are', he asserted, 'theoretical reasons why Mass Culture is not and can never be any good. I take it as axiomatic that culture can only be produced by and for human beings. But in so far as people are organized (more strictly, disorganized) as masses, they lose their human identity and quality.'[38] He chose to compare mass art with chewing gum, decried the introduction of sound into films as signalling the end of any imaginative intensity in movies, and spelled out his own apocalyptic gloom in sub-headings which announced, 'THE FUTURE OF CULTURE: DARK', 'THE FUTURE OF MASS CULTURE: DARKER'. But, more recently, there has been a strong resistance, not only to Macdonald's casual dismissal of material which he apparently regarded as unvariegated and formulaic, but also of the whole categorising process itself.

Terms like 'high' and 'low', 'elite' and 'mass', are misleading in so far as they prejudge a number of issues and derive from a particular view of society. They confuse description with evaluation. Just as the various formulations for class divisions emerged throughout the nineteenth century (in ascending order from 'working class' to 'upper class'), thereby reflecting the steady rise of the bourgeoisie, so descriptive terms to summarise the connection between class and taste evolved in the first decades of the twentieth century (in reverse order, starting with 'highbrow' and descending through 'middlebrow' to 'lowbrow') as a means of discriminating between the supposedly pure values of the intellectual élite and the debased standards of those below them. But, interestingly enough, the terms have almost invariably been used pejoratively, so that at a time when social divisions were being eroded by rising living standards the class war was now very clearly enacted in terms of taste — 'highbrow' meaning hopelessly abstruse and effete, 'middlebrow' implying work with pretensions beyond its achievement, and 'lowbrow', devoid of intellectual content — pap.

Part of the difficulty over the meaning of the term 'popular culture' arises from the differing meanings attributable to the word 'popular' itself, for as the OED makes evident it can mean both 'intended for and suited to ordinary people. Adapted to the understanding or taste of ordinary people,' or 'prevalent or current among, or accepted by, the people generally.' The latter includes everyone, the former excludes all but the 'ordinary'. Hence popular culture is sometimes presented as that which appeals only to the commonality ('mass culture') or to the average ('middlebrow'), thus confirming the social fragmentation of society, and sometimes as a phenomenon cutting across class lines. For some, therefore, it is a simple opiate, for others a subversive and liberating force, linking those of differing social and educational background.

There is a further difficulty still in that the word 'culture' is susceptible both of a general and a specialised meaning. In the former sense it implies the attitudes and values of a society as expressed through the symbolic form of language, myths, rituals, lifestyles, establishments (political, religious, educational); in the latter it is closer to the meaning implied by Matthew Arnold and defined by the OED as 'the training, development, and refinement of mind, tastes, manners: the condition of being thus trained and refined, the intellectual side of civilisation'. And though, as Arnold recognised, the two meanings are by no means entirely distinct from one another, his focus tended to rest on the particular symbolic embodiment of this intellectual aspect of existence to be found in the arts. Thus, by analogy, popular culture is sometimes defined as the attitudes and values of those excluded from the intellectual élite and expressed through myths, rituals and lifestyles specific to this excluded group, and sometimes as the popular, as opposed to the intellectual, arts. The scope for misunderstanding is obviously vast. Hannah Arendt can, for example, justifiably deny the existence of mass culture, regarding it as a simple contradiction in terms, only so long as she rests her case on a narrow definition of culture; while Clement Greenberg can maintain that middlebrow culture, as he calls it, 'attacks distinctions and insinuates itself everywhere, devaluating the precious, infecting the healthy, corrupting the honest and stultifying the wise',[39] only if he is prepared to propound a circuitous definition by which what is bad is middlebrow and middlebrow is what is bad.

The term 'mass society' is of course itself inherently misleading for society is in fact a series of shifting and temporary alliances, and it can be argued that, far from being the cause and product of fragmentation, popular culture celebrates these moments of consonance. It is, in other words, a social and moral gesture. Though people from different classes, income groups and educational backgrounds may not meet in an art gallery, or at the opera or a poetry reading, they may well do so in the cinema, at the World's Fair or at a football match: these, then, are presented as today's epiphanies. If culture implies a connection with former ages and hence enables the individual to relate to the continuing development of mankind, popular culture is thus seen as producing a non-linear connectiveness across classes. It provides a means to share a common experience in the present; a lateral rather than a linear bond. Hence where Yeats had described art as 'the social act of a solitary man',[40] popular culture becomes the social act of solitary men.

But just as Spengler had seen the city, with its aggregated masses, as providing only a parody of community, so the communal modes suggested by the media are, perhaps, more apparent than real. Far from creating a global village with shared values expressed in a common visual and verbal symbolisation, the city-world of today and the media with which it addresses itself may be seen as creating only the imagery and not the substance of communication. Thus the film is the first mass art in which people are gathered together in communal buildings in which the communal element is unimportant. Television, similarly, groups the family in the posture of group contact only to interdict the contact which that configuration implies. Symbol without content. When the teenager plugs the transistor into his ear, he necessarily unplugs from those around him;

the juke box, in order to function, must make conversation ineffective. Progressively, society falls back on visual images, distrusts language, fills the air with Muzak to avoid silence, and plumbs the individual psyche in preference to chancing a human relationship which implies an avoidable vulnerability.

Mechanisation and the growth of the city have turned society on edge in more ways than one. Not only did they undermine a class system which was itself the basis of traditional culture and which had in part been structured on the physical distribution and hence political emasculation of workers, it also took a people horizontally scattered and communicating laterally and reassembled them vertically in tenements and skyscrapers (Spengler, who pre-dated most modern high-rise buildings nonetheless drew attention to tenement blocks such as the Insula Feliculae in classical Rome). Even horizontal transportation has begun to cease to offer an opportunity for personal interaction as the automobile conveys a solitary individual from one vertical plane to another, from apartment to office block and back. And this is not only the reality of the contemporary world or Spengler's grim presentiment for tomorrow, it has also formed the basis of those utopian city plans produced by such visionary architects as Sant'Elia and Le Corbusier who have traced out in their drawings a compartmentalised world in which huge transportation lanes intersect living areas at different heights and angles, separating both vertically and horizontally. And since vertical communication is especially difficult, technology becomes a necessary corollary of vertical living. The telephone and then radio and television become as necessary as did the flushing toilet, the electric light and the air-conditioner. And these in turn contribute to a homogenisation of surroundings which is another product of the city, for the architect, released from his former constraints, no longer feels bound by climatic or environmental conditions. And hence an international style is born.

Yet, thus released, the architect can deploy the devices originally developed to facilitate vertical living, to define a radically new and potentially liberating approach to structure. As Reyner Banham has said of Las Vegas, 'structure is the least dominant element in the definition of symbolic space. What defines the symbolic places and spaces of Las Vegas — the superhotels of The Strip, the casino belt of Fremont Street — is pure environmental power, manifested as coloured light.'[41] Aware of the dangers implicit in urbanisation and technology, we are already learning to recognise their liberating power; conscious of the spiritually debilitating nature of much popular culture, we are also becoming aware of its potentially subversive and energetic impulse in other work (some films, television programmes, science fiction novels and cartoons) which, though generated by commercial compulsions, may at the same time reflect the genuine doubts and aspirations of a people who feel ever less control over their personal and social environment, and, indeed, generate a confidence which may enable them to confront such fears and ideals without capitulating. There is at any rate no basis for as undiscriminating an assault on the press and its electronic descendants as Arnold, Spengler and Leavis were prepared to launch and there is little justification for regarding certain forms (the western, science fiction, detective fiction) as inherently inferior. An aesthetic of popular culture is only impossible if you begin with a definition as limited as that implied by Dwight Macdonald and Clement Greenberg. It is, in fact, salutary to remind ourselves of the consistency with which both individual artists and entire genres, dismissed in their own age as trivial and brutalising, have by degrees been admitted into the ranks of the tradition which Arnold had regarded as so self-evident and immutable. Pascal, for example, denounced the theatre as a dangerous distraction which stood as a threat to Christian life, while the novel, itself a product of the very social forces which Arnold so deplored, accomplished its rise to respectability during the course of two hundred years. The film has done the same in fifty.

As for the impact of American popular culture on Europe, this is certain to remain considerable. With a home market in excess of two hundred million, and with financial resources greater than those of any individual European country, the United States is bound to continue to produce most of the world's films (contraction in the industry notwithstanding), much of the world's popular literature and a large percentage of its popular television programmes — US producers now export more than 100,000 programme hours a year, while nearly twenty per cent of total television transmission time in Western Europe consists of American-made programmes. As a result of its economic and political ascendency it will continue to set the standards for patterns of consumption, athletic prowess, lifestyles, dietary habits, social behaviour and moral standards. But, as the British historian, Denis Brogan, has pointed out, the spread of popular culture is not simply the invasion of American values for 'the Americans are telling Europe something about themselves, not about America. When, Georges Duhamel pessimistically wrote his "Scènes pour la vie future", he cannot have foreseen how soon France, the French people, would turn to "Americanism", which is simply the life of the new industrial societies that England (not the United States) created. This is the most democratic of cultures.'[42] Moreover, in crossing the Atlantic, in spreading downward through South

America, northward through Canada, or westward across the Pacific, American popular culture suffers a sea-change. Detached from the physical and psychic realities which gave it birth, it assumes a new identity. Changing shape at each cultural interface, it becomes, in effect, a Superculture, a reservoir of shifting values and images splashed like primary colours across the consciousness of the late twentieth century.

Democratic or totalitarian, bland or vital, popular culture both expresses and shapes our perceptions of a half desired environment in which the unexpressed becomes expressible and the unattainable is within the grasp of all. If we are to understand ourselves we cannot afford to be too casually dismissive of the distractions with which we fill so much of our time. For not only may these hold a key to the more substantial realities which we thus evade, to the fears and dreams of which they are in part an expression, but their own configuration forms a part of the process of communication, part of the cosmology of symbols, with which we seek to make sense of ourselves and our environment.

Towards a Definition of Popular Literature

LESLIE A. FIEDLER

Any essay in definition which begins with a term in common use courts disaster, since it seems initially to encourage certain expectations which it must finally frustrate. Let me say at the start, therefore, that by 'popular' I do not mean necessarily or primarily what is most widely read, much less what is read by 'everybody'; and by 'literature' I do not mean what is customarily 'studied' in classes in literature, certainly not university classes in English Literature or American Literature or Comparative Literature. Indeed, I use the term 'Popular Literature' only because the misapprehensions occasioned by each of the two words cancel each other out, because it is a contradiction in terms. What I shall be discussing are the kinds of songs and stories which have tended, since the invention of moveable type, to be 'ghettoized', which is to say, excluded from classes in 'literature', and endured only as long as they clearly know their own place. Such a description of my subject matter is, however, already a rough or preliminary definition. When I have rendered it as clear and patent as any commonplace, I will be done.

I reserve the term 'Folk Literature' for orally transmitted song and story before the time of Gutenberg which must be discussed in a quite different historical and cultural context. I do not, however, restrict the term 'Popular Literature' to what is transmitted by print, applying it also to lyrics and narratives transmitted orally by post-print electronic devices: using it, in short, for everything in the realm of 'mass-communications'. But this means everything deemed unworthy, whatever its medium, by the critical establishment created since the Gutenberg era, of being ranked with those 'classics' (Epic, Verse Tragedy, etc.), originally preserved by the painful process of manuscript copying in a time of quite limited literacy. Such 'unworthy' works could not, of course, be denied publication, at first in book form, then as movies, radio or TV plays; because Gutenberg and post-Gutenberg technology, which began by making the publication of anything and everything possible, ended by making it compulsory. As everyone is aware by now, book-publishing and the mass media tend to become even more voracious, demanding an unending supply of raw materials to be transformed into culture-commodities. If the mother of popular literature is mass-production technology, the midwife which gives it birth, and the wet-nurse which suckles it is the 'free enterprise' market-place. But such fostering is not disinterested; since books, movies and TV shows make large profits for the few who 'own' them, even as they put bread and milk into the mouths of many who work for them — including, of course, authors.

What cannot be banned from the market-place, however, which is to say, from wide circulation and, sometimes, financial success, by a self-perpetuating body of reviewers and critics, could, it turned out, be excluded from libraries and classrooms at all school levels. It could, in short, be denied the quasi-immortality bestowed by such critics on the 'Classics', and a small number of Modern works which are in their opinion of equal merit. Sometimes, indeed, it seems as if the self-appointed guardians of culture demand that works which attain market success *pay* for that good luck by being thus banned. Or to put it more circumspectly, institutionalized criticism has sought to identify the 'popularity' it cannot hamper with aesthetic or formal inadequacy, which, presumably, it alone can judge. The touchstones of such judgment have come to be called 'standards': presumably universal or at least long-term values, which prove more often than not the prejudices of a particular class at a particular historical moment. At its worst, therefore, which is to say, at its most shamelessly elitist, such criticism has moved toward the theory that there is an inverse relationship between literary merit and market-place success.

To be sure, certain Romantic, Populist, Democratic and Socialist critics have found it embarrassing to sustain the view that the art-forms preferred by the majority of the people are the least admirable, the least worthy. And to salve their consciences, they have invented the paranoic theory of the corruption of the Innocent Masses by the Degenerate Masters of the Media — agents, presumably, of the ruling economic classes. In fact, however, such 'masters' spend their professional lives in vain pursuit of popular taste, which they not only do not make, but do not even understand — and surely (as anyone who has watched their efforts at first-hand can attest) cannot predict. There is also a condescending corollary to the theory of the Seduction of the Innocent: a corollary which maintains that it is possible through education to purify the taste of the betrayed masses, to deliver them from their bondage to horror, porn and sentimentality, by showing them the 'truth'. In practice, this view amounts to the belief that the people can and should be unbrainwashed, or rather re-brainwashed by enlightened schoolmasters, or the rulers of enlightened states, or their cultural lackeys, into recognizing what is really, *really* good for them — which of course such schoolmasters, rulers and lackeys, have known all along.

It is hard to say who deserves credit for having invented this theory and its corollary, which come to us primarily as nineteenth century products though they somehow persisted until nearly the end of the twentieth, growing ever more untenable and palpably absurd. It is tempting, in a way, to give the credit to Matthew Arnold, re-reading whom recently I decided — son of Israel that I am — to enlist in the ranks of Philistia for the rest of my writing life. But Karl Marx had staked a claim early on in *The Holy Family*, which includes an enraged elitist attack on one of the greatest popular writers of the mid-nineteenth century: a novelist who managed to reach a large working class audience with a hectic mixture of hardcore violence, soft-core pornography, flagrant senti-mentality and Utopian Socialism. I am referring, of course, to Eugène Sue, particularly the Sue of the *Mysteries of Paris*, not yet informed by the followers of Fourier that he was a 'friend of the people'. In his later *Mysteries of the People*, he becomes too explicit, too doctrinaire; but in his early work, he is one with the masses in their inchoate erotic-terrific dreams of liberation.

But if Sue was falsified in his own self-consciousness by the theorizing of the *Phalange*; in the consciousness of his contem-poraries and ours, he was even more drastically falsified by Marx, who taught us first to regard him, and all like him, as purveyors of junk, panderers to the misled masses. What I am trying to say, is that popular literature is not, as a category, a type, a sub-genre, the invention of the authors of the books which we have been taught to believe 'belong' to it, but of certain theorizers after the fact. It exists generically in the perception of elitist critics — or better, perhaps, in their mis-perception, their — usually tendentious, sometimes even deliberate — misapprehension. It will, therefore, cease to exist as a category when we cease to regard it in the way we have been misled into doing. Clearly, what we consider 'serious novels' or 'art novels': works, say, by Henry James or Marcel Proust, Thomas Mann or James Joyce, are indistinguishable, *before the critical act*, from 'best-sellers' or 'popular novels' by Jacqueline Susanne or John D. MacDonald, Conan Doyle or Bram Stoker. Despite peripheral attempts to sort them out before the fact by invidious binding or labelling, by and large, they are bound in the same boards and paper; edited, printed, distributed, advertised and peddled in quite the same way.

Moreover, even if the fashion were to change and universal ghettoization were to be instituted *ab ovo,* they would remain *finally* the same; since they can happen to us, become a part of our consciousness, our vicarious experience, in one way only. We do not have different processes for ingesting works which transmit image, idea and feeling via print or the post-print media, depending on their critical status. We may think back on them differently, but we absorb them in quite the same fashion. How then did we ever come to distinguish one from the other? And more importantly, why did we once (some of us, at least, are now through with all that) ever want to separate out, to classify and rank, not merely what is more skillfully executed from what is less, i.e., the better from the worse; but also what has the loftiest of ambitions from what is humbler in intent, i.e., the high from the low? How finally have we come to believe that 'literature' is divided not just in terms of quality but of kind, which is to say, in terms of status and audience?

Initially, men of goodwill, at least, read or listened to all song and story before thus classifying it. But we have reached a point at which some among us aspire to ghettoize certain writers, certain books, certain whole sub-genres of the novel before reading them. Indeed, in a world where division of labour and delegation of responsibility have been carried to absurd extremes, certain professionals and sub-professionals have been trained to do that job for the rest of us. In the United States, for instance, and elsewhere I suspect, librarians have learned to relegate some books, as they arrive on the order desk to ghettostacks as 'Juveniles', 'Teen-Age Fiction', 'Detective Stories', 'Westerns', 'Science Fiction' — or to a super-Ghetto, locked and guarded, as 'Pornography'. Moreover, judges for our major Fiction Awards, the Pulitzer Prize, for instance, and the National Book awards, are preconditioned to assume, sight unseen, that 'Juveniles' and 'Science Fiction' are simply not to be considered for the major prizes. And, I have been told, the jobbers and wholesalers of books tend to sort out certain disreputable kinds of novels, including Science Fiction, which are not to be sent to 'serious' bookstores: the major distributors and sellers of books. Finally, there are more marginal fictions which do not make it to this level of discrimination, being excluded from even temporary storage and discriminatory display by most American libraries. This ultimately untouchable category includes 'paperback originals' of all kinds, and most notably comic books; though the latter, among children and young adults at least, are probably the most widely read of all narrative forms.

Such generic pre-censorship — or, if that be too strong a term, pejorative pre-classification — provides an easy way out for relatively unsophisticated and fundamentally insecure librarians or bookstore clerks. And who can blame them, trapped as they are in an unworkable system; since even the 'experts', highly educated and well-read critics, find it difficult to indicate the cut-off points on the Gutenberg continuum which separate High from Low or, as certain more ambitious graders of literature were fond of trying to do a decade or two ago (*mea culpa!*) — High from Middle from Low. In the light of all this, it pays to remember that the novel as such was considered by many formalist critics, in the years just after its emergence as a major genre, Pop *per se* — quite like Comic Books or Soap Operas now. And since the promotion of the genre to the ranks of accepted literature, despite the fact that it is quite clearly more closely related to the movies, TV serials and comic books than Poetic Epic or Tragedy, critics have been forced to play ridiculous sorting-out games: distinguishing 'serious novelists' from 'mere entertainers', and 'Best Sellers' from 'Art Novels'.

Such attempts have been compromised by the fact that over and over there have been cases of borderline writers, embarrassingly like what their own times have defined as 'Pop', but endowed with energy and skill, invention and mythopoeic power which will not let them be confined to the limits of any critical ghetto. I am thinking of such stubbornly unclassifiable 'geniuses' (the term itself is an evasion) as Dickens and Twain, Cooper and Balzac, perhaps even Samuel Richardson, father of them all. For the sake of such writers, élitist 'standards' have been bent a little, shame-facedly adjusted or hypocritically ignored, by critics unwilling to abandon either those standards or the writers who challenge them. To have one's cake and eat it too is the choice always of the cowardly or the confused. But some of the critics involved, Samuel Johnson, for instance, that embattled formalist who boldly indulged his perhaps inconsistent taste for Richardson, cannot be so easily dismissed.

Why were they, then, so reluctant to give up categories so clearly unviable? And why, even more distressingly, are some of our critical contemporaries, admirable in other respects, unwilling to do so? The answer lies not in the closed circle of 'aesthetics', but in a larger historical and social overview, which begins by investigating the moment at which modern criticism came into being. If we look hard at the mid-eighteenth century, when it all properly began, it becomes clear to us that the notion of literary standards, along with the emergence of the critic-pedagogues as their official 'enforcers', is a product of the cultural insecurity of the rich merchants and nascent industrialists, who were just then taking over control of society in the Western World. Wielding first economic and then political power seemed to them not quite enough to satisfy hungers bred during their long cultural exclusion. They wanted also to dominate literary culture, as had the ruling classes whom they superseded. They demanded, therefore, first and foremost to be the chief consumers (delegating this function to their wives and daughters) and sustainers (this function they reserved for their male selves) of song and story, which for them had become almost exclusively identified with print and the 'book'. But they desired also to be its judges, the guardians of the 'values' which it embodied and re-enforced.

But this they proved incapable, either in their own right or by delegation to the distaff side, of doing — certainly not with the insouciant self-assurance of the feudal aristocracies who had imposed their taste in this area, at first despite, and later even on and through an established clergy which theoretically despised all 'literature'. Unlike their predecessors, the new ruling classes were born with a sense of insecurity which has since grown indurated rather than being mitigated by time and the habit of command.

They were even, perhaps especially, insecure about the Pop forms which first assumed a central importance with their political rise. The earliest and most notable of these, is of course, the novel itself, which reflected in its archetypal plots the communal dreams of the New Class; and embodied in its very shape and substance, those dreams made paper and ink and boards, a commodity, in short, to be hefted and bought and sold. The incarnate myths of the bourgeoisie are commodities, even as the market-place and technology are its collective unconscious. Yet they did not, could not in the nature of the case, understand on the level of full consciousness the significance of the technology which they controlled, or the new methods of production and distribution which such technology made possible. Yet these were to replace the handcrafted *objets d'art* of the aristocracy with mass-produced and mass-distributed goods; and to transform the economy of culture from one of scarcity to one of plenty.

If the printing-press was, indeed, the first mass-production machine invented by Western society, the modern or bourgeois novel was the first literary genre invented to be produced and reproduced on it. Earlier forms, whether the products of a high minority culture, like Epic, Tragedy and the Lyric, or of folk culture, like fairy tales or ballads, came to lead a second life in print. But the novel was born with and for Gutenberg technology. It has, therefore, changed not superficially but essentially, with every technological change in that area, as well as with every new development in marketing: the invention of stereotyping, the perfection of techniques for making cheap paper, the creation of libraries, private and public. Even the displacement of stagecoach travel by the railroad made a substantial difference in fiction, as men grew accustomed to moving from place to place in an environment which made reading easy, and the Railroad bookstall was developed to satisfy the new need for disposable travel literature. It seems possible at this moment that even as print-technology created the novel, post-print technologies may destroy it; and so Marshall McLuhan, among others, has been insisting. Although his most dire prophecies are clearly not being fulfilled, since even boys and girls continue to read books, sometimes in front of the television screen itself, clearly the novel is being challenged at least, forced to accommodate and adjust by new media which tell tales with greater speed and efficiency to a wider audience than can (apparently) ever learn to read print with real ease. Even among those with Gutenberg skills, their prestige and glamour have been undercut by the electronic media, which transmit speech directly into the ear and images to the eye without the intervention of printed words.

All this, however, was unsuspected by the emergent bourgeoisie, who remained for a long time unaware that insofar as they controlled the technology of print, the machines which reproduced the works of literary culture, they controlled that culture, too. Nor did they suspect that the market-place, which was also in their hands, determined which works of art would persist and be remembered, by winnowing not the 'good' from the 'bad', perhaps, but certainly the more popular from the less. The bourgeoisie were blinded by obsolescent mythologies of Art, which envisaged 'poetry' as the creation of a lonely genius and his Muse, rather than the product of technological man and his machines. Consequently, they thought of literary 'survival', or as they insisted on calling it still, 'immortality', as the result of critical consensus rather than the workings of the market-place. Believing in the division of labour in all fields, they appointed 'experts' to prepare themselves by the study of the Classics, and to tell them (to 'brief' them, we would say these days) whether novels were O.K. in general; and if so, which were more O.K. than others.

Obviously, they did not always take the good advice they sought. Quite often, in fact, they continued to read what their critical mentors had taught them to regard as 'trash' — defiantly in the case of sentimental-pious 'trash', shamefacedly and secretly in the case of pornographic 'trash'. But they did snatch such work from the hands of their children, especially their daughters, when they caught them reading it. In the light of this, it is clear that the function of modern critics and schoolmasters whose subject is literature was from the start rather like that performed by the writers of Etiquette Books, Dictionaries and Grammars. Like the latter, the former responded to the cultural insecurity of the eighteenth century middle classes by providing 'rules' or 'standards' or guides to 'good behaviour'. The new rich wanted to know which fork to pick up; how to spell things 'right'; when, if at all, it was proper to say 'ain't'; and also what books to buy for display in their libraries or on their coffee tables.

At first, the critics had to compete in establishing 'values' or 'standards' in the field of literature with the clergy, who were also assigned by their uncertain masters the task of guiding them right. It was unclear on both sides, and doubly unclear to those caught in the middle, into whose territory literature properly fell, the schoolmaster's or the parson's. Indeed, as long as the critics themselves continued to maintain — borrowing the notion from their pre-Gutenberg predecessors — that literature must 'instruct' as well as 'delight', it proved impossible to separate the domain of Art, in which critics were the 'experts', from that of Prudence, in which the clergy had the final word. And who, in any case, was to mediate between aesthetics and ethics: the critic or the pulpit-moralist?

Since in the hierarchal value system of the bourgeoisie the ethical ranked higher than the aesthetic, it was more than a century before any critic dared confront the power of the church head-on, by asserting the creed of 'art for art's sake'. More typically, critics and pedagogues alike tried instead to beat the moralists at their own game, by dividing all of art along essentially Christian lines into what was Serious, Elevating, Uplifting and of High Moral Purpose, on the one hand; and what was trivial, debasing, vulgar and of no redeeming value, on the other. But such ethical distinctions turned out, to no one's surprise, merely to reinforce distinctions made on presumably aesthetic and formalist grounds, i.e., in the name of Greece and Rome rather than Jerusalem and Galilee. Finally, however, the literary experience confounds moral distinctions, even as it does those based on formal elegance, beauty of structure, precision of language, control of tone, avoidance of sentimentality and cliché or whatever criteria are currently chic. Think of the writers presumably to be excluded from the Canon on ethical grounds who have been smuggled into respectability by bending or adjusting moral 'standards', or simply by lying to oneself or the political guardians of morality, or both. And think especially of how in recent days duplicity has become the rule in courtrooms, where the most eminent literary critics rise to defend banned works ranging from the

Kama Sutra to *Justine* to *Deep Throat*, by claiming for them underlying moral qualities.

Having just seen Shakespeare's *Titus Andronicus* in public performance, and having noted the amoral, indeed anti-social responses in myself and those who sat beside me, I would head the list of such smuggled ethically subversive writers with the name of Shakespeare. But the 'Bard', as his more pious apologists love to call him, has been so successfully 'kidnapped' by the forces of respectability that I will pass him by; urging the reader interested in prudential questions in the realm of art to reflect instead on still unredeemed and perhaps unredeemable figures like the Marquis de Sade, Sacher-Masoch, Cleland, De la Clos, Jean Genet and Hubert Selby, Jr. Such a tack would make clear that the key to the whole question lies in pornography, especially that Porn which treats centrally, sometimes even obsessively, deviant or sado-masochistic sex; the official name of the latter coming of course from two of our selected list of subversive writers. Such works represent the very pole of Pop — Pop at its most disreputable, disturbing, and unredeemable.

To them I shall return in conclusion; but first I must explore a little a profound difference between our own age and that in which criticism was born; the well-advertised Death of God and the slow erosion of Christian morality, which has debouched in the even better advertised New Sexual Morality of the dying twentieth century. Oddly enough (and this unpredictable event casts real light on the subject) those developments have not served to mitigate the conflict between Art and Prudence, or to undercut the distinction between Belles Lettres and Pop. On the contrary, in their initial stages at least, they tended rather to exacerbate the former and to reinforce the latter, as is exemplified very clearly by the line which runs from Matthew Arnold to Henry James and D.H. Lawrence to F.R. Leavis. They are, despite their disagreements on other fronts, crypto-Puritans all of them: convinced that with the death of traditional religion, Art in general and Literature in particular had to become the Scriptures of a New Faith, the Culture Religion. And to do so, they taught each in his own way, it had to subscribe to 'High Seriousness' and to be measured by rigorous 'Standards'.

Such standards were entrusted to a priestly brotherhood of critics, who feeling themselves the sole legitimate heirs of both the lay and clerical taste-makers of the past, sought to establish a New Canon, which would exclude philistine, vulgar, trivial or otherwise heretical stuff, even when, or rather especially when it was enjoyed by the unwary many. What won their supreme contempt, however, was the counter-Canon sponsored by a naive counter-Clergy, unaware that their orthodox God was dead, and the ethics of bourgeois-sentimental Christianity along with him. Only through the exponents of the Higher Morality of Art did the true apostolic succession descend. Only they could loose and bind under the New Dispensation.

In America, the Arnoldian line was even more unabashedly élitist and genteel; for it represented, in a land which had boasted no other aristocracies before it, an attempt to define one based solely on being at ease in the world of High Culture. And it found itself from the start confronting a less accommodating bourgeoisie in the form of its own literal as well as metaphorical fathers: ministers or Senators or merchants. I am alluding, of course, to the line of descent which runs from Arnold through Paul Elmore More to T.S. Eliot to Cleanth Brooks and other genteel Fascists of Southern origin. Furthermore, their epigones of the second and third generation, who have not been exposed from birth to the reactionary mythology of the South — by and large Eastern and urban in origin, the sons or grandsons of European working class or petty-bourgeois Jews, who have made it or failed trying — such epigones sought to achieve on the level of culture the sort of success their immediate forebears had yearned for in the economic and social arena. Such culture-climbers found the University a congenial place in which to establish themselves, by their ability to distinguish between Art and pseudo-Art, Belles Lettres and junk, Serious Literature and the crap their fathers and mothers continued to read. Moving to ever higher levels of exclusivism, they devoted their lives to the explication of notably obscure works in terms even less available to the mass audience than those texts themselves. It was at this point that obscurity, or at least high density and opacity tended to become — along with symbolism, irony and the rest — the accepted hallmarks of High Art: touchstones for judging the works of the past, and guides for producing new works worthy of classroom exposition in the future.

With the second and third generation of 'New Critics', at any rate, élitist criticism was almost totally academicized in the United States; which is to say, the University had become the chief, almost the sole guardian of 'taste' and 'Standards'. This meant the establishment, *de facto* at least, of a new definition of both High and Popular Literature. The term 'literature' came to be used exclusively for proper or serious books, others being condescendingly labelled 'para-literature', as if they were abortive or failed attempts at achieving a status to which often they clearly did not aspire. But there was a certain destructive circularity in the new definition of 'literature' as what was taught in University classes in Literature; since what was taught in those classes was, presumably, 'literature' to begin with, i.e., what had been taught in earlier classes on the subject. But how did it all start, and when will it end?

Even after the recent loss of prestige by the old 'New Criticism', our Universities, especially in their Departments of Literature, continue to function as the last bastions of élitism; finding newer, more fashionable versions of formalism to justify the hierarchal ranking of books. What has seemed particularly attractive has been the latest embodiment of French Neo-Classicism called 'Structuralism', which flourishes even in the publicly supported institution of Mass Higher Education in America, both in the politically Rightist form it has assumed passing through Johns Hopkins — and in the Leftist version, which comes to us directly from Vincennes and the Collège de France. It seemed quite proper that critical élitism and nostalgic Southern Agrarianism be linked. But it is more than a little disconcerting to find hierarchal formalism allied to Marxism in currently chic *gauchiste* forms.

Yet from the start, as I have already indicated, Marxism proved to be profoundly, essentially élitist in the realm of art. Indeed, all ideologies which presume man to be a rational animal, whether actually or potentially, end up in such a trap; for to such ideologies art seems to play an ambiguous, if not a downright disruptive role in the state. It is all art which they fear, and, indeed, at an earlier stage of things, they concentrated their fire on 'Highbrow' or 'Avant-Garde' or 'Experimental' art, i.e., élitist art in its modernist phase. More recently however, as Modernism has been tamed, the attack has shifted (think of the war against 'pornography' in the United States, and that against 'Science Fiction' in the Soviet Union) to the more vulnerable and unredeemably subversive popular arts; which is to say, art untamed, uncastrated, unpurified — anarchic and dionysiac, vulgar, obscene and blasphemous; To all 'rational' believers in Law and Order, whether 'Red' or 'White', 'East' or 'West', the enemy is no longer *Ulysses* or the *Wasteland* but *Deep Throat* and *Beyond the Valley of the Dolls*; no longer surreal chain poems or *The Andalusian Dog*, but comic books, soap-operas and TV commercials.

The need to distinguish between High Literature and Low, and to denigrate or ban the latter persists beyond the historical moment which gave it birth, because it is based on a human response which existed before that moment, and which may cease only with the disappearance of man. Superficially it may seem the creation of an age characterized by the dominance of the bourgeoisie and the development of mass-production, mass-distribution and mass-communications. But essentially it represents, in a new form, the ancient distrust, fear, even hatred of the arts in general and literature in particular. That feeling has, in all ages since the invention of speech, plagued men who are ill at ease with their animal inheritance, the impulsive or irrational aspects of their own psyches; and it has assumed special virulence ever since the Gutenberg Revolution. For a while, however, it looked as if a compromise had been reached between haters of literature and its writers. Even mad, bad poetry, which, as utopian reformers and rationalists have been telling us ever since Plato, 'waters the emotions', seemed under control at last. First in Ancient Greece, and then again in post-Medieval Europe, poets — instructed by philosophy and theology — paid lip service at least to the principle of Law and Order, to which their craft is essentially antithetical. Like 'good niggers', they had 'learned their place': their proper function in the large polity, which is, of course, to instruct and delight; and especially to instruct delightfully those not yet mature enough for grimmer forms of mental discipline.

Since nothing is forbidden to poetry, it remains free, of course, to instruct and delight *among other things.* And sometimes it seems, in fact, to perform primarily these two socially desirable tasks,·though not always as decorously as schoolmasters and critics are deceived into believing. Behind the obsequious smile of the 'good nigger' so patiently striving to please 'ole massa', that is to say, lies the subversive grin of the mocker. Certainly, instruction and delight are not the exclusive or essential functions of literature, as even some dissenting élitist artists have been driven to insist. When, however, high art in pursuit of other ends, goes Dada, it is forced to learn from the popular arts: Krazy Kat or Charlie Chaplin, the Marx Brothers or the makers of soup-can labels. Indeed, it is the so-called 'weaknesses' of Pop which make for its strength in this area; since it is essentially unable either to instruct or delight: being, on the one hand, notably weak in *ethos* and *dianoia*, and on the other, not very strong in *architektonike.* Even in the realm of Aristotelian *mimesis*, it is likely to be less than adequate; since it prefers fantasy to the representation of our shared human lot, either as it is or as it ideally should be.

Yet Popular Literature moves us all the same, both those of us who also respond to High Literature and those of us who subsist entirely on it. Indeed it may, by this very token, move us all the more, touching levels of response deeper and more archaic than those which abide distinctions between instruction and delight, much less the division into High and Low. If we are interested in *how* it moves us — and how, presumably, *all* literature moves us beyond or beside or below the level of social utility — it will repay us to look briefly at three forms: genres or sub-genres of Popular Literature, of which élitist critics remain distrustful or downright contemptuous, though they have traditionally been favourites of the mass audience. These are:

1. Sentimental Literature, particularly as it has developed from

novels written by the first women imitators of Samuel Richardson, down through such late nineteenth century bestsellers as *The Lamplighter* and *The Wide, Wide World*, to present-day 'soaps', the daytime serials on television;

2. Horror Literature from, say, M.G. Lewis's *The Monk*, down through *Varney, The Vampire, Frankenstein, Dr Jekyll and Mr Hyde* and *Dracula*, to the Horror Comics and *The Rocky Horror Show* of this moment;

3. Classic Pornography from Cleland and the Marquis de Sade, to Frank Harris, *The Story of O* and *Fritz the Cat.*

It is possible, of course, to combine all three, as they are combined in the Kung Fu movies starring Bruce Lee; such a film, for instance, as *Fist of Fury*, in which the single erotic scene is clearly a last-minute addition to make sure that the whole range of popular taste is satisfied. Moreover, there is a real sense in which all three of these forms can be regarded as varieties of pornography or titillation-literature: handkerchiefly or female-oriented porn, erotic or male-oriented porn, and sado-masochistic, or universally appealing porn. The last can also be thought of as juvenile-oriented porn; but this amounts perhaps to saying 'universal', since almost everyone is willing to indulge the child in himself, while many are wary about giving rein to what persists of the other sex in their male or female bodies. Terror, indeed, seems sometimes the only form capable of crossing all conventional role boundaries: not only generational and sexual, but ethnic as well (I have seen black and white kids, along with adults of all hues and genders, responding to Bruce Lee movies), and class lines, too. But some types of erotica seem limited in appeal not just because they represent, say, the fantasies of men rather than women; but because they appeal only to readers of a certain social status and educational level — like limericks, for instance, which are apparently an exclusively bourgeois form.

In any case, the pornographic classification seems appropriate in the light of the fact that all three sub-genres aim at 'watering the emotions', rather than purifying or purging them by way of the famous Aristotelian process of 'catharsis'. Indeed, the whole baffling and unsatisfactory theory of catharsis seems to me at this point a pious fraud perpetrated by the dutiful son of a doctor; drawing on the terminology of his father's socially acceptable craft, in order to justify his own shameful taste for what seemed to more serious thinkers of his time exactly what pop literature seems to their opposite numbers in ours. Greek Tragedy, as a matter of fact, aimed at evoking precisely the responses stirred by Sentimental and Horror Porn in all ages, responses which Aristotle called honorifically 'pity and terror'; though Athens of the Golden Age banned the portrayal of sexually exciting scenes from the stage — presumably because they could not be ethically neutralized, like those which stir shudders or tears, even in a ritual setting.

For the sake of the popular drama which he loved as I love soap-operas, Aristotle found it strategic to pretend that the thrill of tragedy and the release of comedy could be subsumed under the rubric of instruction and delight. In our era, however, it seems advisable to readjust the balance by insisting that the plays of Sophocles and Euripides, quite like the three forms of pornography I am considering, at their most effective, cause the audience to get out of control, 'out of their heads', as the modern phrase has it. If such works teach us anything it is *not* to be wise; and if they provide us with pleasure by making us blubber, shiver or sustain an erection, it is a pleasure on the verge of pain. We need, therefore, another term than catharsis to say how we are moved, a term less anal and more erotic; for whatever Aristotle may have urged in his age of genital repression, metaphors of a child on the potty (or even at the mirror) will not do for us. We need to redefine literature in terms of images based on the aspiration of the soul for the divine and the body for other bodies.

Such images are to be found in the single surviving work of one we call 'Longinus', though that is not his name: in an essay we call 'On the Sublime', though the last word is a misleading translation, which allowed 'Longinus' to be co-opted and compromised by eighteenth century formalists. That perhaps-Christian critic used the word *ekstasis* to describe the effect not of popular or debased art alone; but of all art at its peak moments — from the tag 'Let there be light and there was light' in the Scriptures of the barbarous Hebrews, to the most precious poetry of the enlightened Greeks. And what is incumbent on us now, it seems to me as I reach the end of definition and move on to advocacy, is to take a cue from Longinus by creating an approach to literature which will if not quite abandon, at least drastically downgrade both Ethics and Aesthetics in favour of 'Ecstatics'.

Once we have made *ekstasis* rather than instruction and delight the center of critical analysis and evaluation, we will find ourselves speaking less of theme and purport, structure and texture, ideology and significance, irony and symbolism, and more of myth, fable, archetype, fantasy, magic, and wonder. And certainly, when we have granted that the essential function of story and song is to release us temporarily from the limits of rationality, the boundaries of the ego and the burden of consciousness, by creating a moment of privileged insanity, compatible with waking awareness as the analogous experience of dreaming or 'tripping out' are not, we will be out of the trap; delivered at long last from the indignity of having to condescend publicly to works we privately relish; and relieved of the obligation to define, as I began by doing in this essay, distinctions which were from the start delusive and unreal.

The Implications of Cultural Uniformity

MARSHALL McLUHAN

> *How pierceful grows the hazy*
> *yon,*
> *How myrtle petalled thou;*
> *For Spring hath sprung the*
> *cyclotron:*
> *How high browse thou, brown*
> *cow?*
>
> (Walt Kelly)

An old advertisement, long popular in the United States proclaimed: 'You feel better satisfied when you use well known brands.' If this pronouncement applies to the ordinary person, does it follow that a member of the élite would feel better satisfied when he used unknown brands? It might be a very complex inquiry to discover what kinds of power and satisfaction are 'put on' whenever we assume any of the 'masks' of popular language or culture. A popular form from one context may suddenly acquire a very élite quality in a different context. Conventional erudition might well astound a group of commercial salesmen, while the same lore would be a 'drag' in an academic group.

The problem of 'cultural uniformity' has not the same meaning now, under conditions of rapid movement and change, as it had in the slower industrial world of the nineteenth century. In terms of the present exposure to environments of electric information, stereotypes of many sorts and conditions are simultaneously available to a wide diversity of cultures. The question arises, then, whether the same figure, say Coca-Cola, can be considered as 'uniform' when it is set in interplay with totally divergent *grounds* from China to Peru? The user is always the content, at least in the traditional Aristotelian view that the 'cognitive agent itself becomes and is the thing known'. The structure of perception may come from the thing known, but the experience and the satisfactions which the structure yields, naturally depend upon the user. The 'meaning' of anything, on the other hand, is the way in which it relates to the user; and this fact ensures that a high degree of chaos and confusion will always result from a wide diversity of users. Thus, it might be suggested that the use of American stereotypes in the United Kingdom yields a widely different experience and 'meaning' from the use of the same stereotypes or *figures* in their American *ground*. The interplay between the *figure* and the *ground* will produce a wide range of different effects for the users, even when the same *figure* is repeated in the same *ground*.

One of the conflicts of a progressive and rapidly changing world concerns the use of surrounding services which have been obsolesced by daily innovations and discoveries. A vast new industry has been born from this conflict, and its name is 'Camp', and its motto is: 'Throw something lovely away today. Help beautify junkyards'. Despite the grotesque aspect of 'Camp' as the incessant revival of that which has scarcely had a chance to register its appearance or existence, it has already been itself obsolesced by the popular technology of the video replay. The instant replay, available mainly to the audiences of sporting events, offers, as it were, the meaning minus the experience, reversing Mr Eliot's observation that 'we had the experience but missed the meaning'. The instant replay is the *meaning* in that it is less concerned with the input of experience than with the process of perception. The instant replay, indeed, offers not just cognition but re-cognition, and leads the mind to the world of pattern recognition, to aftersight and foresight.

I am going to return to my suggestion that the stereotypes of American culture have a very different character and quality from their users in different cultures. To illustrate this fact, I propose to use the icon or image of the American motor car. It was while thinking about some of the differences between the United Kingdom and the United States that I encountered one very large difference in preferences of spatial orientation between the UK and the USA. Americans, for example, will not tolerate advertising in theatre or cinema. One way of putting it, is to say that North Americans go outside to be alone, and go inside to be with people. There is little or no privacy in the American home. This massive yet subliminal stereotype of uniform idiosyncrasy in North American behaviour and preference, is in sharp contrast with the United Kingdom and European stereotype of going outside to socialize and going inside to be alone. North Americans are little inclined to go outside to socialize or to converse; and at the theatre or at the cinema or at a night club, they expect to be alone with their 'dates'. Any intrusion of public advertisement is as unwelcome to North Americans when they are outside, as to Europeans when they are inside. The European, on the other hand, will accept ads in theatres and cinemas but resist them on radio and TV. The North American will tolerate ads at home on radio and TV which he will not permit in the theatre or cinema. So far as one can track down reasons for the North American attitude to the outside as private, it seems to come to rest at the door of the initial approach to the North American wilderness as an enemy to be tamed and subdued. From the beginning, the North American settlers had technologies which prompted a kind of 'crash programming' of the continent. Always going outside to be lonely hunters or explorers, and going inside for protection and security, seems to have established a massive syndrome of spatial and psychic attitudes which are unlike those of other continents.

The North American's role as 'settler', determined to impose his private will on Nature by means of advanced technology, may have created his habit of going outside to be a self-reliant and lonely hunter, which persists in the American design and use of the motor car for privacy, to this day. The American car is the main embodiment of this extrovert attitude that constitutes the Americans as a 'lonely crowd', deeply resistant and resentful towards all forms of public transit, even when they use them.

D.H. Lawrence, in his introduction to Edward Dahlberg's *Bottom Dogs* may well have misread the entire American attitude to the out of doors and to social life, by imposing his British idea of uniformity on the American. He read the American need for privacy when out of doors as a metaphysical revulsion from human contact as such, completely unaware of the *figure-ground* relationship whereby the American finds indoors the warmth and sociability which the European cultivates outside the home. It is true that Lawrence perceived the American as *figure* against the *ground* of a vast and recalcitrant continent. However, Lawrence transferred his British feeling for inner and outer spaces to a world which long before had radically reversed the older use and meaning of these forms:

'This is, roughly, the American position today, as it was the position of the Red Indian when the white man came, and of the Aztec and of the Peruvian. So far as we can make out, neither Redskin nor Aztec nor Inca had any conception of a "good" god. They conceived of implacable, indomitable Powers, which is very different. And that seems to me the essential American position today. Of course the white American believes that man should behave in a kind of benevolent manner. But this is a social belief and a social gesture, rather than an individual flow. The flow from the heart, the warmth of fellow-feeling which has animated Europe and been the best of her humanity, individual, spontaneous, flowing in thousands of little passionate currents often conflicting, this seems unable to persist on the American soil.

Instead you get the social creed of benevolence and uniformity, a mass *will*, and an inward individual retraction, an isolation, an amorphous separateness like grains of sand, each grain isolated upon its own will, its own indomitableness, its own implacability, its own unyielding, yet heaped together with all the other grains. This makes the American mass the easiest mass in the world to rouse, to move. And probably, under a long stress, it would make it the most difficult mass in the world to hold together.'[1]

In a word, Lawrence assumes that the privacy and solitariness of the American when out of doors, or when he is away from his home, would proclaim that 'they smell in each other's nostrils'. Extroversion, he failed to see, is the mode of American privacy, not the American mode of society. The American extrovert is not trying to be sociable, but private, Prufrock style.

In the same way, the source of the American cult of hygiene and the American horror of halitosis and the acceptance of uniformity, wherever it exists, is the extension of merely *visual* values to every facet of the environment. On the other hand, the great surge of uniformity and social hostility which Lawrence deplored in all the democracies of his time, 'this repulsion from the physical neighbour that is now coming up in the consciousness of the great democracies in England, America, Germany' — this quality of avoidance and non-involvement came at the end of the great industrial and consumer world and just when the electric age began to dominate and to diminish the private person and to programme our experience. It is a matter of personal annihilation which appears as thematic in Bunuel's film *The Discreet Charm of the Bourgeoisie.* All of the private rituals of the upper middle class are plausibly portrayed by Bunuel as continually interrupted by exterior powers from the new environment. The middle class had devised an exclusive world of visual, which is to say, continuous and connected activities and values, which have become quite inconsistent with the instantaneous and discontinuous forms of the electric service environment. The America which D.H. Lawrence deplores is the one that carried the industrial production rationale, and the consumer values of nineteenth century England, to an ultimate destiny of uniformity and collapse; for the new personal involvement of the electric age is indeed the nemesis of American visual values, for these latter had fostered detachment and remoteness.

Today, in America has arisen the question of the quality of the consumer way of life. Among the TV generation values of spontaneity and diversity, and the demand for personal involvement in role-playing rather than mere job-holding have begun to threaten the

American way of life. Nothing has been more representative of the American response to the new age of Radio and TV than the development of Jazz and Rock music. It is no accident that the sounds of both Jazz and Rock originated in the American south; for without the hidden *ground* of 'Elizabethan' English in the oral tradition of the American south, there could be no Jazz or Rock. I am going to suggest that the indispensable condition of all music is speech. It is the spoken word in which the *figures* of song and dance find their *ground.* Moreover, I would like to suggest that changing sounds and rhythms of the environment in a highly technological age enter the common speech in undeveloped areas and emerge as popular music for the metropolis. Without this process of trans-formation, it might well be that we could not live with our technologies. What I am trying to convey is that the complementary responses of an intensely visual and mechanized culture to the electric age was an oral and musical response. The visual uniformity of the industrial world was succeeded by the spontaneity of the electric and acoustic world.

There is a striking observation about the American countenance that may well be related to the American quest for private identity outside the home. It is in *The Dyer's Hand* where W.H. Auden describes a long familiar situation which is changing rapidly today. He cites Henry James's 'so much countenance and so little face' by way of epigraph, and proceeds to develop the theme of the American mask:

'Every European visitor to the United States is struck by the comparative rarity of what he would call a face, by the frequency of men and women who look like elderly babies. If he stays in the States for any length of time, he will learn that this cannot be put down to a lack of sensibility — the American feels the joys and sufferings of human life as keenly as anybody else. The only plausible explanation I can find lies in his different attitude to the past. To have a face, in the European sense of the word, it would seem that one must not only enjoy and suffer but also desire to preserve the memory of even the most humiliating and unpleasant experiences of the past.

More than any other people, perhaps, the Americans obey the scriptural injunction: "Let the dead bury their dead."

When I consider others I can easily believe that their bodies express their personalities, and that the two are inseparable. But it is impossible for me not to feel that my body is other than I, that I inhabit it like a house, and that my face is a mask which, with or without my consent, conceals my real nature from others.

It is impossible consciously to approach a mirror without composing or "making" a special face, and if we catch sight of our reflection unawares we rarely recognize ourselves. I cannot read my face in the mirror because I am already obvious to myself.

The image of myself which I try to create in my own mind in order that I may love myself is very different from the image which I try to create in the minds of others in order that they may love me.'[2]

When the American goes outside to be alone, he does not put on either a visual mask, a costume or a vocal dress, but speaks with his private voice. Elsewhere, it is normal, in socializing, for speakers to use some sort of 'standard' speech. Not so in America. The need to use a merely private and untrained speaking voice is as deeply engrained as the habit of the unschooled and unrecording countenance, so that the American has great difficulty in 'putting on' any sort of audience. It is much easier for him to put on a microphone, or a camera, than a public. And it is the involuntary insistence on the private voice and the private face that accounts for the absence of social caste or class in America.

As popular humour soothes multitudinous abrasions in daily life, popular arts serve to tune the sensibilities to new degrees of environmental tolerance. A popular phrase among the hippies was 'Turn on, Tune in, Drop out', indicating a process of confrontation, resolution and rejection of environmental pressures. In *Man's Presumptuous Brain* A.T.W. Simeons points to a great gap in the human nervous equipment that may well serve as a comment on the hippie phrase:

'In man's pre-human ancestors the close and harmonious co-ordination of cortex and brain-stem was a highly satisfactory means of assuring survival and evolutionary prosperity, as it still is in all wild-living mammals. But when, about half a million years ago, man began very slowly to embark upon the road to cultural advance, an entirely new situation arose. The use of implements and the control of fire introduced artifacts of which the cortex could avail itself for purposes of living. These artifacts had no relationship whatever to the organization of the body and could, therefore, not be integrated into the functioning of the brain-stem.'[3]

Man's new artifacts of speech, clothing, and weapons changed his relation to his environment and changed the environment itself. However, man's responses to his humanly modified environment were seldom adequate:

'The brain-stem's great body-regulating centre, the diencephalon, continued to function just as if the artifacts were non-existent. But as the diencephalon is also the organ in which instincts are generated, the earliest humans found themselves faced with a very old problem in a new garb. Their instinctive behaviour ceased to be appropriate in the new situations which the cortex created by using artifacts. Just as in the pre-mammalian reptiles the new environment in the trees rendered many ancient reflexes pointless, the new artificial environment which man began to build for himself at the dawn of culture made many of his animal reflexes useless.'[4]

The uniformity of the new man-shaped environments engendered many irrelevant reactions to 'sensory messages that no longer called for a bodily state of emergency. . . . Ancient dangers that artifacts rendered harmless . . . put the diencephalon in a state of alarm.' These blind panic reactions led to a censorship which 'began to be applied to the reactions themselves. . . . This meant that instincts and bodily reactions thereto could be operating without any conscious knowledge of the fact, whenever there were cultural reasons for repressing them.' This subliminal strategy or 'second censorship' is the one which seems to be employed in pushing unwelcome or inconvenient perceptions down into an unconscious mode of awareness. William Empson has described the role of the semi-conscious navigator between worlds, in his 'Arachne' which opens:

> 'Twixt devil and deep sea, man hacks his caves;
> Birth, death; one, many; what is true, and seems;
> Earth's vast hot iron, cold space's empty waves:
>
> King spider, walks the velvet roof of streams:
> Must bird and fish, must god and beast avoid:
> Dance, like nine angels, on pin-point extremes.
>
> His gleaming bubble between void and void,
> Tribe-membrane, that by mutual tension stands,
> Earth's surface film, is at a breath destroyed.'[5]

Finnegans Wake is very much concerned with the resonance in the 'tribal membrane' and the drama among the instincts and the artifacts of language and technology, leading to the awareness of the electric role in 'waking' or retrieving the old tribal man. The role of art, as separate from the service/disservice environments created by technology, may well be to bridge the million year gap between the end of evolution and the take-over by the environments created by human artifacts. The function of art in re-tuning jangled sensory modalities that have been phased out by innovations, has steadily gained recognition in the past century. The crucial function of art for social conduct raises almost as many hackles as the moralist does when enjoining uniformity. St. Paul in Philippians 1:27 exhorts them to uniformity: 'That ye stand fast in one spirit, with one mind, striving together for the faith of the gospel'. This passage can remind us that uniformity gets most of its pejorative meanings from specialism and fragmentariness. That is to say, superficial uniformities of the parade ground or the assembly line or the press or pornography, depend upon some human feature or aspect in isolation from context or *ground.* Pornography, for example, is only possible in highly specialist and fragmented communities, losing all interest and appeal where deeper integrities and awareness are permitted.

Uniformity, then, can be considered as a trivial form of integrity. In the same way, the moralistic approach to problems of communication tends to stress the fragmentary aspects of the 'content'. The moralist will attack the world of advertising as 'manipulating' people, ignoring the fact that the media of print and photography and broadcasting to say nothing of the mother-tongues, have profoundly altered the perceptions and sensibilities of our world without any showing of accountability to anybody. The moralist, in relation to the media, is well indicated in the old rhyme:

> 'You hang the thief
> Who steals the goose from off the Common,
> But leave the larger felon loose,
> Who steals the Common from the goose.'

While screaming 'Stop thief!', the moralist is distracted from the larger felonies. Indeed, the moralist is inclined to thrust into his subliminal world the larger issues which do not lend themselves to specialized scoriations.

The role of art may be to tune the human senses and faculties in new strategies of relevance; without which tuning and re-programming by the arts, man becomes a robot. That is, he becomes 'adjusted' and sinks into the lethargy that Dean Swift saw as the bane of the stereotype and uniformity. The fact that the stereotype may produce the somnambule rather than an alert, critical intelligence, need not conceal the value and function of the world of the stereotype as one of inexhaustible resource and corporate perception.

T.S. Eliot spent much of his life exploring the means of 'up-dating' the human sensibility. Sometimes he mentioned the situation with regard to which the up-dating of sensibility and language were to take place, as when he spoke of the sounds of the typewriter and the influence of the internal combustion engine on changing poetic metres. It is in his essay on 'American Literature and Language' that he makes an explicit declaration in this matter. He discussed innovation and imitation, noting that: 'A true disciple is impressed by what his master has to say, and *consequently* by his way of saying it; an imitator − I might say, a borrower − is impressed chiefly by the way the master said it. If he manages to mimic his master well enough, he may succeed even in disguising from himself the fact that he has nothing to say.' It is in this context that he proceeds to the matter of 'up-dating':

'It is possible, on the other hand, that the influence of Mark Twain may prove to have been considerable. If so, it is for this reason: that Twain, at least in *Huckleberry Finn*, reveals himself to be one of those writers, of whom there are not a great many in any literature, who have discovered a new way of writing, valid not only for themselves but for others, I should place him, in this respect, even with Dryden and Swift, as one of those rare writers who have brought their language up to date, and in so doing, "purified the dialect of the tribe".'[6]

The world in reference to which Dryden and Swift 'up-dated' the English language was the new and intensely visual one of Gutenberg and Copernicus and Newton. The 'up-dating' process involved the shedding of the glories of Baroque rhetoric in favour of a direct colloquial gesture; and the new world in reference to which Mark Twain 'purified' the English language was the world of the railway and the telegraph and the steamboat. Mark Twain's twang and slang and visceral gesture went with a large mythic pattern, remote from the urbanity of eighteenth century logos. At high speeds of information, visual awareness yields to acoustic involvement in the world of the simultaneous and of the 'auditory imagination'. Indeed, the entire work of Pound, Eliot, Joyce and Yeats testifies to a recovery of acoustic structures of inclusive awareness, while much of the critical scholarship of our time relates to the retrieval of acoustic structures of knowledge and experience which are also attested to in the world of Jazz and Rock. Nothing could be more explicit or relevant in this regard than Eric Havelock's *Preface to Plato*, or Lain Entralgo's *Therapy of the Word in Pagan Antiquity*, or Parry and Lord's *A Singer of Tales*.

A major development in the physics of this century is the discovery that the chemical and physical bond of matter is not the connection but the 'resonant interval'. This same discovery was central to the work of the symbolists for whom the collage and the mosaic superseded narrative structures. Eliot's well-known review of *Ulysses* specifies this structural form:

'In using the myth, in manipulating a continuous parallel between contemporaneity and antiquity, Mr. Joyce is pursuing a method which others must pursue after him. They will not be imitators, any more than the scientist who uses the discoveries of an Einstein in pursuing his own, independent, further investigations. It is simply a way of controlling, of ordering, of giving a shape and significance to the immense panorama of futility and anarchy which is contemporary history.'[7]

Mr Eliot is here describing the acoustic and resonant method used in all of his own work. Yeats had made use of the same discovery earlier and describes it in his comments on 'The Emotion of Multitude'!

'I have been thinking a good deal about plays lately, and have been wondering why I dislike the clear and logical construction which seems necessary if one is to succeed on the modern stage. It came into my head the other day that this construction, which all the world has learnt from France, has everything of high literature except the emotion of multitude. The Greek drama has got the emotion of multitude from its chorus, which called up famous sorrows, even all the gods and all heroes, to witness, as it were, some well-ordered fable, some action separated but for this from all but itself. The French play delights in the well-ordered fable, but by leaving out the chorus it has created an art where poetry and imagination, always the children of far-off multitudinous things, must of necessity grow less important than the mere will. This is why, I said to myself, French dramatic poetry is so often rhetorical, for what is rhetoric but the will trying to do the work of the imagination? The Shakespearian drama gets the emotion of multitude out of the sub-plot which copies the main plot, much as a shadow upon the wall copies one's body in the firelight. We think of *King Lear* less as the history of one man and his sorrows than as the history of a whole evil time. Lear's shadow is in Gloucester, who also has ungrateful children, and the mind goes on imagining other shadows, shadow beyond shadow, till it has pictured the world. In *Hamlet*, one hardly notices, so subtly is the web woven, that the murder of Hamlet's father and the sorrow of Hamlet are shadowed in the lives of Fortinbras and Ophelia and Laertes, whose fathers, too, have been killed. It is so in all the plays, or in all but all, and very commonly the sub-plot is the main plot working itself out in more ordinary men and women, and so doubly calling up before us the image of multitude. Ibsen and Maeterlinck have, on the other hand, created a new form, for they get multitude from the wild duck in the attic, or from the crown at the bottom of the fountain, vague symbols that set the mind wandering from idea to idea, emotion to emotion. Indeed, all the great masters have understood that there cannot be great art without the little limited life of the fable, which is always the better the simpler it is, and the rich, far-wandering, many-imaged life of the half-seen world beyond it. There are some who understand that the simple unmysterious things living as in a clear noon light are of the nature of the sun, and that vague, many-imaged things have in them the strength of the moon. Did not the Egyptian carve it on emerald that all living things have the sun for father and the moon for mother, and has it not been said that a man of genius takes the most after his mother?'[8]

This account of the parallel structure without connections is very helpful in understanding the role of the popular arts as a parallel or counter-culture to the establishment of any time. Yeats here explains why it is possible for extraordinary effects to be attained by quite trivial themes and gestures. The tendency of the establishment is also to look for the significant in the manifest *figure* rather than in the inconsiderable *ground*. Shakespeare's double plots permitted the most trite and popular forms of his time to achieve unexpected intensities.

It should not be surprising to discover that underlying any *figure* of cultural uniformity there might well be a *ground* of great diversity and discontinuity. However, before having a look at this possibility, I should like to point out the obvious uses of uniformity, whether in taps and plumbing, or in words and speech. Coherence and ordinary viability depend upon the maintenance of a great field of clichés and stereotypes, and there would be little satisfaction in confronting a hardware world of plumbing in which each situation presented unique and ingenious designs which required great attention before they could be made to perform. When a machine breaks down, there is, of course, the great advantage of study and discovery which ensues, and the same is true in various ways with the uses of language. If machines yield the secrets of their construction only as the result of breakdown, it is possible to discern the same principle at work in language and society. At the opening of their work *The Human Nature Industry*, Ward Cannel and June Macklin canvass the theme of the 'Word-of-the-Year'.[9] Among the qualities which characterize the Word-of-the-Year 'is that it be used by the people who tell it like it is'. The word for 1968 was 'relevant', and 'the word was very popular so it was held over for another big year'. The function of the Word-of-the-Year 'is that it make some order out of the disarray and disrepair in the human condition, or at least indicate what should be fixed first'. The fact that many of these words have a career of twelve months is somewhat more mysterious than the fact that 'a Word's career is over when it falls into the hands of management (1938) and is either merchandized or measured. . . . By the time a Word gets in, it is already on the way out'.

The dynamics observed here concerning the Word-of-the-Year as a principle of uniformity and coherence in the flux of verbal fashions, extends also to many other social patterns. For example, *Le Défi Américain* (Servan-Schreiber) was a popular book just at the moment when American industrial and managerial procedures had reached a moment of obsolescence and reversal, and *The Lonely Crowd* by David Riesman and others, was a study of 'the changing American character' just at the moment when the lonely, extrovert American was beginning his 'inner trip' and his retreat from goals and objectives under the impact of TV. My own book *The Mechanical Bride* took as theme 'the Love Goddess Assembly Line' with the car as bride, just when the prior American economy and culture was altering its stress from industrial hardware to the world of design and software. In the same way, the 'Women's Liberation' movement appears as a struggle to attain masculine jobs and status, just when the entire organisation chart of specialised jobs is dissolving into complex role-playing. For America, the electronic revolution from industrial products and consumerism to information and custom-made services, is a reversal of the entire way of life, with goals and directions suddenly yielding to roles and *figures*. America has found the paths of industrial uniformity and continuity no longer to its taste. Living in a new environment of instant electric information has shifted American attention from specific goals to the cognitive thrills of pattern recognition, a change most obviously manifested in the TV service of the instant replay. The same pattern of reversal in the transition from the industrial to the electric age appears in the role of Sputnik (1957) in placing the planet inside a man-made environment.

B.J. Muller-Thym, the well-known analyst of management procedures in the United States, pointed out years ago that the electric speed of information movement reversed the pattern of mass production into the custom-made:

'B.J. Muller-Thym was historically among the first to note that the form intrinsic in automation ultimately is not standardization but variety, because all mechanical processes with variable dimensions can be programmed by tape to manufacture a customized product, where every changeable item can be tailored precisely to the buyer's specifications. Muller-Thym's favourite example is the single machine that can "make up to eighty different kinds of automotive tailpipe as rapidly and cheaply as you can make eighty of the same one," and he notes that most extras and other variables on automobiles are nowadays assembled precisely to the individual customer's order.'[10]

As the technologies of men converted the planet into a garbage dump, Sputnik pushed this process to the reversal point, bringing in the age of ecology and programming. Arnold Toynbee had named this coming pattern 'etherealization', and Buckminster Fuller had seen it as 'doing more and more with less and less'. The flip point in this process comes on the telephone, for example, when the 'sender is sent'. You and your interlocutor are simultaneously in London and Tokyo, or New York and Berlin. When the sender is sent, the reversal of the transportation idea of communication is complete. Until recently, it was customary to think of communication as a form of transportation of data from point to point, but with the data simultaneously in both places, there has occurred a change of form that has affected American feelings for space and personal relations. Since the time when TV began to bring the exterior world inside his home and to take his personal, domestic world outside into the environment, the American has returned to conventional space feeling.

I would now like to return in this connection to what I earlier said concerning the American attitude to the motor car as private space which permits Americans to go outside to be alone. The uniformity of American culture with respect to this longstanding pattern of going outside to be alone and inside to socialize is currently reversing as TV brings Vietnam to the American domestic space and puts the domestic space outside on network programmes. American attitudes to space and time have undergone radical change in the past decade and new uniformities are shaping up complementary to, and perhaps even contradictory to, the previous conventions. As noted earlier, the forms of a culture become patent at the moment of exit, and if this fact is referred to as the use of the rear-view mirror, it may achieve new poignancy from the French phrase for this mirror, *'la glace derrière'*. The quality of experience attained by the *'glace derrière'* is as ambiguous as the mirror itself. John Knowler devotes a nostalgic chapter of *Trust an Englishman* to 'the posterior shrine' and the meeting point of many motifs and uniformities of British culture.[11] Indeed, *Trust an Englishman* is a kind of whimsical replay of some of the patterns of British culture as a kind of wistful look in the rear-view mirror, reminding us that what is actually to be seen in this mirror is not so much the traffic that has passed us by, but that which is catching us up.

This fact may remind some people that the world of fashion, in the arts and in entertainment alike, depends a great deal on the selective revival of times past. Hamlet, who must have appeared as a revival of medieval 'royalty' in 1603, was even more acceptable to the nineteenth century as an aesthetic object retrieved from a decaying medievalism. At electric speeds, every kind of human past is present, exactly in the manner in which T.S. Eliot discerned the prehistoric and contemporary simultaneity of the life of words:

'What I call the "auditory imagination" is the feeling for syllable and rhythm, penetrating far below the conscious levels of thought and feeling, invigorating every word: sinking to the most primitive and forgotten, returning to the origin and bringing something back, seeking the beginning and the end. It works through meanings, certainly, or not without meanings in the ordinary sense, and fuses the old and obliterated, and the trite, the current, and the new and the surprising, the most ancient and the most civilized mentality.'[12]

One of the paradoxes of auditory and acoustic structures is not only their discontinuity and simultaneity but the creative roles which they offer for stereotypes, a fact which appears in Parry and Lord's account of the formulaic procedures in the oral epic. It is the same in the world of Jazz, where, again, performance is creation and composition at the same time. Without the stereotypes and formulas there could not be the participation of the public in the creative act. The same features are presented by Eric Havelock in *Preface to Plato* as inseparable from poetic composition in the oral tradition of the ancient world.

What I wish to draw attention to is the fact that electric simultaneity restores the conditions of oral tradition as never before, impelling us to reconsider the nature of uniformities and stereotypes, both verbal and non-verbal.

American English in Europe

DAVID CRYSTAL

> *American is understood*
>> (sign in a London shop window)
>
> *Kippers sur toast*
> *Fried egg avec chips*
>> (menu in a Le Havre café window)

The language of popular reactions to linguistic borrowing is itself worthy of study. Its tone is largely pejorative; its style metaphorical and dramatic; and this is nowhere more violently in evidence than in the case of the influence of English — particularly American English — upon the languages of Europe. Newspaper reports, television programmes, even learned papers refer to the phenomenon in terms of 'invasion', 'sixth column' and 'infiltration', the English vocabulary 'ousting' and 'strangling' the native word-stock. A recent attack on foreign influences on Spanish in the paper *ABC de Madrid* by Salvador de Madariaga is headed *El castellano en peligro de muerte* ('Spanish in danger of death'). A British paper complains about the American 'barbarization of the Queen's English', adding (ironically) that we should 'preserve the tongue that Shakespeare spoke'. *Parlez-vous franglais?* is the title of a polemic against the influence of English on French, in which the author inveighs against 'anglomanie', 'anglofolie' and 'américanolâtrie'.[1]

As H.L. Mencken shows very clearly in the opening chapters of his classic *The American Language*,[2] Americanisms have been reviled almost as long as America. What is less well-known is the extent of the struggle by American authors to get free from their own feelings of inferiority about their distinctive English. Only after the emphasis placed upon it by such writers as Noah Webster did one find an attitude of pride which led to the development of the expression Mencken used as the title of his book, and which was so fiercely supported by Finley Peter Dunne's Chicago-Irish barman, Mr Dooley: 'When we Americans are through with the English language, it will look as if it had been run over by a musical comedy!'

Yet despite its history, the impact of American English on the languages of Europe (as opposed to on British English) is a largely twentieth century phenomenon. In 1921, the anthropologist-linguist Edward Sapir, in his influential book *Language*, was of the opinion that the influence of English upon other languages was negligible. Nowadays it is perhaps the most obvious feature of the European linguistic scene. But it is difficult to generalise. The influence of one language upon another is no constant thing, and reflects very much the mutual influence of societies upon each other, and in particular their political policies. As Mencken says (p.31), 'This war upon Americanisms naturally has its pitched battles and its rest periods between. These rest periods tend to coincide with the times when it is politic, on grounds remote from the philological, to treat the Yankee barbarian with a certain amount of politeness'. Linguistic purists tend to forget this elementary point of language principle, that language does not exist in a vacuum, but reflects a particular social context and set of cultural values, and that attitudes to language normally reduce to attitudes towards the social realities underlying them. It will undoubtedly be the case, then, that many of the attitudes we encounter towards American English in Europe, while voiced as attitudes towards the language, will be the surface reflection of deeper (and sometimes unconsciously held) attitudes towards the American way of life as a whole. A South American teacher once wrote that in his country optimists teach their students British English, pessimists American English. But this is a statement about politics, not applied linguistics.

To establish the facts about American English, however, is by no means easy. To begin with, one has to pierce a web of stereotyped views which obscure the situation. To many purists, anything that they consider 'wrong' with their language may be ascribed to American influence. There is, for instance, a traditional view that sentences in English ought not to be ended with prepositions, and that to do so is to fall a victim to Americanisation. But whether a sentence should end with a preposition or not is a question of style, not American influence: it was in fact raised as a problem by John Dryden and his contemporaries, who were trying to relate norms of English grammar to those found in Latin — and this was less than a generation after the Pilgrim Fathers landed! It is nothing to do with specifically American English at all, and the topic has in its time been as controversial in the United States as it has in England.

More important than this is the methodological difficulty of distinguishing American from other kinds of English, especially British. How can one be sure that a word borrowed by French, let us say, was borrowed from America directly, and not borrowed from

England (which earlier might have borrowed it from America)? In the absence of detailed etymological study of many of the words involved, it is usually difficult to be sure whether one is talking about British or American influence; and indeed most of the publications on the subject fail to make any such distinction, but talk generally about 'anglicisms' or 'English loan-words', without any further claims about provenance (as in Blancquaert, 1964). The same point applies to the influence of any one language upon another, of course (for example, how many of the loans in Italian have come direct from England, and not via France? cf. Rando, 1969), but it is particularly crucial for the study of English, where currently large numbers of words are involved, and the assumption about Americanisation is so loudly and fiercely voiced (as in Etiemble, 1964).

The difficulty of drawing any consistent distinction can be easily illustrated by listing the words labelled thus in the dictionaries. For example, Giraud et al (1971) distinguish 'americanisms' from 'anglicisms' in their French dictionary. (They also cite a category of 'anglo-americanisms', but give only one example, *poster*!) Apart from this, their lists are:

americanisms:
acculturation, action painting, american way of life, black capitalism, body stocking, boom, brainstorming, building disease, col-blanc, drive-in, drugstore, drugstoriser, musical, play-boy, popart, pop music, reconversion, soul, yippie, zoom

anglicisms:
attaché-case, badge, be-in, best-seller, birth control, boom (sense 2), *brain power, check-up, club-house, cool, doping, dressing-room, engineering, establishment, feed-back, flower power, flash, gadget, gap, happening, hardware, has been, house-organ, impulse goods, incentives, jamesbonderie, jet, lay out, leadership, Living Theatre, management, marketing, mass media, merchandising, new-look, new thing, non-stop, package (deal,* etc.*), panel, patchwork, performance, planning, play-back, remake, rewriting, show, skin-head, smog, software, spot, standing, stress, take off, thriller, timing, togetherness, underground, VIP, workshop*

It is impossible to see from these lists what criteria have been used to place, say, *musical* in one category and *flower power* in the other; and perhaps as a result of this problem, most dictionaries, while they often have a label available for marking Americanisms as such, hardly ever use it (as in Harrap's 1970 *French-English Dictionary of Slang and Colloquialisms*).

Having made these cautionary points about the definition of Americanism, it is possible to sidestep the etymological question to a certain extent by adopting a working definition which contains a psycholinguistic principle. By an Americanism, I understand a linguistic usage whose American origins are capable of demonstration (by the usual etymological techniques) and are *still generally recognised in the popular mind.* Thus there is nothing psychologically American any longer for most British people about such words as *briefcase* or *bingo* (listed by Mencken as American), whereas there is generally an active association for such words as *vacation* and *apartment.* On this basis, it is possible to classify Americanisms into five broad categories.

1. Usages where the American term is unused in Britain (it may or may not be understood), though the phenomenon referred to is shared by both, e.g. *sidewalk, diaper.*

2. Usages where the term is familiar, but its sense differs in Britain (again, it may or may not be understood), though the phenomenon is shared by both, e.g. *billion, block, biscuit, gas* (= petrol), *trunk* (of a car).

3. Usages where the term or sense refers to an American 'institution' (in the broadest sense, including geographical, political, botanical, etc. phenomena) and could be used in Britain, but only when referring to that institution, e.g. *baseball, senator, alumnus, dollar.*

4. Usages where term, sense and phenomenon are shared, but the occurrence is more normal in the United States than in Britain e.g. *hi, can* (of fruit), *French Fries, low gear.*

5. Usages where there are still definite overtones of American origin, but there is no obvious difference in frequency of use between Britain and the United States, e.g. *coke* (= coca-cola), *O.K.*

Items will of course shift from one category to another as time passes, and only categories 1-3 provide really clear cases of Americanisms. But even if we restrict ourselves to these usages, there remain a number of unanswered questions to complicate further our discussion of this topic. In particular, it is by no means obvious how many there are, or whether American-British linguistic differences are increasing or diminishing. Most of the published lists of differences are small, and tend to concentrate on certain central topics, e.g. terms belonging to education, cars, foodstuffs. In a radio discussion made jointly for the BBC and the Voice of America a few years ago, Albert Marckwardt and Randolph Quirk took the view that the sum total of these differences was in fact quite small, and was moreover diminishing.[3] Certainly, there is a strong tendency for the American usage to become widely known in England, for obvious reasons to do with the general influence of the popular media; but it should also be pointed out that certain areas of Anglo-American difference have never really been studied, so that currently available lists are certainly underestimates. In particular, there have been few studies of the more colloquial styles of speech, including the idioms and sociolinguistically restricted expressions (as in 'There you go', said by a waitress to a customer at the beginning of a meal); and when one considers the rapid development of new urban dialects, American Negro English, and so on, it seems clear that any claim about the present state of Americanisms is premature. One recent study accumulated some 5,000 British-American lexical differences with little difficulty.

The last methodological clarification concerns the notion of 'usages', in the above classification. So far, the examples have all been of vocabulary. But if we look at American English as a whole, and ask in what respects it might influence another language, then clearly other aspects of language structure need to be considered, not simply vocabulary. As an initial step, four main kinds of linguistic influence can be distinguished: pronunciation, orthography, grammar, and vocabulary. The last is by far the most common process, but the others ought not to be ignored. American influence might thus be demonstrated in European languages if the forms used showed a clearly American usage under any of these headings. For example, if a language borrowed a phrase in which the verb *gotten* appeared, an American source would be immediately apparent, as the British equivalent is *got*. In this way, we could argue for the use of specifically American pronunciations, or spellings (as in *center* instead of *centre*). There are clear examples in vocabulary. In Spanish, the term for 'government', traditionally *Gobierno*, is often replaced by *Administración*, which is evidently American in origin. Likewise, in Norwegian, *truck, gasspedal, senator, convertible*, and *derby* (hat) have all been cited. *Pedala gasa* turns up for 'accelerator' in Serbo-Croatian. *Drugstore* is widely known. And many of the items listed below display American origin in the clear senses of categories 1-3 above.

But not all of them. When one looks dispassionately at the question of American English influence in Europe, bearing this methodological discussion in mind, it does seem possible to make some headway in the task of distinguishing Americanisms from English loans in general. However, when popular attitudes to these loans are taken into account, the distinction becomes blurred, and indeed is regularly ignored in the foreign press. Most of Europe identifies English as American English, and the criticisms reflect this assumption. It therefore seems important to take the stereotype into account in presenting any analysis of the situation, and as a result the classification below contains examples of English loan-words from both American and British sources, the point being that, whatever the etymological reality, it is quite possible to find any of them — even *pub* — being referred to as an Americanism from time to time.

It is not difficult to classify English loan-words in Europe: the categories will obviously reflect the areas of greatest cultural influence. One may dispute the actual headings used, and sometimes it is difficult to decide into which category an item should go; but some such classification is essential, as the various categories attract different degrees of comment. Sporting terms, for example, are generally assimilated with little comment, whereas some of the consumer terms below have attracted fierce opposition. The examples within each category have all been taken from a real context of use in one of the main languages of Europe; but most of the items are common to all. The spellings given are as in English: they do not reflect the orthographic changes which often apply when a language makes a loan-word conform to its spelling-rules, e.g. *boxing* becoming *boksing* in Norwegian, *goal* becoming *gowl* in Spanish, *whisky* become *güisqui* in Maltese.

1. Sport, including general terms for events, results, standards, etc., as well as items belonging to particular events: *comeback, semi-final, walkover; forward, offside; deuce, volley; knockout, clinch; photo-finish, jockey; bobsleigh, baseball; go-kart, goalie.*

2. Tourism, transport, geography, etc.: *picnic, sightseeing, hitchhike, stewardess, travellers cheques; stop, motel, taxi, runway, crash-landing, agency, antifreeze, jeep, scooter, clutch, defroster, fullspeed, joy-riding; navy, tanker; canyon, coyote.*

3. Politics, commerce, industry, etc.: *senator, briefing, goodwill, new deal, pressure group; big business, marketing, boom, top secret, lockout, sit-down-strike; sterling, dollar, cent.*

4. Culture, entertainment, and the mass media in general: *musical, jam session, blues, boogie woogie, top twenty, juke-box, hi-fi; cowboy, happy ending, Western, vista-vision; Miss Sweden* (etc.), *pimp, striptease, brain(s)trust, polish, show; group, yeah-yeah-yeah.*

5. People and behaviour: *fair play, snob, smart, ladylike, sexy, sex appeal, crazy, cool; gangster, mob, hold-up; baby, nigger, grand old*

man, cowboy, boy scout, freelance, reporter, stand-in; doping, drugs, hash, snow.

6. Consumer society: *jumper, make-up, nylon, derby; barkeeper, bartender, bootlegger, smoking, grillroom, pub, snackbar, long drink, coca cola, coke, juice, cocktail, sweet* (wine), *bacon, hamburger, kingsize, ketchup, hickory, aspirin; air conditioner, penthouse, WC; pickup, tape, LP; camera, film, poker, scrabble; shopping center, supermarket, self-service, drive-in; kleenex, Christmas card; bestseller, lay-out, science fiction, thriller, royalties; bulldozer, excavator, pipeline.*

7. Miscellaneous: *allright, OK, up-to-date, weekend, fifty-fifty.*

The influence of English upon grammar is more difficult to trace. It is as a rule uncommon to see loans of any syntactic complexity being introduced into a language, unless they are quotations taken as wholes, or stereotyped expressions (such as *All rights reserved*). The most complex syntactic expressions illustrated above have been compound noun phrases, for example *shopping centre, show business, angry young man, pin-up girl* (all used in Dutch, for instance), or the examples listed at the beginning of this paper from French, to which might be added *eye-liner avec eye-shadow.* An interesting grammatical feature is to see whether a loan-word's inflections accompany it into the foreign language. According to Zandvoort (1967), English verbs in Dutch usually adapt to the Dutch verb inflections (e.g. *fixen, relaxen*), whereas nouns often keep their English plurals, as in *drink:drinks* (for Dutch *drank*, pl. *dranken*). German sometimes takes over the English *-s* (as in *callgirl:callgirls*), sometimes imposes its own pluralization rules (as when nouns in *-er* stay unchanged in the plural, e.g. *Teenager*, pl. *Teenager*), and sometimes allow both (Carstensen, 1965, cites both *Skilifts* and *Skilifte*, for example). There also seem to be different preferences for loan-words of different classes from language to language – for example, French seems to borrow more *-ing* forms than other languages (*smoking, camping, parking*). Italian goes in a great deal for blends using its own system of affixes, e.g. *weekendista, pongista* (from 'ping-pong'), *newyorkese*, and the remarkable *cocacolonizzare*, based on 'colonize' (see Klajn, 1972: p.98).

Occasionally, too, it is possible to see more general syntactic pressures operating on the basic grammatical rules of the language, and affecting word order, ellipsis, and other processes. In Spanish, for instance, translations of book-titles from English often show the influence of English syntax: for example, the standard form of 'A study of . . .' would be *Estudio sobre . . .*; but one will often see the indefinite article used, thus: *Un estudio sobre . . .* Zandvoort (1967) cites a number of instances affecting Dutch. In Dutch, one can use adjectives as nouns more freely than in English, for example, 'the sick man' would normally be *de zieke*; but constructions of the type *de zieke man* are also found, when prompted by some specific equivalent in English (as in the phrase 'the sick man of Europe'). Again, the standard equivalent for 'Waiting for Godot' would be *In afwachting van Godot*; but it has emerged as *Wachten op Godot*. Formulae are also affected; in Spanish a standard invitation might say *El senor X y senora*; but one often nowadays sees *El senor y la senora X*, under the influence of English word order. The process of anglicization of word order, inflection, etc. seems to have been taken to extremes in Yiddish, a Jewish language originating in Germany, and originally displaying many of the features of that language, but now incorporating a great deal of American expression (especially in those dialects used in the United States). Feinsilver (1970) sees this as an inevitable linguistic process, and in fact predicts the change of Judaeo-German to Judaeo-English — and when one considers some of her examples, it seems that that day is not far off (e.g. *Vy you dunt taket a nap? Di baby sleepet already.*).

In spelling and pronunciation, it is usually difficult to see the results of English influence, as the borrowed forms rapidly assimilate to the native language patterns. Consonants and vowels get altered to their nearest values in the native language (e.g. *club* sounds more like 'clop' in Dutch), and new rhythms and intonations take over, so that words are often split up differently from English (Zandvoort cites *folk-lore* becoming *fol-klore* in Dutch). The written form is more resistant to change, but as we have already seen, many words come to be used in the orthographic patterns of the new language. This is only to be expected. European languages are on the whole more 'phonetic' than English — that is, they have a more regular sound-spelling correspondence: words like *sightseeing* would provide major reading difficulties, and they often undergo regularisation and simplification as a result. There are nonetheless types of word which tend not to change — proper names, for instance (e.g. *Lenin* is often seen in Spanish, though the normal rules require *Llenin*). As a result, it is often easier to see Anglo-American influence on a European language than to hear it.

Now that we have looked at the main processes involved in the exercise of English influence abroad, we may return to the central cultural questions. What accounts for the explosion of English loan-words in modern Europe? And how can one explain the ferocity of the objections illustrated at the beginning of this chapter? Let it be said once and for all that there would be no loan-words at issue at all if some section of the societies involved did not will it. There can be no superimposed plot, with language. Controlled attempts to neologise, to change linguistic habits in the mass, have always failed, as the history of the European Academies of language has shown. So who wants Americanisms? What is their function? No complete analysis has ever been made, but as one reads the relevant studies, it is clear that they have no single, simple purpose.

The obvious reason for their existence, of course, is to point to the universal interest of certain features of the American way of life — sport, music, and so on — which produce a set of values considered to be modern, fashionable, and desirable among the younger, trend-setting generations of European society. To that extent, the criticisms made are as much directed at these values, and the phenomena themselves (pop music and the accompanying behaviour) by people for whom these values do not appeal, as at the language itself. Depending on your point of view, therefore, English loans can be either a good or a bad thing. If you are pro-American, or pro-British, then they will be seen to have a positive role to play in facilitating contact, mutual understanding, and so forth. If you are antipathetic, or anxious to preserve a strong sense of cultural identity for each of the European groups, then English loans will tend to be opposed.

This reasoning accounts for much of the emphasis, perhaps, but it is too much of a simplification to explain everything. Within the general division of opinion referred to, there are more subtle linguistic forces at work shaping popular attitudes to English loans. For one thing, not all loan-words are considered equally good or bad. Most people accept the inevitability of English words being introduced whenever a new term or sense is formed and there are no native equivalents. There is no point in trying to coin an Anglo-Saxon translation of *sputnik* in English, and likewise, when one is faced with a mass of technical or scientific neologisms, or of words expressing notions wholly restricted to America or Britain, objections normally do not arise. The opposition comes when English words are used unnecessarily, in the view of the European speaker, or where his native language is forced out of its normal syntax and idiom. By 'unnecessarily' here, one means cases where the native language already 'has a word for it', or where one could easily have been constructed out of native elements. Lorenzo (1966: 66), for example, objects to words that 'supplant perfectly healthy Spanish words' — for example, replacing *fabrica* by *planta* (for 'factory'), or *en realidade* by *actualmente* (for 'actually'): this for him is 'the object of proper condemnation'. Likewise, Zandvoort (1967) instances the replacement of *maretak* by *mistletoe* in Dutch. It is cases like these which attract the majority of criticisms, and lead to the violent vocabulary of the opening paragraph of this chapter.[4]

But there are other reasons accounting for the various strengths of criticism which one can observe around Europe. Regardless of one's overall attitude towards the United States, internal factors in a country have a definite role to play in determining whether a country will treat the question with relative equanimity or with ferocity. Doubtless it is a question of personalities as much as anything else. One influential writer (such as Etiemble in France) or group (such as the Society for Pure English in England earlier this century) can promote a national feeling. Without Manuel Criado de Val's weekly programme on Spanish television devoted to language problems, in which the influence of English is regularly criticised, there would be much less noticeable controversy in Spain on this topic. Lorenzo (1966) in fact considers television to be such a significant influence on Spanish attitudes in this respect that he devotes a separate appendix to it. But in addition to this, one might say with some certainty that countries in which a guardian of the purity of the language, in the form of an Academy, is strong, are obviously going to be more articulate in their opposition to loan-words (particularly of the 'unnecessary' kind) than countries where no such institutions exist. Again, countries where there is a low level of teaching about the native language are likely to find a low sensitivity among people towards the kind of language being used and the kind they would like to see.

Then there are more insidious reasons. For example, a correspondent from Spain once argued as follows: 'the press has been used for many years now to hide rather than to inform, for political reasons, and the style of many articles on current affairs is almost incomprehensible even for educated people. The less educated public is therefore likely to regard irregularities in grammatical construction (or foreign loan-words) as something in the same class as the larger number of things that they do not fully understand'. On a different tack, Norman Eliason thinks that:

'the low status accorded American English is due in part to the prejudice against it more or less actively fostered in the schools. Much of this prejudice is a direct consequence of using as the basis of instruction Received Standard, that is, the kind of English which is the birthright of a limited and diminishing class of Englishmen exemplified by Sir Anthony Eden or which is acquired in public schools like Eton.'[5]

And lastly, one might illustrate the widely-held view that English

words give a 'snob value' to the 'upper middle-class' foreigner's use of
his language, and criticism thus varies in proportion to the survival of
such a class in European society. (This must be similar, one supposes,
to the larding of one's own speech with expressions such as *élan, joie
de vivre, sine qua non,* etc.) This is something which has been
claimed by Gooch (1971) in relation to Spanish; and also by a
Danish commentator in the Norwegian *Morgenbladet* (28 October
1960), who argued: 'the exaggerated use of English words, where
Norwegian words are just as good, seems snobbish . . . and it leads to
ludicrous situations where people are compelled to use words which
they can neither pronounce nor understand'.

But not everyone is critical. The market researchers, for example,
have had a great deal to say about the merits of English loans. It was
reported in the Norwegian paper *Aftenposten* (25 October 1960), for
example, that a Finnish firm sent out some coffee for the home
market in tins with a Finnish text. Sales were poor. The firm then
had new labels made with a text in English on the same tins, and
sales rocketed. Again, Zandvoort (1967) reports on a case where the
leader of a youth club in a Dutch town obtained a considerable
increase in the active interest of the boys once he had given his club
an English name. This kind of association of ideas is of course quite
universal — witness in English the use of French for names of
restaurants, night-clubs, and so on — but it is certainly a major
process in the impact of English abroad.

Who, then, can claim the credit, or (depending on the point of
view) take the responsibility for the English invasion? According to
the Norwegian paper *Dagbladet* (30 January 1960), 'journalists at the
news agencies bear the chief responsibility for the ruination of our
language', and it cites examples of English proper-names for
geographical areas being used instead of those already available in
Norwegian, e.g. *Jutland* for *Jylland.* Certainly the influence of the
major international news agencies, such as API and Reuters, should
not be underestimated here, as a large proportion of the items in the
European press comes via these agencies, and translation standards
bend before deadlines. But it is not as simple as this. Some papers,
such as *Der Spiegel,* seem to go out of their way to use American
expressions; for others, the opposite is the case. To discover why
would involve us in an excursus into the sociology of journalism. But
there are in any case other factors, which do not involve the press at
all. For example, it has been argued that a main source of influence is
the specialist (especially the student) abroad, who, having learned a
specialism with all its accompanying vocabulary and slang, returns to
his native country to find no equivalents for this knowledge, and
introduces the English terms as needed — a tendency to be discerned

as much in television production as in biochemistry. Or again, it is said that there are more English loans used in countries that have had a high and relatively regular rate of emigration to the United States. Some also claim that English has gained favour, especially since the Second World War, in some countries as a less pernicious alternative to being swamped by German. Norman Eliason, in almost jingoistic vein,[6] considers the direct influence of Americans in Europe — in particular the G.I. — to be particularly significant.

Even from this brief survey, it should be clear that the influence of American English on European languages is a complex phenomenon, and one which can hardly be studied separately from a vast array of cultural, national and political factors. But there are no grounds here for an Anglo-American linguistic chauvinism. With increased commitment by Britain to Europe, large-scale borrowings *from* the main European languages are inevitable, and have already begun.[7] Randolph Quirk made the point succinctly, in a 1970 conference in Luxembourg sponsored by the London Institute of Linguists: 'where anxious purists in France have been deploring Franglais in recent years, we shall perhaps hear retired colonels in Britain complain of the 'Fringlish' or 'Engleutsch' which is drowning the native wood notes wild'. Fifty years ago, recalling Sapir, the influence of English in Europe had hardly been noticed either.

Mediated Environments
or: *You can't build that here*

REYNER BANHAM

This paper proposes that, with only rare exceptions, the influence of US architecture on European architecture through normal channels of architectural influence, has been virtually non-existent — but that the influence of certain American scenes or environments, as transmitted through the media of the popular arts, has been extensive, little understood and usually misapplied.

The wrong place to look
The obvious places to look for US influence on European architecture would be in types of buildings that serve particularly American industries, or actually brandish the word 'American' on their nameplates. The obvious period to look for these would be during the first great craze for Americana in the nineteen twenties. Yet if one actually investigates the style and layout of the three most obvious categories of buildings — filling stations, movie palaces and 'American' bars in grand hotels, the results are, at first sight, bafflingly negative.

Filling stations, for instance, serve a typically American type of industry, both in themselves and in the vehicles they fuel. But in an equally typical American manner, the tradition of the industry has been one of minimum capital investment; the tanks and pumps were installed in a kind of architectural vacuum, and where architecture was applied it was usually to *prevent* the station looking American. That is, in an attempt to protect local character or amenities, the required buildings had to follow the approved *Heimatstil*, as on the *autobahnen*, or a fake vernacular, as in the bungaloid half-timbering and thatch occasionally seen in the Home Counties around London.

Only very recently has the deliberate use of architecture as a promotional device by oil companies begun to produce what might be mistaken for an American influence — and even here appearances can deceive. The architecture of some conspicuously 'designed' Esso outlets is in fact Italian, the sites having been taken over from AGIP; Shell's *Canopus* programme is also of European origin; only the style of the new Mobil outlets with their cylindrical pumps and variations on the theme of a circular canopy is a pure import from America and, ironically, it represents a standard of taste which no educated European could condemn, and most would admire — especially when they know it to be the work of Eliot Noyes, late of the Museum of Modern Art and other blameless bodies.

But all this is a matter of the last ten, or even five, years. We are talking about the sixties, not the twenties. If we now go back to the twenties, suitably warned, to look at movie palaces, we shall find a situation similar in effect, though very different in substance. Their rise, during the twenties, corresponds to a period when US architecture was in something of an intellectual slump, but US environmental technology was riding high. The machinery to project the films, reproduce the sound, control the lighting, operate the mighty organ and air-condition the interior was nearly all of US origin or based on American developments. Its effect on the basic layout of cinemas was fundamental and visible — the elaborate and extensive grilles flanking the proscenium arch had to be there to serve both the ventilation and the sound-system.

Yet the form and decoration of those grilles would have been the same had the United States never existed. American architecture had passed that extraordinary phase of precocious creativity that produced the first phase of architectural influence on Europe chronicled by Leonard Eaton in his brilliant book *American Architecture Comes of Age*,[1] and apart from one or two timid domestic-scale imitations of Frank Lloyd Wright in Holland, the United States was exporting nothing architecturally. In the field of fancy-dress architecture and fantasy, European styles held sway on both sides of the Atlantic — the debts of the Granada Tooting are to Spain direct, not by way of Santa Barbara and the Spanish Colonial revival in California.

As far as the exteriors of the movie palaces are concerned, the condition of non-Americanisation is even more conspicuous. European cinemas had pioneered the use of neon tubes and similar display lighting devices, the first being in Leicester Square, London, in 1913.[2] The overall architecture of the exteriors was not usually all that fantasticated — and you wouldn't really expect it to be, coming from the drawing boards of men with names like Harry Weedon and Walmsley Lewis — and its main debts, in England, were usually to the 1925 *Art Déco* of Paris, or to the later, more rectilinear Expressionism of the same period in Germany and Holland. Most of the Odeons in England were as much refugees from Nazi Germany as were most of the art-historians.

And after all that it must seem pure gratuitous sadism to do a demolition number on American bars. By their very style and title they must have been conceived by non-Americans. Even if the names of the cocktails were American and the bartender black they were mostly pure Art Déco — as are the few examples that actually got built in grand hotels in the States! It only remains, really, to record that the man who designed the first one, in Vienna in 1907, was the architect, Adolf Loos, who had been to the United States and was much affected by what he saw there. The bar — and it still survives to prove my point — was designed, however, in a style he could have learned without crossing the Ringstrasse, let alone the Atlantic.[3]

More like back-projection
This may seem a very negative introduction to the subject, but it is important to establish (a) that historically obvious places to look for US influence are the wrong places, and (b) that historically customary methods for estimating and locating influence are the wrong methods. The reason why I feel this paper to be apt to this present discussion is because the architectural historian must go outside the normal channels of fine art transmission of ideas and images if he is to see where and how the influence of the United States on Europe has been exercised in architecture, and must look at the channels of popular art — more specifically at Pop-Art, as the term first came into use in the fifties.

Let me make two further points about this. Both are concerned with the physical nature or substance of architecture, which is massive, permanent and fixed to the ground. Architectural influence is not exercised by moving the artefacts about, nor significantly by moving the architects about. Direct professional influence is exercised more than any other way via professional publications, most notably a select band of monthly glossy magazines. These half-dozen publications exercise uncommon power in deciding who shall see what (I speak from experience of some extraordinary incidents while I was on the editorial staff of the *Architectural Review*, and they are incidents that I know can be paralleled in the editorial history of other magazines) and which aspects of what is selected shall be presented to the readers. Further back down the line there is earlier selectivity exercised by correspondents in the field, and the visual filtering effect of the talents and interests of the photographers who record the work in the first place. Given all this, one should not be too surprised, I suppose, that the works of Rudolph Schindler, for instance, an architect of world class working in California, should take an average of six years to get published in the New York magazines and forty to appear in European ones!

Compare these time-lags with the virtual instantaneous communication in the Pop media, and you will see that whatever aspects of architecture and environmental design can be managed by those media will be far better known to the general public than will architectural matters to architects. But architecture remains intractable material for the pop media because of its very physical nature. Whereas the material of pop is highly styled, transient, mass-produced and mass distributed, serious architecture in our time has been under-styled, permanent, and — above all — produced one at a time at the place where it is to be used. Admittedly, America with its pre-fabricated tract houses and mobile homes has gone further than any other country in breaking this rule — yet the moment a mobile home comes to rest, its inhabitants start anchoring it to the ground with porches and gardens! So that while one can assemble an exiguous list of exceptions to the rule that there is no Pop architecture in Europe, and very little in the United States, the list is notable chiefly for its exiguousness.

Another considerable matter here is that many US building types are irrelevant to Europe or nearly so. I think I have seen *both* the two drive-in theatres operating in Europe! And the number of motels in Great Britain would not add up to an economically viable chain in the States. At a detailed level, of course, much has been transferable — the United States set the standards of plumbing we look for in European architecture fifty years later. But much of that detail falls below the normal threshold of architectural or popular attention.

Thus, the nearest thing that many of us will ever see to the architecture of Mies van der Rohe is our local laundromat. On a quick check of new or re-fronted shops in our immediate neighbourhood I ascertained that, out of a cluster of some thirty, twenty-one showed American influence, and of these eleven were specifically Miesian. *Where* they showed this influence was in the metal glazing bars and trim, ventilating grilles and frameless door mountings around their windows; the Miesian ones, specifically, used similar (in some cases exactly so) metal sections to those used by Mies, all ultimately derived from the standards built up for Sweets Building Catalogue by Professor Lönberg-Holm at Ann Arbor in the thirties (it was only where the pieces of metal met that you could tell you weren't dealing with Mies). And there's nothing new about this; the first laundromat where this fact struck me was on the Ile de la Cité in Paris in 1953!

As I say, however, this building goes on below the threshold of normal attention. But how does American architecture perform above that threshold in the Pop media where I claim its main influence to lie? The answer is that it performs less *in* the media than *around* them. American architecture is the building blocks out of which are assembled the environments in which the action of Pop takes place, a kind of continuous back-projection behind the superstars, the dreamboats, the supergroups, the filtertips, the Superflies, the muscle-cars, the Untouchables and biodegradables.

Muzak was never like this

This, however, does not mean that US architecture functions as a kind of visual Muzak. There are very good physiological and psychological reasons, I suspect, why nothing visual can ever perform that subliminal role — the architecture in the pop media certainly doesn't. The Odessa Steps (to take a momentarily out-of-context example) are like a real place, even to those who have never seen more than that particular clip from *The Battleship Potemkin.* So are the storm drains of Los Angeles even to those who only know them from the closing sequences of *Them.* And suddenly to find yourself in one of those Pop-canonised environments, like the ramp down the Santa Monica palisades, produces a shock of recognition which I think must be peculiar to the motion-picture arts.

One of the reasons for this is certainly that the movie medium also gives, unwittingly, instructions on how to behave in these environments. Most movie buffs could find their way through the corridors of Alcatraz or down death row at San Quentin in the unlikely event of finding themselves there. Most can cope quite adequately with a rather more likely piece of the US built environment — because it is a slightly exportable piece. There is hardly a major city in Europe that does not boast somewhere a Western-style Hickory-pit Chuck-wagon Steak-house or locally mis-spelled equivalent, all random cedar planks and brand-burnt lettering. It has double-hung chest-high swing doors of course, and everybody, staff and customers alike, knows exactly how to go through them, where to put the hand, how to place the feet, the attitude of the head, and we all know where they learned all that stuff! What's particularly revealing is the way the staff use such doors, since they will usually have both hands full. In a similar circumstance in an industrial environment, where double-hung swing doors are not uncommon for fireproofing or other reasons, a person with both hands full uses the back to swing only one door, usually the left if one is right-handed, and comes through half sideways half backwards, protecting whatever is in their hands. But apart from perhaps Buster Keaton, did you ever see the hero of a Western movie enter the saloon leading with the left shoulder and looking down and to the right? And neither do the waitresses in your local Lariat Room!

Andy Hardy in Harlow New Town

Now, at this level it can be argued in some detail that US building, if not architecture, as represented in the Pop media, has actually affected the design of architecture and environments in Europe. I propose to take four examples as the basis of this discussion: one seemingly too trivial to be believable, the second historically documented, continental in its distribution and possibly lethal in its consequences; the third involves a manner of interpreting a particular kind of environmental change which was going to happen anyway, but is perceived in a special way because of its distribution via the media; and the fourth represents a divided image of paradise and disaster, a dream-nightmare that came true, mortally true, for some Europeans in 1973. The second and third examples don't depend particularly on the moving picture arts, as we shall see, but the first one emphatically does. It has to do with front gardens; it can best be introduced obliquely, thus.

My first teaching stint in the United States was at Carbondale, Illinois — a suburb of nowhere with a campus attached. Describing the local scene with its neat white houses set among neat shrubbery and trees behind neat front lawns to an architect friend on my return, I saw him having a flash of revelation. 'You mean,' he said 'like Andy Hardy country!'

This is a very common response in my generation. The image of an ideally openfronted society without garden fences came to us first as the setting of a seemingly endless series of misadventures of scapegrace Mickey Rooney in the household of lovable old Judge Hardy. That well-manicured middle-American suburbia, seen through the coated lenses of Hollywood genteelism, became for better or worse the ideal landscape of our formative years. I still recall how impressed we were to discover that there was, as of 1939, one suburban road with fenceless front-gardens in Norwich — impressed not only because it matched the dream image, but because it was so rare in Britain at the time. By about 1955 however, it was becoming much less rare, since most of the New Towns were built to this formula, with open greenery in front of the houses, and fenced gardens only at the back.

Now, there were all sorts of reasons why places like Harlow New Town were laid out like this, not the least being the professional ambitions of landscapers on New Town staffs, and the desire of the ex-officers who ran the New Towns to eliminate the 'slovenly appearance on parade' of independently operated or neglected front gardens. But the idea of the open front lawn had to be sold to all sorts of other people, including the inhabitants, local councillors, administrators, and in retrospect I doubt whether it could have been done — and gone on being done — had not Hollywood in general and Andy Hardy in particular, established the open front lawn as an image in good currency even among those who had never seen it in the original grass!

Cities of the future — past and present
The Andy Hardy proposition is not a very portentous one; but the next two are, since they have affected our whole understanding of possible cities of the future, and can therefore be seen to have guided very large-scale architectural and town planning decisions. The images here are of New York and Los Angeles; their critical influences have been exercised in the nineteens and twenties in the case of New York, the sixties in the case of Los Angeles. New York here means, specifically, the silhouette of Lower Manhattan seen from the sea, from the Jersey shore, from Staten Island, or anywhere else it could be seen as a whole. The world had seen nothing like it before, and little since — not even the far more picturesque outline of San Francisco today with its office towers stalking right over the ridge has displaced that incredible skyline, that solid cluster of skyscrapers rising to a central peak in a three-dimensional bar-graph of escalating land-values.

It is true of course that this was the first sight of America beheld by immigrants arriving from Europe, but for that very reason it must have become known in Europe by some other means, since so few of the immigrants ever came back. What did transmit the image of lower Manhattan back to Europe seems to have been illustrated magazines. We have good anecdotal and circumstantial evidence for this,[4] but a systematic and itemised iconography has yet to be done. It would be difficult to make such a study exhaustive because of the ephemeral nature of illustrated magazines, but as every celebrity or new ocean-liner to arrive in New York was photographed against that unmistakable skyline, there should be no lack of material even in quality magazines like the *Illustrated London News*.

In addition to this direct transmission, there is a fictive image also in early science-fiction illustrations, say to *The Sleeper Wakes* by H.G. Wells, which may be set in the London of the future, but looks and sounds remarkably like New York in the twenties. The *Strand* and its Continental equivalents ought to provide a rich lode of this second-order imagery. The third order of imagery will be found in architectural publications, beginning with the projects for Milan in the year 2000 exhibited by the Futurist architect Antonio Sant'Elia in 1914.[5] The image as presented by Sant'Elia has already gobbled up that of the Chicago Loop, with its elevated railways at the feet of the skyscrapers, and much of the science-fiction overtones from Wells. But those were specialised addenda; the status of the skyscraper city as an image in good currency always goes back to half-tones of New York in the printed mass-media, newspapers and magazines. Once established as a third-order image in currency it was almost unstoppable. For radical innovators from Paris to Moscow it was the image of the future city that their own cruddy old decrepit metropolises could only become after they had been razed and remade anew. From Le Corbusier to the illustrators in the *Daily Mail* it was the Standard Metropolitan Future, to mangle Herman Kahn's terminology only slightly.

In fact, no European metropolis has ever achieved that Manhattan silhouette. Legal, topographical, financial and political differences make it impossible. There are towers, but they are scattered, even when they were planned as a group, as in the Hotorget in Stockholm. But the most sensational difference is that where the towers exist, scattered across some urban prospect in Europe, at least half of them will not be commercial office blocks at all, but social housing. As J.M. Richards said in 1958: 'Many people have in mind a vision of the skyscraper townscape of the future comprising glassy towers rising gracefully into the sky.'[6] But most of them are concrete, not glass, because most of the people who have in mind that vision are the architects and housing committee chairmen of major cities like Manchester or Coventry or Glasgow or London, because there is more than a particle of truth in the slander that those who were killed in the Ronan Point collapse were sacrificed to the architectural profession's obsession with tower-blocks. And since all the objective, economic, social and structural justifications for tower-blocks had long since withered away, we are left only with the visual and symbolic. And since the visual qualities of Ronan Point were nil, we are left only with the symbolic — the image of tower-cities as the symbol of the better future.

The seventy-year life of that symbol as an image in good currency is one of the cultural phenomena of our time. The other two I propose to discuss are much younger, and potentially more short-lived. That of Los Angeles as a city of the future is an image of the early sixties. Significantly, the meaning of the image has reversed its polarity in ten years, without any change in the image itself, which remains one of a city festooned in freeways. The content of the image, however, is a very curious one. The freeways serve the automobile and a local dream of universal mobility, but that dream is almost intransmissible because the actual experience of moving about on the freeways is difficult to render comprehensibly in the most apparently obvious medium, the moving picture. Instead, the image of the freeways has been mediated for us via a still picture (and I intend no joke about traffic jams) emphasising the static mass of the civil engineering involved, particularly in the multi-level intersections.

This is quite a sophisticated still, normally requiring the use of a helicopter and — in the definitive *Time-Life* version — a fish-eye lens. Fifteen years ago this was an image of the good life: 'Dig those crazy Los Angeles Freeways' say old postcards you can still buy, and as an image of the good life it inspired many European traffic engineers and motorists, for whom the equivalent local prototypes would have been too embarrassing to recall, because of their connections with Hitler and Mussolini.

But with rising hostility to urban motorways in particular, it has now become a standard image of evil. However inapplicable it may be to conditions in West London or Glasgow or Stockholm or Urbino, the activists' cry of *homes before roads* owed much of its impact to the mental contrast, reliable as a conditioned reflex, between *local* homes and *Los Angeles* freeways, since few of the activists or their hearers had ever seen a major urban motorway or motorway intersection outside the mass media.

The city of nobody's future
The reversed polarity of the Los Angeles image may derive not only from specific local causes concerned with motorway problems, it may also be part of a totally shifted image of America, which is even better exemplified by the determination that Las Vegas shall not happen here. The successive mediations of the image of Las Vegas are such recent history that they are open to historical scrutiny in a way that none of the preceding images are, and since I had some involvement in them, I think I have some responsibility to try and clarify what happened.

The key period lies around 1965-66, but the image of Las Vegas had been freely available via the media well before that, from movies that go back even before *The Las Vegas Story*, and from widely-seen TV series like *Route 66*, all so long ago that young James Bond must seem a real Johnny-come-lately. All, however, combine to enforce the master image of the giant illuminated sky-signs along the Strip and Fremont Street at night. This is not an environment that can be rendered in any single view — the casinos on the Strip are scattered over some miles and must be cruised in a car; furthermore, each illuminated sign goes through a more or less complex sequence of programmed transformations in time and colour. For purely technical reasons, then, this has to be an image of the era of Cinemascope and Technicolor.

It had, in fact, barely reached its definitive form by the mid-sixties, and what then made it characteristic was its formlessness and tastelessness — by the standards of established culture, that is. The scatter along the strip had no discernible plan; the signs were simply commercial art raised to an intense pitch, while the establishments they advertised were basic motels with added gaming rooms. Whereas the great image of Manhattan had been of an undesigned but distinct form composed of designed elements of architecture, that of Las Vegas appeared to be an indistinct and undesigned formlessness composed of elements that fell below the threshold of architectural attention.

Furthermore, the resultant form in New York was patently monumental and related to the more durable aspects of conventional cities, in spite of its radical implications. Las Vegas appeared neither monumental nor durable; not only were its buildings flimsy, but the whole scene could be destroyed by a power cut. The difference is underlined by looking at cataclysmic versions of the two cities as presented in the Pop media. After the Bomb and the Neutron Flux, New York would make — in the classic definition of architecture — 'magnificent ruins' that would stand long after the degraded remnants of the human race had destroyed themselves in some appropriate science-fiction trauma. But of insubstantial Las Vegas after the nuclear holocaust there would remain nothing . . . nothing except, as in that memorable last track of Stan Freberg's brilliant first LP, the echo of the folk singer ('Los Voroces was a mighty city, and it worshipped a silver bird . . .') and the coyote howling in the naked wilderness. . . .

The Las Vegas environment then was a classic Pop artefact, as that term had come to be understood by the end of the fifties — an expendable dream that money could just about buy, designed for immediate point-of-sale impact, outside the canons of Fine Art. But it was also an unmediated image, still contained within the matrix of Pop culture and impinging on nothing else. The change began in the summer of 1965, when Tom Wolfe published *The Kandy-Kolored Tangerine Flake Streamline Baby*,[7] in which he reprinted his famous essay on Las Vegas. Only it wasn't famous then because it had still to make its full impact, and that only came with re-printing, because it then reappeared in company with an introduction to the whole collection which returned to the Vegas theme in order to drive home what had become by then Wolfe's main preoccupation – the irrelevance of established fine-art standards of judgement to what was actually happening in America. In order to emphasise this point he went beyond the straight celebratory description of the signs which had appeared in the original piece, and now insisted that they were the normal design-style of North America, pitting them against the Baroque of Versailles[8] at one extreme, and the abstract modernism of Mondrian and Moholy-Nagy at the other. He was claiming thereby that they were to be considered at the same cultural level as the canons of visual art taught in Liberal Arts Colleges in the States or in art-history courses in Design Schools in Europe.

The challenge could not be ignored. In December 1965 I altered my North American itinerary in order to take in Las Vegas for the first time, and I may have been one of the first to do so. But I was very far from the last, and by the summer of '66 it was required viewing for all architectural students visiting North America, even if they hadn't actually read Wolfe, but just got the word on the student grapevine. Las Vegas was well and truly sprung out of the purely Pop context, re-mediated by Wolfe, and was now part of the general European discussion of town planning and aesthetic control. Effectively it re-polarised that discussion because, for anyone who found anything good in the Vegas environment, established procedures of town planning and standards of aesthetic control had to be wrong. The place didn't so much flout those standards – simple opposition would have left the argument with its original polarities – it simply ignored them, which made new polarities necessary.

It fell to me to make the first comments on this situation in a European magazine, in 1967.[9] Reviewing *Kandy-Kolored*, and taking my cue from Wolfe's class-conscious oppositions of taste, I raised the question of why there would never be a Las Vegas in England, and answered it to my own satisfaction by pointing out the entrenched power of the planning establishment to prevent it. Furthermore, I supposed that if anything like that were to happen in Britain, it would be indoors, where it could not offend the eyes of the *culturati*, as Wolfe called them. However, the idea of an English Las Vegas clearly intrigued a number of people at that time, and in 1969, together with Cedric Price, Peter Hall and the paper's editor, I contributed to *New Society*[10] one of a set of studies of what might happen if certain areas of England were opened to Strip-type development. This time the planning establishment felt required to take notice, and we were subjected to a matching set of stony-faced put-downs by most of the leading mouthpieces in the field. The area of the image's relevance had been extended, but the final effect, I think, was to alert the preventive arms of British planning to the possibility that someone might actually try to do a Las Vegas on them, and thus increased their vigilance against its happening.

In the meantime, and perhaps more significantly, Robert Venturi and Denise Scott-Brown (also inspired by readings in the *Kandy-Kolored*) had published the first version of their definitive study of the architectural and planning consequences of Las Vegas in *Architectural Forum*,[11] the New York architectural monthly. This was the very opposite of the blanket condemnation the *Forum*'s conventionally-trained readers presumably expected. Against the grain of conventional planning wisdom, the two writers applauded the profusion of shameless illuminated signs, the total independence of those signs from the architecture of the buildings to which they referred, and the total independence of those buildings from urban planning as normally understood. Claiming to have discovered a 'Significance for A & P parking lots', they announced that 'Billboards are almost all right!'

This may sound like Americans talking to Americans, but the international standing both of the authors and of the magazine meant that their views were heeded or rejected throughout the international architectural community. Also, their re-packaging of both the argument and the imagery in the conventional formats of school studio work, and the colour-slides normal to art-historical teaching, meant that the image had been mediated yet again. At the same time, Venturi's publication of designs based on Las Vegas procedures — his famous decorated sheds — meant that we had arrived at third-order imagery, like that of New York in 1920, and that it might prove equally unstoppable.

But 1970 was not 1920, and the Las Vegas image now came under discussion, indeed under fire, from thinkers and theorists of a totally different calibre to those involved in the days when it had been part of a private British conversation around Bedford Square or Long Acre. As a result, Las Vegas became not only a planning problem but — by the time Tomás Maldonado had finished — a political paradigm of capitalism as well.[12] Against the 1968 image of the Strip as a working exemplar of a more flexible and less absolutist style of urbanism than that proferred by European theorists from Ebenezer Howard to Le Corbusier and Doxiadis, there was now ranged the counter-image of Las Vegas as the total surrender of all social and moral standards to the false glamour of naked commercial competition.

This effectively returned the argument to where Stan Freberg had left it in 1957 — the bomb had been the last attempt of the Casino El

Sodom to outbid the floor-show across the Strip at the Hotel Gomorrah, where they had just re-staged the Arab-Israeli war 'live every nite!' But whereas Freberg had been addressing himself to a fairly limited circle of hip insiders in the Pop world, Maldonado had raised the stakes to the level where only top planners, architects and design theorists could play, and the ante was the fate of Western civilization . . . or something.

Like most high-level dialectics, this had become a largely theoretical affair with little direct application to any particular places in Europe or America. Yet, somewhere along the way a very direct and painful practical application had been triggered – indeed a mortal mediation of the Las Vegas image. If people died in the collapse of the Ronan Point tower-block because, in some way, tower blocks were a manifestation of the architectural profession's determination to build the city of the future in the image of New York, then it can equally be argued that those who lost their lives in the Summerland disaster in the Isle of Man in 1973 did so, in part, as a consequence of the determination of our Establishment that there should be no Las Vegas in Britain.

As I prophesied, Las Vegas could only happen here if it was kept safely indoors, and as Warren Chalk pointed out in a sympathetic study of Summerland long before the tragedy, Summerland was simply Las Vegas inside out:

> There is a complete conceptual reversal of those examples of Las Vegas casinos, like the Stardust . . . with its constantly changing façade all done in lights with an immediate 'I must go inside there' trick that is not sustained once across the threshold. And somehow the reversal works. Bland outside, once inside it's a very different all-happening scene.[13]

Bland on the outside because that is what British planning decorum is supposed to require, in opposition to the all-action exteriors of the Stardust, Dunes or Golden Nugget. It was folded back over itself seven storeys deep because one cannot, in Britain, think of land as something cheap and endlessly available. As a result, a small fire that would have been a minor diversion in a parking lot on the Strip in Las Vegas became a holocaust on the sea-front in Douglas, Isle of Man. Literature and art only rot your mind; buildings can kill you.

Imagery, mediated and latent
Exaggerated? Yes, but only to clarify the point. Imitation of Las Vegas was not, at any stage I can ascertain, a conscious intention of

the designers of Summerland. It was always Disneyland, and it is to Disneyland that Warren Chalk turns for comparisons throughout almost the whole of his article. But Disneyland is not an image in its own right; it consists almost entirely of brilliant simulations of other environments, other places. It contributes no original imagery to our stock — even the Matterhorn with a hole in it must have been done, somewhere, by René Magritte. But when Chalk needs an image, even a reversed image, to characterise the whole place, it is (and rightly) Las Vegas.

In all discussions of the architecture of pleasure, the townscape of fun (or even the urbanism of doom) since 1966, the imagery of Las Vegas lies latent, retaining much of its original meaning and power, mediate it how we may. And so, too, do the other urban and architectural images we have borrowed almost unwittingly from the United States. So, while we patiently trace our witting borrowings by subjecting them to the established methods of art-historical scrutiny, noting an overhanging roof from Frank Lloyd Wright here, or a well-turned glass and steel corner from Mies van der Rohe elsewhere, we may be totally missing the point about American architecture's effect on Europe.

High above our bent and scholarly heads as we pore over our book-learning, tower the glittering images of the popular arts, like the signs along the Las Vegas strip. Cow-Country Baroque they may be, but not for nothing are they called 'The Lively Arts' — or 'The Deadly Arts' if we mediate and re-mediate them (as at Ronan Point, or Summerland) until their original meanings have been obscured. Much as we may despise the convention-bound planning authorities who insist that 'you can't build that here', these authorities may have a truer appreciation of the real import of American building than those who know it only in the abstracted and mediated forms in which it is usually handled in all forms of scholarly and sub-scholarly discourse, from colour-supplements to history seminars.

The Influence of American Foods and Food Technology in Europe

MAGNUS PYKE

The two most important articles of food introduced into Europe from America were potatoes and maize. When potatoes were first brought over in the sixteenth century, and for almost two hundred years thereafter, they were treated with suspicion by the peoples of Europe. They were reputed in Switzerland to be the cause of scrofula and almost up to the nineteenth century were in France claimed to cause fever. In Germany, Frederick the Great was compelled in 1774 to use the Swabian gendarmerie to enforce their consumption. 'The things have neither smell nor taste, not even dogs will eat them, so what use are they to us?' read the message sent by the citizens of Kolberg.[1] But while the compulsion of the Emperor overcame their misgivings and provided the benefit, up till then unavailable, of a reliable source of ascorbic acid (vitamin C) during the winter months the effect elsewhere in Europe of this import into Europe of a food from the New World was less fortunate. The adoption of potatoes by the Irish as a foodstuff eminently suitable to their social circumstances — easy to grow in the Irish climate, simple to cook, combining readily with the milk from the family cow and, above all, not easily destroyed by the landlord's agents evicting a tenant from his holding for non-payment of rent — led in due course to a major social disaster. When for the three consecutive years of 1845, 1846 and 1847 the weather was unseasonably humid and warm and the crop failed due to the depredations of the fungus, *Phytophera infestans*, about one and a half million people died of famine. The social structure of Ireland was thus damaged to a major degree and has, indeed, not fully recovered to this day. (Salaman has discussed the social influence of the potato on the Irish Community.)[2] The society of the United States, to which great numbers of such Irish as escaped the famine emigrated, was also permanently changed thereby. The potato, a food native to the Americas, is one illustration of the potent influence which an exotic imported commodity may exert on a European community.

Maize also, the so-called Indian corn, when introduced into Europe, taught to the poor of these nations, as it did to those of the European colonists of the United States, the lesson already known to the Red Indians, that a food commodity or the process required to prepare it for consumption, may possess unexpected, even disastrous, results if imposed on another community unpractised in its use. Eaten as corn meal or the like as a primary foodstuff, maize gave rise to the disagreeable, even dangerous, disease of pellagra.

The harmful social effects on European society of these two quite different foods, potatoes and maize, appear to have arisen from the readiness with which they could be fitted into economically impoverished communities and through their very convenience as a cheap source of energy value. Maize also brought harm to impoverished communities in Italy, particularly in Lombardy, France, Spain, Rumania and Corfu, quite apart from Egypt and the United States itself. Simultaneously deficient in the vitamin niacin, and the amino acid, tryptophan, maize when used, as potatoes also had been used, as the main staple of an inadequate diet for socially depressed populations, led to generalised malaise. Work became unbearable; people suffered from headache, giddiness, diarrhoea and discolouration of the skin, which form the characteristic indications of pellagra. (As a component of the meat-based diet of Red Indians in America, where it was indigenous, the low levels of niacin and tryptophan in maize were immaterial.)

If it is accepted on the basis of these examples that the introduction of primary foodstuffs from America into Europe can produce profound social effects, the influence of American methods of food processing when applied either to foods already widely distributed outside America or to others not extensively recognised outside the Western Hemisphere, can produce effects on Europe equally significant. It is clear that a number of characteristically American foods as well as American methods of food processing are to be found in Europe. At the same time other foods, widely consumed in America, have not been accepted in Europe and have made no impact there.

Some years ago I put forward as a speculative postulate for a 'dietary law' the proposition that 'if there is nutritional need for an article of diet, the free play of social forces within a community will in due time cause that article to be invented'.[3] It could similarly be argued that only when an innovation from America fits, in some way that it is not possible to foresee in advance, into the social context of Europe, will that food or food process exert a significant influence there.

Buzzell and Nourse carried out a detailed study of the fate of all the innovations in food manufacture launched on to the United States market over the decade 1954-1964.[4] They reached the conclusions, firstly, that of all the allegedly novel products only 7 per cent were in fact new and that even when the most experienced companies, employing the most highly qualified research staff and the most resourceful marketing experts and spending substantial sums of money on test marketing and promotion, decided to launch a new food they were entirely unable to forecast which of three eventualities would occur. One pattern of events was 'steady growth'; that is to say, the product immediately proved acceptable and became increasingly so as time progressed. The second pattern observed by Buzzell and Nourse was described as 'peak and decline'. Sales first increased, then remained steady for a while and then, after a year or so, fell away. The third sequence of events was 'steady decline'. Regardless of the wholesomeness of the food or of the amount of effort devoted to its dissemination, such popularity as it initially enjoyed consistently dwindled.

These phenomena can be interpreted, as they were seen by Buzzell and Nourse, in terms of economics and business administration. On the other hand, an alternative interpretation would be to view those products that were accepted as fitting into the evolving social fabric of the society to which they were newly available. Among these signally successful products aimed at American society were de-hydrated potato, increasing in popularity eighteen-fold within the decade, frozen dinners increasing by 483 per cent, and semi-moist canned pet foods. The difficulty of forecasting beforehand whether new food products aimed at the American market will or will not influence the social scene appears to be paralleled when a food product, developed to fit the needs of American society, is newly introduced into the different social environment of Europe.

Breakfast cereals
In certain respects, cornflakes and the diversity of other so-called 'breakfast cereals' of the same category epitomise the basic characteristic of American foods, which themselves reflect American style and philosophy. Ideas about right and wrong when extended to food, not only comprise views about the suitability or unsuitability of eating certain articles of diet, but are also concerned with eating

behaviour which itself constitutes a major factor by which the social coherence of a community is maintained. Cornflakes and a whole series of similar products, including Nuttose, Grapenuts, Malta Vita, Cero-Fruto and many more, were developed as part of the religious philosophy of the Seventh-Day Adventist community then settled at Battle Creek, Michigan. The original idea was that such food products were in some way peculiarly pure and could therefore appropriately be eaten straight out of the box and without further handling or preparation by those people most earnestly in search of spiritual purity.[5] At the same time a great deal of attention was given to the mechanical details of the process by which these breakfast cereals were manufactured in order to produce a uniform, palatable and, consequently, commercially saleable commodity. It followed that the social change which breakfast cereals can be argued either to have brought about or, alternatively, assuming that the change was already happening, of which they were an indication, was only partly due to their purported religious significance and was perhaps to a much larger degree inherent in the technical ability, manufacturing skill and heavy expenditure on advertising undertaken by their devout — but business-like — American originators. The social change in the United States by which a rural population eating 'corn pone' and maize-meal mush became converted into a business community with a vigorous marketing policy eating cornflakes occurred abruptly. The style of twentieth century urban life, in which people increasingly believed in the inevitability of devoting the major proportion of their lives to industrial employment, called for exactly the qualities that cornflakes provided; the cooking of maize in bulk in a factory rather than the preparation of saucepansful of porridge in a multiplicity of individual kitchens; service direct from the container rather than from a cooking pot or serving bowl which would subsequently need to be washed; stability, allowing the packet to be put by in a cupboard without having to be covered or kept cool, thus allowing it to be taken out by a single individual living alone. In addition, manufactured breakfast cereals were well suited to be eaten quickly by an individual in a hurry as distinct from a group of people enjoying a meal together. This perhaps is the central feature in their properties as an American innovation underlying their success both in the United States where they originated and in certain European countries into which they have been introduced. A bowl of porridge was something a housewife served at a family meal. A packet of cornflakes is better suited to the needs of an individual living alone or at least employed alone, separate from corporate family endeavour, under the impersonal pressures of an office or factory.

As one of the first and most successful examples of a 'convenience' food, cornflakes fitted admirably into the American scene in which the population had quite abruptly ceased to be rural and had become urban and in which it was expected that most women as well as men would engage themselves in activities linked to the acquisition of money rather than to social activity within their family circle. To what extent the vigorous promotion of breakfast cereals of American origin in European countries affected the social development of such communities or was merely a reflection of what was occurring there as in the United States is difficult to decide. In Great Britain, cornflakes and the like almost completely displaced indigenous breakfast foods even in Scotland. However, in Latin countries where, while industrialisation has increasingly been embraced, social organisation remains more strongly family-orientated and custom retains the 'continental breakfast', packeted cereal food products have made less impact.

Coca Cola and ketchup
One of the most remarkable effects which American food technology has exerted on European culture is the penetration into the dietary habits of European nations, as it has in many other parts of the world, of drinks of the 'cola' type. It could be argued that these products of American ingenuity, depending as they do on technical expertise in their formulation, bottling, labelling, distribution and advertising and on American business genius in the powerful effort behind their dissemination and marketing, represent almost the only totally original and non-natural foodstuff. The concentration of caffeine of 200-230 p.p.m. in the most widely distributed brands provides 100 mg. in a half-litre glassful which compares with 150 to 250 mg. in one or two cups of tea or coffee and clearly constitutes one of their attractions. Nevertheless, there appears to be no rational explanation of why the particular flavour of cola formulations should have led to their general acceptance, not only by consumers in the United States, but also by members of the diverse societies making up the population of Europe. One hypothesis to explain the wide consumption of these drinks in Europe could be that the insistent, sustained and skilful publicity maintained by the powerful American manufacturers has been successful in breaking down resistance to the initially unfamiliar taste. In addition, the mildly stimulating pharmacological effect of the caffeine satisfied people's needs for a social analgesic which has now taken its place side by side with wine, spirits, coffee and tobacco.

Whereas the acceptance of cola drinks by European consumers

represents the penetration of a product possessing an entirely novel taste, the parallel introduction of tomato ketchup could be taken as an example of the way in which a powerful commercial effort succeeded in persuading people to buy an article which they previously prepared for themselves. Tomato ketchup, it appears, firstly possesses taste and smell, already esteemed by the target community and, secondly, is of uniformly acceptable quality and is presented in a convenient package, available in its manufactured form at all times, and not just in season. The American firms marketing ketchup in Europe provided a product which possessed all these qualities.

It may be considered that tomato ketchup, a condiment, like cola drinks which are consumed as a mild stimulant without thought of food value, exerts little social effect on the European consumers who eat it. That these characteristically American products are widely consumed abroad is, however, of significance in spreading uniformity — a feature of the current technological age. As will appear later, the means used to produce and harvest the substantial tonnage of tomatoes used in the mass production of ketchup exert a further, and more significant influence on European society.

Food technology and mass production
Many of the processes underlying what could be considered today to be characteristically American foods and peculiarly American examples of food technology did not, in fact, originate in the United States. Nevertheless, in most instances they owe their current qualities to a large degree to the influence of American technique and the drive of American organising genius.

Canning, conceived in France and brought to a state of industrial practicability in Great Britain in the nineteenth century, was advanced to a high degree of efficiency and diversity in the United States in the twentieth century. The basic principles which are the hallmarks of American food processing (characteristic labels and vigorous advertising) may not, indeed have originated in America at all. The single individual who could claim to have done for the marketing of food what Henry Ford did for the motor car was Thomas Lipton. Born in Glasgow in 1850, he began work as an errand boy at the age of 10, emigrated to the United States at 14, returned to Glasgow at 18, opened his own shop at 21 and by the time he was 28 had not only established a chain of shops in a number of Scottish towns but had invented the system of prepackaged branded commodities, the success of which in due course transformed him into a titled yachtsman and a millionaire.[6] But regardless of its origin, the invention of mass production in the manufacture of food had a variety of social consequences. In European countries, as elsewhere, it was perhaps inevitable that the earlier bond linking locally grown foods with what people expected to eat — even in large cities such as Paris and London where produce markets were until recently located close to the city centres — should slacken with the growth in population. Branded products, among which canned foods predominated, appear to their purchasers divorced from any particular or recognisable rustic environment and to be simply articles of commerce. Amongst such products canned baked beans can be cited as a leading example.

Canned baked beans which have come to be in Europe one of the most characteristic examples of the food products derived from America, developed from the pork and beans once widely popular in farming communities in the United States. The pork content was gradually withdrawn and the recipe most generally favoured became beans in tomato sauce. This retained substantial popularity in the United Kingdom and elsewhere in Europe until the remarkable circumstance arose in which baked beans were more widely consumed in Europe than in America, their country of origin.

But the main social significance of baked beans was as the forerunner of a long series of canned foods. Whether or not American manufacturers originated the methods by which they were produced or the means by which they were standardised, advertised and marketed, American firms undoubtedly played a leading role in popularising such products now categorised as 'convenience' foods. Canned products of all sorts: meat, fish, vegetables and particularly fruit were followed by 'quick-frozen' products of high quality, attractively packaged, widely advertised and distributed through a chain of retail shops equipped with appropriate 'deep-freeze' storage facilities. Although once again the technique for freezing foods and keeping them frozen is based on the discovery of thermo-dynamics, made by a Frenchman named Nicolas Carnot, in 1824,[7] credit for the modern development of the frozen-food industry must go to Clarence Birdseye who, stimulated by a visit to Labrador where he saw fish, frozen as hard as wood, used for food, set up the first freezing plant in New York in 1928. Between 1940 and 1966, the weight of frozen vegetables rose from 92 to 3,415 million pounds, of frozen poultry from 48 to 2,528 million pounds and of frozen fish, meat and fruit from 30, 14 and 225 to 971, 842 and 756 million pounds respectively.[8] And besides the commercial marketing of individual convenience items, the new techniques made possible an equivalent increase in complete dinners, sold frozen and only needing to be heated. All these techniques, originating in the United States and vigorously marketed by American businessmen, have spread across the industrialised communities of Europe. There have been several social consequences.

One of these has been a significant change in shopping habits. When food retailers still purchased their supplies in bulk — flour and sugar by the sack, tea in a chest, butter in a keg and cheeses whole — the local store was a place of resort. It was a social centre as well as a distribution point. Standard articles, prepackaged and preserved by canning or freezing in a large-scale modern factory are distributed with more efficiency, even if with the loss of social intercourse, in an equally efficient large-scale supermarket. Hence it is reasonable to suggest that one of the effects American food technology has had on the character of European society has been to accelerate the extinction of the general store on the street corner, of the specialised butcher, baker, greengrocer and dairy and to substitute the supermarket. Great Britain, moving forward a decade behind the United States, possessed 175 supermarkets in 1958, 367 in 1960 and 4,800 in 1971.[9]

As the leader in prepackaging, canning, freezing and to a lesser degree, for example in the development of instant coffee by dehydration, the United States could be said to have played some part in the change in the social coherence of the family, for which advances in food technology have in some measure been responsible. In the time of our grandparents, family meals, both in the United States and Europe, were co-operative undertakings. A series of operations, the peeling and preparation of potatoes, perhaps even the killing, plucking and cooking of a chicken, the stock pot. in Britain the boiling of a suet pudding, in Italy, France or Germany even more elaborate and time-consuming operations were all put in train and so managed to culminate in 'dinner time'. Convenience foods have not only abbreviated the preparations needed for a family meal, they have made such a meal a dietetic irrelevance. People can now prepare and consume prepackaged commodities individually. Although the 'TV dinner' is less common in Europe than it is in the United States it is starting to appear.

The influence of American ideas about health and nutrition on European behaviour
Although it is recognised in Europe and America that food provides both pleasure and nourishment, Americans have attached more importance than Europeans to the contribution their diet makes to health and nutrition and have been quickest to change their diet in relation to what they have thought to be the dictates of nutritional and medical science.

It is interesting to note that one of the first and most enthusiastic protagonists of a diet influenced by beliefs about the healthiness or unhealthiness of particular food items, namely, Dr Sylvester Graham, was propagating his views in the nineteenth century, before the days of modern knowledge of nutrition. His two-volume book *Lectures on the Science of Life* was published in Boston in 1839. 'The public tables of our steamboats and hotels', he wrote, 'almost literally groan beneath the multitudinous dead that lie in state upon them embalmed and decorated like the bodies of Egyptian potentates emitting their spicy odours to disguise their natural loathsomeness'. But it was to bread that Dr Graham paid the closest attention and it is his teaching about this article of diet that influenced, first American, and subsequently European diet. He adduced a number of facts to support his hypothesis that bread made from washed whole grain coarsely ground was particularly wholesome. Graham bread and Graham crackers are still current in America and undoubtedly stimulated the continuing use of brown bread by European consumers.

In the twentieth century, when current views on the nutritional requirements for health were becoming established, American workers were again more enthusiastic than those in Europe in taking up the new ideas. Whereas many American workers interpreted the available biochemical evidence as supporting the daily need by an adult for 75 mg of ascorbic acid (vitamin C), students in Europe considered 30 mg or less to be sufficient. To obtain the larger amount, American nutritionists recommended the consumption of a daily glass of orange or grapefruit juice for breakfast and this recommendation was vigorously supported by the citrus growers of Florida and California. Although citrus juice has never attained the widespread popularity in Europe that it enjoys in the United States, there is no doubt that American influence has led to its acceptance on quite a large scale in Europe and that such technological developments as canned and dehydrated citrus products are also to some degree bringing about a change in dietary habits in Europe.

The reciprocal influence of the most firmly established example of an artificial food, namely, margarine, on the dietary patterns of Europe and America has been quite complex. Margarine was invented by a Frenchman, Hippolyte Mège Mouriès, in 1869. When the initial problems of manufacture had been overcome, it became a popular article of diet primarily in the Netherlands. Of today's total production of some five million tons a year, most is still produced in Europe, with Holland as the principal manufacturer. The production of margarine in America was for many years hampered by restrictive legislation designed to protect the dairying industry from competition with butter. This legislation took several forms. A popular device which continued until comparatively recent times were varying decrees insisting either that margarine should not be coloured at all or that it be produced in some bizarre shade of blue or pink.[10] In due course when technical means were found to enable the use of almost any type of oil in its manufacture and soya-bean oil became a significant ingredient, the monolithic opposition of American farming interests was breached and margarine production in America gradually increased. It is interesting to find that restrictive legislation similar to that once in force in the United States continued in Australia and New Zealand into the 1970s.

The first stage in the history of margarine, extending over a full century, can thus be seen to have been an example of food technology exerting an influence on the American diet. (Margarine was initially developed as a butter substitute to supply the needs of people unable to afford the more expensive butter.) The second and current phase was due to the serious increase in coronary heart disease amounting almost to an epidemic among middle-aged men in countries where such men took comparatively little exercise. Their diet was ample and rich in fat, and the proportion of fats containing fatty acids the chemical structure of which was 'poly-unsaturated' was comparatively low. Fats low in poly-unsaturated fatty acids are characteristically firm and solid at normal ambient temperature as are those suited to the manufacture of margarine, the consistency of which is most like that of butter.

The high proportion of American citizens possessing motor cars led to a considerable decrease in the amount of exercise taken; the ample diet most Americans ate made them vulnerable to obesity and heart disease; and the special interest Americans take in what they believe to be scientific findings about health all led to a need for change in their dietary habits. For these reasons, American manufacturers took the lead in developing soft, so-called 'chiffon' margarines usually sold in tubs. Whereas traditionally margarine had been produced to simulate butter as closely as possible in appearance, taste and nutritional value, the new products were marketed as improvements, both in their appearance and convenience and, more particularly, in their nutritional value. This claim could primarily be based on their being made of fats rich in poly-unsaturated fatty acids. The success of this approach was attested by the fact that more margarine is eaten in the United States than butter. The influence of this American acceptance of soft margarine on the diets of Europeans was demonstrated in two ways. Firstly, medical authorities in Sweden, Norway and Finland issued recommendations paralleling those of the United States Food and Nutrition Board and the American Medical Association,[11] which advised people to reduce the proportion of saturated fatty acids in their diet. Secondly, consumption of soft margarines in Europe increased considerably, prompted partly by the medical arguments in their favour and partly by vigorous sales campaigns on the part of their manufacturers.

The influence of agricultural engineering as food technology
Although European scientists and technologists have made significant contributions to the rapid modern advances in agricultural technology, American workers have been in the forefront of the progress that has been made. This has brought matters to the point where it is no longer possible to define the frontier between the contribution made to the finished article by the producer and that made by the processor. Both are concerned in an integrated operation which has been variously described as 'agribusiness' or 'factory farming'. Poultry farming has been converted from an agricultural process into an industrial operation. American scientists led the way in the selection of birds of the appropriate genetic strain which would produce broilers exactly suited to the needs of the supermarket. They pioneered larger and larger processing units until million-bird establishments were not uncommon. Similar mechanisation and automation has been applied to dairy and bacon production. Horticultural crops have been similarly adapted to the needs of food technology; carrots can be grown to a size exactly suited to the cans in which they are to be packed. Peas too are produced for mechanical harvesting and shelling for immediate freezing. Prior to the work done between 1952 and 1962 at the California Agricultural Experimental Station, tomato growers in California used to recruit 40,000 workers to pick the 125,000 acres of tomatoes grown each year. Now, since G.C. Hansen succeeded in breeding a variety of tomato plant capable of resisting the stresses of mechanical harvesting and C. Lorenzen designed a machine to cut the plants at ground level, shake off the fruit, discard the vines and convey the tomatoes directly to the processing factory, almost all the tomato crop from 1969 onwards has been picked mechanically and the 40,000 workers have lost their jobs.[12]

The lead set by American food producers has been followed in Europe although to what extent the same trend would have taken place of its own accord cannot be assessed. It seems justifiable to assume, however, that the influence of American example, that is of the philosophy of the supremacy of technological advance and economic efficiency, has been a potent factor in what has occurred. If this is so, it is an example of a major social change brought about in Europe by American methods of food production. The same methods and machines employed for harvesting tomatoes in California are also used in Italy and, it may be, for the same American-based firm. The importance of the social influence of these advances in food technology is sharply illuminated in the current plans by which it is proposed that European agriculture should be organised. The European Economic Community, bearing in mind the possibilities offered by technology, set up a commission to devise means by which food could most efficiently be produced and most economically distributed and marketed. This became known as the Mansholt Plan. The French Government set up a similar body to do likewise for French food production. Its conclusions were set out as the Vedal Report.[13] The general conclusions of these two bodies were the same. Technological efficiency in food production as in food processing, both deriving to a significant extent from American leadership, has proved to be so efficient that from 1954 to 1962 the number of family workers on farms in Europe fell by 43 per cent and farm employees dwindled by 25 per cent. For the period 1970-1980, the Mansholt plan foresees a further reduction in farm population by 50 per cent while between 1965 and 1985 the Vedal Report envisages a transfer of 80 per cent of the people working on farms to an industrial urban life. Here is social change indeed. Already by 1972 the number of people in the United States who were unemployed and on relief was greater than that engaged in food production on farms. The forecasts made by the economic planners of the EEC indicate that a metamorphosis from a Europe of primarily rural populations living to a large degree on small family farms to a community of towndwellers employed for wages by manufacturing industry is visualised. To a major degree the cause of this social revolution can be attributed to the adoption in Europe of American ideas and technology.

Action and reaction
While, as has been argued in the preceding pages, particular social changes and a general social trend can be identified in Europe as having been due to American foods and food processing methods, a substantial number of American foods and methods aimed at bringing about changes in Europe have not, in fact, done so. In spite of powerful commercial efforts to popularise chewing gum in European communities, the degree to which its use has become a habit in Europe is limited. The popularity of peanut butter among European consumers has also failed to equal that in America in spite of the efforts that have been made to introduce it.

On the other hand, both hamburgers and 'hot dogs' originated in

Germany and may be considered examples, therefore, of European food products which have exerted a predominant social influence in America.

The word 'cafeteria' is a characteristically American linguistic innovation which undoubtedly exerted influence on European habits. Modern American developments of 'fast service limited menu eating establishments' represent in some respects a further extension of the same principle. Yet the early rigours of the cafeteria system — chairs with a fixed support for the cafeteria tray on one arm and the 'automat' itself — failed to appeal to European consumers. Now it is the Swedish Smörgesbord and the British 'carvery' which are exercising a European influence on the initially American innovation.

Urbanisation and increasing industrialisation are characteristic both of the United States and Europe. Apart from the introduction from America of entirely new foods, the main innovative trend into Europe has been the use of increasingly sophisticated methods of food technology. Although current indications are still insufficient to allow any clear-cut opinion to be formed, doubts as to the wisdom of too rapid and complete a disappearance of small farming units on the one hand and the evident popularity of foods which are not mass produced on the other, raise the possibility that such general influence of American foods and processes as can be seen on European consumers could change markedly in direction in the future.

Advertising: the American Influence in Europe

PETER MASSON and ANDREW THORBURN

The average consumer, sitting in front of his television set in Hull, Haarlem, Hamburg, Helsinki, Hauteville or Herrera, shows little curiosity as to the origins of the commercial now vying for his attention. Nor should one expect it; his concern is a personal one, and his acceptance/rejection of an advertising proposition will depend on his own personal motivation. This is, in fact, the essential requirement of mass communication or advertising; that a common proposition can be made to appeal personally to a wide number of average consumers. That mass communication does take place effectively within any particular national society is a function of a complex of normalising factors, within which mass communication techniques in general and advertising in particular are not insignificant.

Undoubtedly, cultural 'normalising' factors are at work on a supra-national basis, but they are still frustrated by such elements as language, distance and legal structures as well as tradition. The simple transference of American advertising films or copy for mass market goods to the European screen or newsprint has therefore, and not surprisingly, been rare. To gauge the effect of American advertising in Europe through the eyes of the consumer is not therefore meaningful; the mechanism of influence has been far more circumspect.

The origins of the American influence in Europe, and many other parts of the world, must lie in their sociological and economic background. At the risk of oversimplifying by the use of national stereotypes, we can still accept that the American stereotype is different from the European. The former is born out of a relatively young society, based on the pioneering spirit of its early settlers in a society which reacts to challenge and is highly competitive and flexible. It not only accepts new ideas but is constantly seeking them out. It is a society looking to the future rather than the past. It is an environment in which one would expect new product development and the unfettered use of mass promotional techniques.

As early as 1867 estimates of US annual advertising expenditure were $60m, growing to $360m by 1890. By the turn of the century national magazines like *Cosmopolitan* and *McCalls* carried around 100 pages of advertising per issue. Inevitably there were excesses in advertising claims which, even within liberal US society led to regulation both from within the industry (National Vigilance Committee, renamed National Better Business Bureau) and from the Government (Federal Trade Commission) during the first two decades of the twentieth century. But it brought no check on total advertising, which continued to rise substantially, receiving a boost from a new medium — radio — in the mid-1920s, to reach $3,400m by 1929.

At the same time the United States' economy was far outstripping the 'Old World' and its manufacturers were looking to export its ever-increasing range of consumer goods. It is against this background of experience and economic strength that US manufacturers and advertising agencies took their first major marketing steps in Europe. J. Walter Thompson re-opened an office in London after World War One (having first set one up as early as 1897), using the Libby business as a springboard, and in 1927 General Motors gave them a major impetus into Europe. JWT opened an office to handle G.M. business wherever there was a manufacturing or assembly plant. Similarly, McCann Erickson was initially motivated to expand overseas by the needs and requirements of the Standard Oil Company of New Jersey.

It is out of these early hand-in-hand developments that much of the US influence has arisen. Both manufacturer and agency made a point of staffing their administrations with their own people. They brought with them US experience in marketing new products — the ability to take a longer term view for a pay-out plan. They accepted the necessity to educate the consumer and considered advertising to be the essential tool for this. 'It pays to advertise' became the standard American slogan of the nineteen twenties. Many products which are now household names were introduced during this period — Kellogg, Kodak, Ford, G.M. America's real contribution in the twenties was new product development, introduced via the medium of advertising. Advertising became an accepted, and clearly successful, tool in the marketing mix. British and European companies also found that 'it pays to advertise'.

The whole economic system during the depressed years of the 1930s was put under critical examination, not least advertising. Advertising was failing to be the consumer stimulus and prime mover in growth and development that it had been in the twenties. Advertising in itself had to be understood and an effort made to determine what kind of advertising was most effective.

American researchers like A.C. Nielsen, George Gallup and Daniel Starch were pioneers in this field. The techniques they developed provided a valuable assessment of the effects of advertising. These techniques were equally applicable in markets outside the United States, and those expatriate Americans based in Europe after the Second World War wanted those tools. Gallup Poll is now virtually a household name in Europe. George Gallup enfranchised local research companies with his name and techniques. Nielsen on the other hand set up his own retailer research panels step by step throughout most European countries. His success and influence was such that today it is customary in many European countries to examine variations in consumer demand by Nielsen Region. Starch advertising effectiveness techniques still form the basis of most work currently done in this area today.

The years following World War Two saw an enormously expanded US influence in Europe, in terms of economic aid, business concessions, political influence and numbers of personnel. Europe had to be rebuilt, it couldn't afford US consumer goods, there were controls everywhere, not least on newsprint and advertising. The mechanism of American influence changed; it became more indigenous as advertising companies were forced to work within the constraints of the highly controlled European environment. In many ways the influence dissipated and the American in Europe became 'more European than the Europeans'.

The post-war picture in the United States was different, advertising expenditures soared from $3,400m in 1946 to $5,700m in 1950. The ratio of advertising to Gross National Income was still much higher in the States during the 1950s than in Europe. In 1953 it was 2.6 per cent (1.5 per cent in Britain) and 2.9 per cent (2.1 per cent in Britain) in 1959. A new medium had added impetus to US advertising development — television. Within ten years television had become the third largest advertising medium in the United States with nearly 15 per cent of the total expenditure.

Trial and error is involved in the development of anything new and the television medium was no exception: both in the organisational structure and in its use as a medium, Europe had the US experience to call upon. Certainly, some eight years later, British commercial television was able to avoid the excesses of multi-channel networks, advertising domination through sponsored programmes, uncontrolled volumes of spots, and 'unbalanced' programming through the constant pursuit of large audiences. Britain nevertheless maintained television as a flexible and powerful advertising medium. Europe, however, had observed the growth of US commercial television, and the apparent detrimental effect it had on other media (notably magazines and cinema). Most European governments, under pressure from the existing media owners, have severely curtailed and controlled TV advertising to the point where they can only just raise sufficient revenue to finance the television medium. There was little thought of providing a flexible advertising medium. Television's rapid and successful American development had not in this instance helped the advertiser in Europe.

With the development of commercial TV in the United Kingdom, we see a major growth period in total advertising and increased interest in British advertising by US agencies and personnel, and by British agencies in US personnel and techniques. Commercials had to be made, and there had been eight years experience of making them in the States. A whole gamut of experience exchange took place – US creative people coming to work in London agencies (including British ones), US production companies setting up in London, UK personnel touring the States, as well as US commercials being adapted for UK use. In the research field too we saw a major US influence. Television audience measurement is the key (under the British and US systems) to the selling-assessment of the medium. Of the three main contenders for the industry research contract, two were American. The contract was finally awarded to a joint operation by Nielsen (US) and Attwood (UK) known as T.A.M. (Television Audience Measurement). TAM subsequently obtained the contract for measuring the television audience in Germany along with the German company INFRATEST, forming a joint operation known as INFRATAM.

Television was, as it were, a special event in the US/Europe advertising relationship. Whereas the 1920s contribution from the United States was the whole concept and power of advertising, the contribution of the 1950s is embraced by the word 'marketing'. Many of the activities involved in 'marketing' had been used in one context or another by progressive companies long before on both sides of the Atlantic. Procter and Gamble had a brand manager system in the early 1930s, and a lot of work had been done on physical distribution problems in the 1940s by Fenton B. Turck. But credit for a total 'marketing' approach generally goes to Ralph Gardiner in his overhaul of General Electric's horizontal organisation into 126 operating departments, each virtually a business in its own right. During the 1950s in the United States and subsequently in Britain, virtually every facet involved in the process of getting products to the consumer came under review.

Advertising took on a wider role, particularly in establishing a favourable 'pre-selling' climate. Market research gained an acceptance previously denied to it. Selling became a 'profession' and got the required tools. Product design placed the emphasis on convenience and ease of handling. Packaging often became so important that the contents no longer seemed to matter. Any development of this magnitude is subject to excesses and whims, but the 'marketing' foundation was solid. Distribution studies by major companies were producing surprises. Monsanto Chemicals developed a detergent but sold it to Lever. Lever had the marketing capacity to reach retailers, Monsanto did not. Making a product had become a supporting activity; manufacturing could always be farmed out, but marketing could not.

But the key to marketing was plentiful credit, both consumer and commercial, to encourage the adventurous, with a combination of courage and skill, to invade established markets, and to maintain their pressure when the invaded fought back. The parallel to this in the retail trade was price discounting, which wrecked the contented merchants hiding behind 'fair trade' practices and traditional mark-ups. The marketing function was well summed up by Sol Fox, writing in *Printers Ink*: 'The marketing concept is not a method; techniques arise from an understanding of the concept, which is a feeling, a state of mind, a way of looking at business from the point of view of creating and satisfying customers'.

With their new 'skills', products and wealth, US manufacturers were looking further afield for new markets and their US agencies wanted to be able to take them there. If they didn't, some other US agency might do so, and thereby weaken their hold on the US domestic business. The ability to service an advertiser multi-nationally was becoming a criterion for agency selection. By the mid-fifties Europe was freeing itself of control, and surging forward; it became an obvious development area for US advertisers and agencies. J. Walter Thompson, McCann, Young & Rubicam and Foote, Cone & Belding had developed networks in Europe before, or soon after the Second World War. For others, the late 1950s onwards became a scramble into Europe. Share exchanges, outright purchases, new ventures were all ways in which American agencies sought to operate in Europe. Ted Bates (Colgate, Mars, Mobil and Warner Lambert) merged with John Hobson & Partners in 1959 and from there made a dozen mergers in Europe in the next seven years. Similar developments could be observed by Benton & Bowles, Compton Advertising, N.C.K., B.B.D.O., Grey, etc. Later in the sixties the more successful European networks succumbed to American buyers. Kenyon & Erkhardt (US) merged with Colman, Prentis & Varley, Leo Burnett (US) took over the LPE Group of Companies and D'Arcy (US) merged with Masius Wynne-Williams. By 1972 only three of the world's top thirty agencies were not US owned (two Japanese and one British). In each European country about half of the top ten billing agencies are US owned; for example, in Belgium it is six, Britain eight, Netherlands five, Sweden three, Switzerland two and West Germany six.

One might expect therefore that US influence on European advertising over the last ten to fifteen years would have shown a rapid and marked increase. In fact, with the eight to ten year 'start' the US economy gained over Western Europe after World War Two, the major marketing and product developments that were made, and the increasing American ownership or control of European advertising agencies, one would have expected domination by American products and advertising and in consequence adherence to American lifestyles. For better or for worse this has not been the case.

We can only hypothesise as to why US companies have not achieved that impact on the European market-place and lifestyle that they have achieved in other parts of the world, such as Central and Latin America, the Caribbean, South Africa, Japan and Australia. On the whole, US companies have not, in the last fifteen to twenty years, been particularly successful in Europe, even though the parent US company has been exceptionally innovative in new products and marketing in the United States. One may instance General Mills, Hunt Wesson, and Pilsbury with remarkably little European activity, and General Foods and Procter and Gamble with unspectacular results.

The answer must lie in the biggest single scarcity in advertising and marketing — skilled manpower. American agencies could not export sufficient manpower to run at the advertising execution level all the agencies they were acquiring or developing. They had to use local labour. For example, in 1961, out of a staff of 366 in London, Young and Rubicam only had five who were American. The same was true of American manufacturers.

To a large extent the American personnel were swamped by the Europeans; they came to accept that Europe was different, and that they had to change their techniques. This 'European advice' seriously curtailed their activities. Firstly, at a product introduction stage; here the 'advice' would often be that the product was too 'advanced' for the market, research had shown that the consumer saw no 'need' for it, and wouldn't purchase it at the price projected. Secondly, at the marketing level; 'advice' would be that new distribution techniques would upset 'the trade', new packaging would destroy existing corporate/brand loyalty, use of television would be too effective and evoke a negative response from the Government, and a particular style of advertisement used in the United States would be too 'brash' for Europeans.

Whatever the rights or wrongs of these arguments American agency managements and their clients accepted the advice and did it the 'European way'. They renounced the panache, courage, and marketing skills that had achieved so much in their own country and in other parts of the world.

This is not to suggest that the techniques of advertising and marketing that formalised so well in the United States in the 1950s did not get used in Europe. The techniques certainly did and in many cases were significantly developed. What really did not come across (or was dampened when it did) was the entrepreneural and innovatory spirit.

The late 1950s and early 1960s in British advertising agencies were certainly the era of the marketing and research man. Marketing services (including organising salesman activities, merchandising and point of sale material, new product development workshops) and Research services (including the motivational assessment of consumers, as well as head counting studies) became the new wares by which agencies were endeavouring to attract new clients. The logic was to offer these marketing services to clients who had not yet developed them, or to meet skill with skill in the case of a large 'sophisticated' marketing company. The major British agencies which undertook these developments were not without success. The London Press Exchange, with a particularly large spread of marketing services organised in separate profit centres within its group, won the UK Ford account in 1961, in spite of J. Walter Thompson acting for Ford throughout the rest of the world.

Certainly in the United Kingdom this emphasis on research was not new, and in the field of media research it was ahead of the United States in organising data on an industry basis. (The IPA National Readership Study started in 1954, whereas the Simmons and BRI syndicated surveys in the United States were developed in the 1960s.) Subsequent major developments in readership research have come out of France (reading-frequency scales), Sweden (informant classification developments), the United Kingdom (media model developments) and more recently Germany (macro-measurements of advertising effectiveness).

The local staffing of American agencies in Europe has likewise had a limiting influence on US creative work in Europe. Its acceptance has been more by chance than design, but again this does not mean that Madison Avenue was not making the running. Certainly, if the 1950s belonged to the marketing man, the early 1960s belonged to the creative man, with the Bernbach and Ogilvy 'creative advertising revolution'. If one were to try to document the characteristics of this new 'style' one would stress its ability to empathise with and understand the average man in the street and to position the products in terms of his environment. The execution of this involved the use of humour — not 'corn or slapstick', but of a much more sophisticated appeal. But further than humour it involved irreverence — no longer did one have to proclaim the superlative. Avis admitted it was number two, not number one, in the rent-a-car field, and had to 'try harder' and by implication give better service. Copy became much more down-to-earth, and was written as people spoke it. Sex too has played an ever increasing role, seemingly to the point where any conceivable product has some sexual overtone. Finally, we must list creative daring — buying out the space in a whole magazine, or taking a whole page with one sentence of copy.

All these developments crossed the channel but in a piecemeal way, and not especially through the financial structures of agency networks. Their assimilation or adaptation came about through individuals in creative advertising fields. It is perhaps not insignificant as a barometer to note the further move of the Ford UK advertising account. This time, again bypassing J. Walter Thompson, it moved to Collett Dickenson & Pearce, and, in the style of this new agency, in 1966 began to develop some 'creative daring'. A complete change from the 'marketing' approach of the LPE.

The European advertising industry was being shaped, gradually but firmly, in a different way through American influence. While US techniques in marketing and advertising design techniques were not particularly systematically applied, US agency network development has been. American advertisers, with their view of Europe from 3,000 miles away, and their successful history of pulling together their fifty states in marketing terms, inevitably wished to treat Europe as one country.

Western Europe had, however, been developing since World War Two, in advertising and marketing terms, as a collection of individual nations, each representing a distinct market-place. Britain had been taking the lead both in terms of volume of advertising and in terms of developing new methods and techniques of training, much of it, as we have seen, US influenced. Such multi-national advertising as there was by the end of the 1950s tended to be organised from London. The London Press Exchange, for example, had a specialised seventy man agency (INTAM) specialising in overseas advertising, only a third of whose billing, however, went into Europe. A large part of the rest was concerned with the Commonwealth.

The ending of the boom years of the 1950s, the signing of the Treaty of Rome, the infusion of younger management who had learned their craft during the fifties, and the increasing pressure of American advertisers and agencies, led British agency management to look more seriously at Europe. S.H. Benson, Mather & Crowther, Colman, Prentis & Varley and London Press Exchange, to name a few of the leading agencies in the early sixties, were endeavouring to establish their own networks on a scale approaching the larger American agency operations. Lintas and the London Press Exchange (later LPE) actually reversed the process and acquired small US agencies.

For British agencies the going was hard both financially and administratively. British agencies were essentially forced into Europe in order to gain business from the American international companies operating across Europe. The American agencies were financing their development out of their existing (very large) domestic business. British advertisers had not re-orientated to Europe from their traditional Commonwealth business. Those British agencies that bought or set up companies in Europe had to take a fairly short-term view on the payout period. The operations were often financial tightropes, and the development of advertising campaign co-ordination and training plans on a European basis was limited.

To be fair to the British networks of the sixties the intention to raise standards of local branches and to co-ordinate campaigns was there, but the truly multi-national accounts of any size were few and far between. Lintas, insulated by its Lever business throughout Europe, probably made the soundest developments in common standards and training. Masius Wynne-Williams made similar developments by the use of a mobile team of specialists (media, creative, research) assisting and quality controlling planning in each local agency, particularly on Mars Petfoods. The LPE, in a less formal way, did the same for Miles Laboratories (Alka Seltzer). In the main the US agency networks were not achieving any greater degree of co-ordination than the British were in the field of mass market fast-moving goods. While they had many US companies in this field, they did not necessarily handle the business in all European countries. Companies like Procter & Gamble, General Foods and Colgate were running local operations in each country, often with local production and relative autonomy in the advertising and marketing operations. Again, in spite of their major financial investment, we cannot say at the present time that they have led the way in Europe, but they may well be better placed to react to future changes.

Europe is changing in marketing terms. The changes are coming about through the removal of tariff barriers, joint economic and fiscal policy, and a new legal harmonisation on the marketing of goods. That is, the whole marketing environment is changing as is the social and economic structure. Education, greater wealth and travel are great 'normalising factors'. Increasingly, European products and European marketing are becoming a reality.

However, an important requirement (but not an absolute necessity) to European marketing is the existence of European media and thus far the only cross border influence has been due to language similarity (French media in Belgium and Switzerland, and German media into Austria and Switzerland) and the technical considerations of electronic media. (The English language programme on Radio Luxembourg can be picked up in places as far apart as southern Sweden and northern Italy.)

Without doubt, United States general news magazine and newspaper publishers have done most to encourage a total view of Europe as a market. Certainly they have been forced to modify the concept by offering regional or country editions of their advertising magazines (e.g. *Time* Scandinavia, *Time* UK) but the main thrust has not changed from that of truly multi-national media. *Time* has pursued this concept from 1946 in Europe and *Newsweek* from the 1950s and their combined European advertising revenues in 1973 are likely to reach $15m. Other US publishers have taken a similar multi-national view of Europe, but in the more specialised area of business — as in *Fortune, Business Week, International Management.* But these were certainly paralleled in timing and international intent by the British publication, the *Economist.* There are certainly many examples of European multi-national technical journals emanating from the major countries — the United States, Great Britain, West Germany and France.

From this brief review of media development one can begin to see the pattern of 'Europeanisation'. Firstly, at a technical level — technologists need a common medium (and advertising). But more generally, businessmen have common needs, just as the educated, more affluent members of the population have common needs for world news and products to meet their increasingly similar lifestyles — alcoholic beverages, financial services, cars and travel and leisure products. Certainly, these developments are dependent upon the increasing political and economic unification of Europe, but US influence via its publishers has undoubtedly been the prime mover in the market-place.

Of course, European media developments have not been static. They too have observed the market developments in the business field. Series of similar national publications have been started, like *Espansione* (Italy), *Expansion* (France), produced by local publishers in each country in partnership with the US publishers McGraw Hill (publishers of *International Management* and *Business Week*). In the same sphere Vision Europe publishes a common magazine in four languages. Europa Magazine entered the news/leisure field under Dutch management, but has recently been bought by American Express. Other European publishers are beginning to see the merit of offering a European package, and instead of accepting the risk of new publications have embarked on joint marketing ventures — groupings like the top five: *Elseviers Weekblad* (Netherlands), *La Métropole* (Belgium), *Handelsblatt* (Germany), *La Vie Française* (France), *Il Sole/24 Ore* (Italy).

However, these have not, as yet, shown much vitality. Others, like the Europa grouping, have produced a common product which is basically a monthly supplement which appears simultaneously in *La Stampa* (Turin), *Frankfurter Allgemeine Zeitung* (Germany), *Le Monde* (Paris) and *The Times* (London). This common product is marketed by each of the advertisement sales forces of each newspaper under a central co-ordination. Likewise, the Reader's Digest Association, another major US publishing house, has marketed its mass market product in line with European development on a national basis, such that it is now a leading advertising medium in every European country (except Austria). It too is setting the pace with the introduction of a new multinational advertising facility — the Key European City editions. An advertiser can now market in the Key Cities (more wealth, better education, better distribution) across Europe without spreading his advertising to less wealthy rural areas.

Such then are the major influences brought about by the US publishers. Our conclusions must be that the structural and technical effects of the US advertising industry in Europe have been enormous — though very varied as the century has evolved. Yet the US industry has not controlled the situation; it has been contained in Europe by one means or another. However, the Americans are still keeping ahead in the current 'Europeanisation of Europe' with their large ownership of agency networks and their established 'European' media. This challenge will continue to stimulate us in the 1980s.

American Religious Sects in Europe

BRYAN WILSON

There is a marked contrast between the European sects which migrated to the United States and those which, originating there, have spread their influence in Europe. Leaving aside the larger dissenting denominations, Congregationalists, Baptists, Presbyterians, and subsequently Methodists, most of the European groups which went to America went not only seeking refuge, but also to withdraw from an oppressive social order. Many of them were pietist, introversionist groups, who found in America the opportunity (or sometimes experienced the necessity) for the establishment of vicinally segregated communitarian organizations, and the perpetuation of cultural traits which, though distinctly European in style, were, paradoxically, more easily maintained in the New World than in the Old. Such were the Mennonites (and particularly the Amish), the Hutterians, the Ephrata Community, Zoarites, Rappites, the Amana Society, and the Shakers.[1] These groups have exercised very little return influence on Europe with the exception perhaps of the larger and more denominationally-organized groups of Mennonites, (although some, in search of less-sullied social contexts, have diffused their influence to underdeveloped parts of the world: and particularly is this true of the stricter groups of Mennonites who have established colonies in Mexico, Paraguay, Java, and British Honduras).

The American sects that have most influenced Europe have been those that *originated* in the United States, and which have absorbed particularly American styles of religiosity. The lack of a 'return' from the migrating groups (excepting again the major denominations) is to be explained by the fact that those European sects that migrated to

America were seeking refuge, and were therefore not themselves disposed to seek large numbers of new converts: some indeed were distinctly 'ethnic' in style and maintained an almost ethnic barrier to admission. It is the indigenous American groups which manifested the ethos of expansionism; optimism (in respect of recruitment if not in their ideology); pragmatism, in their organizational goals and sometimes in their religious perspectives; and a capacity for rationalization and routinization of religious activities, and certainly of organizational procedures. Some of these characteristics have also marked the influence of the American wing of major denominations on their European, and especially on their British, counterparts, as instanced in the long-term export of revivalistic religion from the United States to the rest of the world, which has affected in greater or lesser degree most of the major Protestant denominations in Europe, particularly the evangelical wing of the Church of England, Lutheranism, and Methodism, and even the originally doctrinally less-receptive Presbyterians of Scotland.[2] Among sects the extent of this particular influence has of course varied, being most marked in those sects that have most connection with the evangelical Protestant denominations — sects which have been labelled 'conversionist' from their emphasis on the crucial importance of a conversion experience (and sometimes also on subsequent emotional experiences in enlargement or reaffirmation of the experience of conversion).[3] But all the American sects that have really exerted influence abroad have shared the aggressive concern for recruitment; the diminution of distinctions between laymen and professionals (and the elimination of sacerdotalism); a strong tendency to the centralization of organization and the replacement of local community structures by a more conscious establishment of 'local branches'; the use of mass media (cheap, or even free, mass distribution of literature; radio; television).

Clearly, not all of these tendencies are equally evident in all movements. Variations in period and circumstances of origin, in ideological stance, and in the extent to which there has been an accretion of subsidiary concerns; all influence the measure in which these general attributes are characteristic. But the broad ethos of American culture and society is found in American sectarianism as in the major American denominations: American sects have less 'sense of the sacred', less sense of the profound distinction between sacred and profane, and less reverence, in religious devotions as in personal styles, than was traditionally the case in Europe.[4]

Several American sects or groups of sects have been influential in Europe. The movements which have exerted more controlled and specific influence widely in Europe are Jehovah's Witnesses, Seventh-

The Western European Membership of American Sects
(compared with membership in the United States)

Country	Population (000,000s) (1972)	Jehovah's Witnesses (1972)	Seventh-day Adventists (1968)	Pentecostals (groups & adherents) (c. 1970)*	Mormons (1972)
USA	205.1	431,179	404,511	2,920,000 (28)	2,133,758
Gt. Britain	53.9	65,693	11,741	137,000 (7)	71,415
Austria	7.5	10,077	2,614	1,200 (1)	
Belgium	9.6	15,224	1,207	6,200 (2)	
Denmark	4.9	13,760	3,988	15,000 (2)	
Finland	4.6	11,340	5,222	70,000 (1)	
France	51.4	45,012	5,010	33,000 (3)	
Greece	8.9	16,158	268	2,320 (2)	
Italy	54.6	25,810	3,311	142,000 (3)	68,020
Netherlands	13.2	21,769	3,228	10,000 (1)	
Norway	3.9	6,106	5,416	70,000 (1)	
Portugal	8.3	9,841	3,579	11,000 (1)	
Spain	33.1	16,672	2,612	1,000 (?)	
Sweden	8.1	13,052	3,787	135,000 (2)	
Switzerland	6.3	8,326	3,846	6,800 (4)	
W. Germany†	61.4	95,975	26,245	65,000 (8)	

(The figure 68,020 is bracketed across the European countries from Austria to W. Germany as a combined total.)

* Numbers in brackets are the number of separate sects whose members together comprise the total. These figures include baptized members and firm adherents, but should be treated with some caution since different movements employ different criteria of membership. The figure for the United States is probably an underestimate. All four movements included in the figures provide only adult members (usually persons of over 14 years). Population for each country is given as the gross figure.

† includes West Berlin.

Sources: For all three movements other than the Pentecostal groups, numbers are provided by the denomination concerned. Figures for the Pentecostal sects are taken from Walter J. Hollenweger. *Die Pfingstkirchen* (Stuttgart) 1971, pp. 367-8, 374-7.

day Adventists, Christian Scientists, and Mormons.[5] Of less influence, but certainly active in Europe, is the Worldwide Church of God (formerly the Radio Church of God), the organization of Herbert W. Armstrong. The most diffuse influence has been that of the Pentecostalists (a generic designation for a very large number of sects which differ on many details of theology and ecclesiology, and, more incidentally, in style, sophistication, and social composition, but all of which share doctrinal commitment to the continuing operation of the 'gifts of the Spirit' as described in the New Testament, and in particular to the significance of 'speaking in tongues').[6] Pentecostalism followed, reinforced, and carried further the influence of the even more diffuse Holiness movement which spread its evangelical ideas of sanctification to Europe in the last half of the nineteenth century. The separated sectarian groups preaching Holiness (as distinct from the undenominational revivalists who made by far the greater impact) established a number of fellowships, especially in Britain and Germany. New Thought, the movement for metaphysical mind-healing, has had some rather diffuse influence through several separate organizations which have their own membership and organized meetings, (the Unity movement is perhaps the largest), but also as a cult among people in other church fellowships, or among people who belong to no organized movement. Several other religious movements which owe their origins to America — for instance Moral Re-Armament and the Charismatic Renewal movement — cannot properly be described as sectarian. Finally, the Church of Scientology, which, in so far as it is a religious movement, may be said to be sectarian, has, in the last two decades, become a widespread psycho-therapeutic organization, in which thousands of individuals have undertaken courses or undergone therapy from accredited practitioners.

Several of these movements regard their local assemblies as 'branches' rather than as autonomous churches, and the procedures in the branches are uniform throughout the world. Thus the Christian Scientists, whose central organization — a Board of Directors — is at The Mother Church in Boston, follow a Sunday service in which the 'lesson-sermon', composed of scriptural citations and extracts from the Christian Science textbook, *Science and Health*, is the same everywhere. The form of the service is identical: only the hymns and local announcements differ. Jehovah's Witnesses use *The Watchtower* as a catechistical source in their meetings, and other literature which ensures uniform and practically simultaneous coverage of doctrines in all their local Kingdom Halls. Even the Seventh-day Adventists, whose services have much more local variation, not only in content but also in style — some being much more 'churchy' than others — use a quarterly of lessons for their Saturday morning Sabbath school meetings which, although local ministers are free to invite their own speakers, follows at least a similar theme in the discussion groups, which are the core of Sabbath school activity.

Thus, although the point does not hold for all American movements, there is among the influences of sectarianism a significant development of unified religious practice, made possible by the use of printed guides to teaching. It has helped to ensure a measure not only of doctrinal unity, but simultaneous concern with particular issues within a given movement at local levels throughout the world. It functions, too, to maintain the ideal of corporate unity in groups which are, in fact, very much larger than the term 'sect' suggests, and which, without such devices, might be faced with dissimilar patterns of development in different cultures and among different status groups. All the groups which use detailed pre-arranged programmes of worship, and which attach importance to uniform procedures, are groups which emphasize that doctrine must be true in every detail. In such movements ideological control from the centre is a protection against schism and centrifugal diversification.

Different as are Christian Scientists, Jehovah's Witnesses and Seventh-day Adventists in other respects, these three movements rely to a very considerable extent on the dissemination of literature to win new recruits. The late nineteenth century, when all of them were founded, was the age of the new mass reading public, and until the turn of the century a very large proportion of all books and periodicals published were religious in tone. All these three movements have used door-to-door canvassers, although Christian Science gave up this particular method of disseminating Mrs Eddy's works at a very early date, preferring reading rooms (every Christian Science church is obliged to maintain one) in which a proper atmosphere of reverent study is created and in which there is no suggestion of a commercial concern with 'sales'. The movement's periodicals and the small number of authorized works, (more usually biographies of Mrs Eddy rather than expositions of doctrine) are available — to be read on the premises, to be borrowed or bought. The colporteur has remained prominent in the Seventh-day Adventist movement. For Jehovah's Witnesses door-to-door canvassing is the vital means of assuring the movement's growth. Mormon missionary work, too, depends on similar activity and whilst a smaller proportion of Mormons are engaged in this work, the young American canvassers who serve for two years in the mission field are familiar figures throughout western Europe.

The literature of the Christian Scientists is written and printed in the United States for distribution throughout the world. The Adventists and the Witnesses operate presses in other countries, but the bulk of their material is written in the United States, and the American style of presentation is evident in the literature of all three movements. The extent to which congregational life follows American patterns differs in the three movements. The Adventists have always favoured a higher degree of local autonomy, and indeed have encouraged their members from different countries to maintain their sense of national, cultural participation, and thus the atmosphere of Adventist churches differs from one country to another. But Adventists rely less on their own literature for the content of services which follow devotional styles and procedures that are more or less conventional in orthodox Protestant denominations, although local congregations are often also the focus of a somewhat separate community life.

Neither the Witnesses nor the Christian Scientists permit local initiative in the content or order of services, or in the lifestyle of congregations. In effect a highly programmed and routinized procedure is followed which bears the strong imprint of impersonal corporate activity. The communal element of congregational life is not stressed, and individual participation is obliged to conform to prescribed times and procedures. Although Mrs Eddy herself occasionally manifested some degree of national and ancestral pride, she also emphasised the objective and timeless quality of the things she taught, thus leaving little room in Christian Science for personal, local, or national cultural styles. The Witnesses reject all local or national allegiances, and see themselves as already a people prepared for the Kingdom of Jehovah soon to be manifested. Their teachings owe less than does Christian Science to distinctively American influences, much as the movement's organization and procedures bear their imprint.

Sects for which literature is central to evangelistic effort frequently produce additional material which is of only semi-religious interest. Clearly there might be a variety of reasons for this development: as a more subtle strategy for presenting their distinctive message; as a way of attempting to provide their converted following with a wider span of approved interests; as a method of keeping large printing houses busy, and reducing overheads by the diversification of the products which the faithful should buy and (in the case of Adventists and Witnesses) canvass. Mrs Eddy, in deciding to publish *The Christian Science Monitor*, which is perhaps the best known and most respected periodical of sectarian provenance, had in mind a newspaper that, whilst reporting the news, would also conform to the precepts of Christian Science, avoiding undue emphasis on human tragedy, on sin, disease, or death, the reality of all of which Christian Science denies. (This policy led the newspaper's war reporters into some curious circumlocutions when, for example, reporting casualties in the First World War.) Undoubtedly Mrs Eddy wished to influence secular society, and to provide her followers with a source of secular information which did not in itself corrupt their thought. Whether she saw the *Monitor* as in itself an agency for recruitment to Christian Science is less clear: the newspaper carries only one relatively short article on Christian Science metaphysics each day. Nor is it entirely clear how *The Plain Truth* fits into Herbert W. Armstrong's conception of the mission of his Worldwide Church of God, a sect that has used literature and radio almost to the exclusion of all other techniques in the recruitment of members. For some time *The Plain Truth*, which is sent free to anyone who requests it, carried vivid descriptions of the events that the movement believed were to occur with the outworking of prophecy. Later, policy changed and the journal became to all appearances a secular magazine preoccupied with social, scientific, and especially ecological, issues. For some years, the fact that this magazine was published by a religious organization was virtually concealed, but policy has now changed again.

Awake is a fortnightly periodical of Jehovah's Witnesses which is much less explicitly concerned with doctrinal matters than *The Watchtower*, the official and essentially doctrinal organ of the movement. Whilst it is always clear that *Awake* is a vehicle for Witness ideology, and draws out the implication for Witness teaching in many spheres of social and civic activity, it certainly endeavours to be a periodical of 'general interest', with appeal to those who are not Witnesses.

The Seventh-day Adventists are perhaps the sect with the largest and most diversified literary output. Its scope reflects the many-sidedness of Adventist teaching, and the wider degree of regional and local autonomy encouraged by the movement. There are, apart from strictly doctrinal magazines which circulate little beyond the confines of the movement, a number of magazines devoted to quite specific concerns, in particular to health. Those devoted to prophetic exegesis, to religious liberty, and to education reveal the strong imprint of the doctrinal stance of the movement on these subjects, but some of the health periodicals appear more general in their concern to disseminate dietetic (and often vegetarian) principles, hygiene, and standards of good living, and abstinence from tobacco and alcohol. A wide range of literature is carried by Seventh-day Adventist colporteurs, workers for whom this is a full-time job.

Different as are the three movements principally considered in the foregoing respects (Witnesses, Adventists and Christian Scientists) all can be said to represent relatively intellectual styles in religion, in the sense that knowledge of teachings, promoted through the printed word, is indispensable for any who seek membership. All of them emphasise, albeit in different ways, .practicality. Pragmatism is a substantive value for Christian Science; it is the key to the organizational techniques of the Witnesses; and even among the Adventists there is an emphasis on practical issues, systematic organization, and highly routinised annual collections of funds for a variety of denominational causes, in which the leaders claim to 'make the Seventh-day Adventist dollar the hardest working dollar in the world'. Christian Science claims to be as demonstrable as mathematics and thoroughly practical. Proper application of the knowledge of God is believed to lead to real benefit in this world, in health, wealth, longevity, intelligence, pleasure, happiness. The Witnesses have developed highly systematic and efficient methods of organizational deployment of personnel for the dissemination of their literature. Mainly by well controlled door-to-door canvassing and the use of thoroughly rehearsed techniques, contracts are made and those interested are offered courses of Bible study. Although the ultimate goals of the Witnesses are substantive — preparedness for God's coming kingdom — their interim activities are highly instrumental and rational. The Christian Scientists manifest a similar value-orientation less in their recruitment techniques than in their actual doctrine. 'Christian Science works' is a slogan which would not make sense applied to the faith of the Witnesses or the Adventists. Yet, different as is the role of doctrine and its legitimations in these movements, both Adventists and Witnesses manifest a highly pragmatic attitude to their affairs.

In many ways, Christian Science represents the first important *organized* attempt to harness religious ideology rationally and systematically to the service of secular goals. Extreme as is the formulation of the values of pragmatism, instrumentalism, and optimism in New Thought groups generally, this orientation was also a growing element in American religiosity in the major denominations in the late nineteenth and early twentieth centuries. The established churches of Europe have been less ready to proclaim that religion is an aid in the attainment of quite specific 'success goals' in the life of the individual, but in the popular inspirational writings of Bruce Barton, Norman Vincent Peale, Bishop Sheen, Ralph Trine and many others, these ideas became the staple religious diet of millions of people in America.[7] They manifest a degree of calculation, the conscious rational use of religious means for secular ends, and egocentrism, which stands in some contrast to the predominant preoccupation of traditional European Christianity with social control, moral constraint, and the maintenance, through religious agencies, of a secure framework of social order. Success goals, although widely represented in the major American religious denominations, have perhaps never been dominant, and their appeal to Europeans of the same denominational persuasions has been slight. In the New Thought teachings, and in Christian Science, however, this pragmatic, instrumental orientation to religion has been widely disseminated in Europe. The significance of the New Thought movements is not easily assessed, although they have operated in all western countries, particularly in Britain, France, and Germany. Their organizational weakness and the lack of emphasis on traditional conceptions of membership, worship and congregational assembly has perhaps reduced the effectiveness and durability of their influence. Of movements in the New Thought tradition, Christian Science alone has successfully adopted the traditional model of religious involvement and church commitment. Christian Science flourished in Britain from its introduction in the 1890s, especially between the two Wars, winning a considerable number of middle class and some influential adherents including several members of the aristocracy, a few MPs, a few high-ranking military, naval, and diplomatic figures. It was never so successful in continental Europe, except in Germany, where it continued to grow well after the Second World War (at a time when its growth appeared to have ceased in Britain). The movement has published no membership figures for Europe, but it is doubtful if, even at its peak, there were as many as 30,000 members in Britain, or more than ten thousand in West Germany, the countries in which it has had greatest influence in Europe. Its adherents in other European countries appear to have included a more than representative number from the middle and upper classes.

When, in the 1960s, the Scientologists moved their main centre of operations to Britain, hundreds of mainly young people were recruited from Britain and other (mainly Protestant) countries in Europe to take courses at the new centres in Sussex and in Edinburgh. The Scientologists have never made public the total numbers enrolling in their courses or seeking affiliation with their Church, but it seems likely that at least ten thousand Europeans have been involved in the movement. Scientology appears to appeal predominantly to people under 40 years of age, and stands in marked contrast with Christian Science and the earlier New Thought cults, the votaries of which have always been predominantly middle-aged and elderly, with a considerable preponderance of women among them. Whereas the earlier movements were preoccupied with bodily healing, Scientology is very much more concerned with mental health and exercises to improve the intelligence, and this perhaps explains the age constituency of each type of movement.

Apart from Scientology, Christian Science and the New Thought groups present the most marked contrast with European religious thought-styles. All other major American sects have shared with European predecessors or contemporaries some doctrinal perspectives. The adventist sects (the Jehovah's Witnesses, Seventh-day Adventists, and Christadelphians — the latter today numbering about 16,000 in Europe, the vast majority in Britain, with small groups in Norway, Germany and France) share certain broad features of pre-millennial prophetic exegesis with some evangelical members of the major Protestant denominations. Details differ, inevitably, but throughout the nineteenth century there were in Britain and in Germany particular groups whose central chiliastic expectations — from the point of view of the outsider, or of less literally-minded Christians — were not dissimilar. In rejecting (or modifying) the idea of the soul, and in placing greater emphasis on resurrection than Protestant orthodoxy has tended to do, these movements chose alternative items from the plethora of the Christian doctrinal inheritance. These issues cannot be said to have been of any particular social consequence, however, important as they were for the cohesion of particular groups and the assertion of their differences from others. All of these sects bear the style of their nineteenth-century origins, and the theories of literal biblicism that were then widespread throughout Christendom. The financial endowment which has been provided for these ideas from America, and the employment of new American techniques for proselytizing, have, of course, contributed greatly to their continuance, appeal, and acceptability in Europe. The Witnesses have considerably and consciously amended their pattern of activities and the character of their group life in the twentieth century, but they remain, (as do Adventists and Christadelphians) a sect which retains many of the characteristics of nineteenth-century minority sectarian groups. Both Witnesses and Adventists have had to come to terms with the size and dispersion of their members: the idea of a sect counting its members in millions was not part of the nineteenth-century conception. In each movement some members have been concerned from time to time at the excessive involvement of their members in certain worldly concerns, but over time the Adventists have developed a somewhat less rigorously sectarian, and a more denominational position, hindered, inevitably, by the core doctrines of the seventh-day Sabbath and Old Testament dietetic obligations.

Perhaps the most important general social influence of these three adventist sects has been their determined position as conscientious objectors to military service. The Adventists are usually prepared to serve in medical corps, but Witnesses and Christadelphians who, in one or other of the World Wars, were eligible for military service, have been almost completely uncompromising in their response. This has given the movements considerable — and in wartime, unfavourable — publicity. It may, however, have done something to promote the cause of conscientious objection and to have made it more acceptable among a wider public, even for those whose objections have not been specifically on religious grounds. Slowly the rights of members of these sects in regard to conscientious objection have been acknowledged in one European country after another since the Second World War.

In other social matters the influence of these three groups differs. Neither Witnesses nor Christadelphians are teetotallers, although they are non-smokers. The Adventists have used their resources to combat the use of both alcohol and tobacco among the wider public, however, which has never been a concern for the other adventist sects. From time to time they have made common cause with other fundamentalists, as part of pressure groups against the liberalization of laws relating to alcohol, and in the attempt to persuade governments to make public the dangers of smoking and drinking. An Adventist five-day cure for smokers has been used by many, some of whom have in consequence become interested in the movement. Christian Scientists and Mormons prohibit tobacco and alcohol (and, like the Adventists, tea and coffee, although this has had little social consequence, and this particular injunction appears to be widely ignored by Christian Scientists). The presence of Christian Scientists in natural legislatures has been periodically useful to pressure groups concerned about smoking and drinking. The three Adventist groups would, generally, avoid involvement in public affairs, and Witnesses and Christadelphians would not accept public office. No such inhibition affects either Christian Scientists or Mormons, although in Europe only Christian Science has recruited from those social classes with much opportunity for careers in political and public service.

Displaying considerable contrast with the rationalizing tendencies of sects discussed above are the numerous Holiness and Pentecostal sects in America. Although some of these are on a large scale (the Church of the Nazarene is the largest Holiness sect, and the Assemblies of God and the Church of God, Cleveland, are among the largest American Pentecostal sects) and hold together many church communities in denominational unity, the emphasis in all of these movements is on personal experience in the local congregation. Ideologically, they are committed to conversion as the central

Christian experience and to subsequent sanctification experiences, and, in the case of Pentecostals, experience of the 'baptism of the Holy Spirit' and the exercise of the Spirit gifts. The subjectivism of these movements and their commitment to emotionally-stirring religious experience limits the extent to which routinization of organization and activities is possible. The more expressive Pentecostal groups have had far greater influence in Europe than have Holiness sects. They provide opportunities for feelingful religion, for greater spontaneity, freer expression, and the indulgence of the emotions than is possible in the more restrained, more intellectual styles of religion of the movements discussed above, in which knowledge of doctrine is of more importance than dramatic religious experience. Pentecostal sects also have their mechanisms of control, of course, but even where a denominational structure develops, it is free, vigorous, and sometimes ecstatic, expression in the local congregation which really distinguishes Pentecostal religion.

American Pentecostalism owed a good deal to the emotional freedom of traditional negro Christianity, and negroes were prominent among its early leaders and converts. Emotionalism, invocations, noisy outbursts and sustained choruses characterized early Pentecostalism. Sermons were often crude and ungrammatical and the jazz styles of negro music were adopted: the decorum and dignity traditionally associated with religious devotion in Europe was abandoned. Pentecostalism was brought to Europe, first to Norway, only a few years after its American beginnings in 1900, and spread steadily. Whilst always less vigorous in style and more pastorally controlled than American Pentecostalism, Pentecostal congregations had a more enthusiastic tone than — revivals apart — was common in even the more conversion-oriented Protestant denomination in Europe. Recruits were drawn almost entirely from the less well-educated working class, mainly in Protestant countries. Using revivalism and divine healing campaigns (rather than the dissemination of literature) as the principal means of recruitment Pentecostalism often drew in volatile people whose commitment was unstable. Its social impact was slight, although Pentecostalists often joined other evangelicals for interdenominational revivalistic occasions, and sometimes provided manpower for various causes, in particular for campaigns supporting temperance and Sunday observance (in Britain), or opposing Roman Catholicism. Although some prominent Pentecostalists were conscientious objectors in the Second World War, the mass of the rank and file were not persuaded to adopt this position. The various Pentecostal sects tended to ignore political affairs, and, although they supported conventional social norms and civic order, in the typical evangelical fashion they

regarded individual conversion as a better basis for social improve-
ment than programmes of social and institutional reform or social
welfare. The social and political orientations of Pentecostalists
(although these have never been given party political expression) are,
in common with those of most other fundamentalists, conservative.
Innovation in devotional procedures is accompanied by profound
distrust of political and social change. This particular combination of
attitudes is perhaps related to the fact that Pentecostal religion draws
heavily on styles and themes of religion as presented to children in
Sunday schools: simple images, free expression, facile dichoto-
mization of right and wrong, all serve to re-evoke childish responses.
'Old time religion', which is what Pentecostalists have often
emphasised, is often the religion of childhood re-awakened by
activities that rekindle old emotions. The literalism, enthusiasm,
emotionality, and social conservatism are linked by their common
inheritance from the individual's past.

In this conservative orientation, sectarian Pentecostalism differs
from the apparent orientations of the neo-pentecostalists of the
Charismatic Renewal movement — in which the gifts of the Spirit
(and particularly speaking in tongues) are, since about 1958,
demonstrated among Catholics and Protestants of various denominations. This movement is not sectarian and so is not our concern
here, although it is an American influence on European religious
thought and practice, and harnesses Pentecostal practice to meet the
widespread contemporary demand for authenticity, immediacy, and
radical spontaneity as a protest against the over-institutionalization
of modern life. The attitudinal correlates of the charismatic
movement are, as one might expect, quite different from those of
'classical' sectarian Pentecostalism.

Although there is a strong puritanical element in American
sectarian religion, this orientation is by no means uniformly adopted
by all American sects. The millennial sects — the Adventists,
Witnesses, Christadelphians — share with fundamentalist groups such
as the Holiness and Pentecostal sects, a somewhat restrictive attitude
towards involvement in the affairs of the world. Social control of
individuals is evident in all these movements, and although the
outsiders' stereotype of sectarianism as joyless, narrow, oppressive,
and censorious, is almost always in error, all of these movements are
anti-hedonistic. Members must gain their joy (which is usually
extolled, either as a present possibility or at least as an anticipation
of joys to be experienced in the next world) in prescribed ways. But
the content of prescription varies considerably, and from an outside
point of view there is a clear distinction between the millennial and
Pentecostal sects on the one hand, and movements such as Christian

Science, Scientology, and Mormonism on the other. Christian Science does maintain a certain control over its adherents, through the particular type of mental discipline and thought control. But, apart from the particular restrictions on tobacco, alcohol, drugs, and the recourse to medicine, Christian Scientists are, within the bounds of conventional morality, generally free to enjoy the world, and their ideology emphasises the happiness which adherents should experience. The focal point of control is less the adherent's activities in the world, than his commitment to truth as prescribed by the movement. Scientology, which in many respects has some resemblance to Christian Science, also tends to leave its members free to participate in the world in their own ways, with an emphasis on the enhanced enjoyment of life which Scientological training itself is said to confer. In this movement, too, there is an attempt to control the individual through re-definition of his situation and by the inculcation of specific mental orientations. There is evidence that, within the inner organization of Scientology, a rigorous code of discipline is maintained in respect of the performance of staff members in gaining recruits for the movement. Those who fail to reach their targets may suffer social ostracism and degradation, but this scarcely affects 'lay' Scientologists. Their social and moral behaviour is of no concern to the Church of Scientology although they would be disciplined for association with 'suppressive persons' — those critical of Scientological therapeutic practice.[8]

Mormonism — no less distinctively American in style than Christian Science — rejects conventional puritanism. Its teaching is optimistic and universalistic — virtually all men will enjoy eternal life. 'As man is, God once was; as God is, man may become', and 'Men are that they might have joy' are Mormon dicta which summarize the movement's soteriological position. Recreation, including sport, dancing and entertainment are not only tolerated but have always been actively encouraged. Salt Lake City had a theatre before it had a temple. Despite the strong social and communal character of their church, Mormons are free to engage in secular business, politics, and social affairs. The Mormon rejection of Protestantism's traditional puritan inheritance may be an important element in the movement's contemporary appeal. Mormon recruitment in Europe, particularly in Britain, Scandinavia, and Germany, was, from as early as the 1840s, considerable, but because of the early policy of inducing converts to migrate to Utah the long-term influence of Mormonism in Europe has not been very great.[9] In the early years the almost pan-American and nationalistic implications of Mormon doctrine reinforced dispositions towards emigration to America: only since the Second World War has Mormonism sunk sizeable roots again in Europe but it cannot, despite considerable growth, yet be said to have had any extensive impact.

Sectarianism is always necessarily a minority phenomenon. Over the long term, the balance of denominational trade weighs heavily in favour of European exports to America. The return flow of religion of American origin to Europe has been modest in comparison, and the movements themselves, although by no means unimportant in their influence, have been small. The significance of American sects, although their impact has been in no sense unified, has been greater than the figures for membership suggest, however. Sectarian religion is more intense than church religion, and its members are more committed and socially more conspicuous. Whereas religion in general, and the majority churches, Catholic and Protestant, lose their social influence steadily throughout the western world, and are increasingly regarded as less and less important, on the evidence of social survey data, the sects, in contrast, continue to exert the strongest hold over their members, and some of them have sustained remarkable rates of growth in recent decades at a time when membership in orthodox churches has been falling both relatively to population, and even absolutely. The Witnesses have been most effective in their overall increase, and in most European countries are growing faster than the rate of population growth. Other movements have had success in particular countries: the Mormons in Britain, and, in the last two decades, the Pentecostalists in Italy.

The most agreeable climate for sectarianism has been in Protestant Europe — and this has been true for Scientologists as much as for Pentecostalists. Catholic countries have until recently effectively resisted the growth of sects, both through church influence on governments, which have been persuaded to maintain restrictive laws and, at times, oppressive measures (especially in Spain), and because in Catholic countries opposition to the Roman Church has been more political than religious. (Anticlerical traditions as such have not been especially propitious for sectarianism, as the figures for France illustrate.) The inroads made by the Pentecostalists in Italy, particularly among the poorer classes and especially in southern Italy, have come through the agency of returning immigrants, who have brought the faith that they have adopted in the United States or Brazil to relatives at home. The success of Pentecostalism there now begins to parallel the early impact that it had in Scandinavia, particularly in Sweden, where it has long been the largest denomination after the state supported Lutheran Church. The license for greater emotional freedom which sectarian Pentecostalism provides has had its greatest appeal among the poorer and less sophisticated sections of the population. The Scandinavian Pentecostalists are now long established; the Italian assemblies of the movement are relatively recently formed: both because of the general Protestant dominance in Sweden and the settled and respectable nature of Pentecostalism there, it may not be untrue to say that this movement is today less sectarian in that context than it is in Italy. The half century lag between the movement's impact in the two countries reflects, perhaps, not only Catholic resistance in Italy, but also something of the lag in social development between Scandinavia and southern Italy.

All sects represent some measure of protest against the cultural lifestyle of their contemporaries, and constitute a comment — whether conscious or unconscious — on the inadequacy of prevailing moral norms or social facilities and opportunities. In that they appeal to rather different social classes, they address themselves to rather different perceived deficiencies. Thus, whereas most sects appeal to the less educated sections of the population, Christian Science, New Thought, and perhaps also Scientology have had more impact among the middle-classes. They are less ascetic and offer wider intellectual opportunities for their recruits. They share with some others, as we have noted, the practicality, rationality of procedure, and the sense of purposive commitment. They are perhaps less implicitly egalitarian than the more radical adventist groups, even though they all offer channels for social mobility through their own organization. New opportunities to take leadership roles, and to acquire status within the community are offered in all these movements. Sects make a strong reassertion of certain abiding human values, and all of them provide specific grounds for hope in an uncertain world, offer opportunities for service and self-expression (even if within a very circumscribed framework) in a cause which offers total, absolute, and final meaning for the individual's life and the course of contemporary society and history.

The Call and Response of Popular Music:
the impact of American pop music in Europe

MICHAEL WATTS

Pop music, popular music, rock: these are all phrases lumped indiscriminately together to describe the music of the mass-think society; yet divisions clearly do exist. If 'pop' is obviously a derivation of 'popular' — in fact, a trade term, initially — the two are patently not synonymous. Popular culture, of which music is only *one* of the major factors — along with movies, radio, television, sport and the literature of tabloid newspapers, magazines and paperback fiction — has an all-embracing nature that reflects the established values of society as a whole. Pop culture, however, which has pop music as its central moving force, is in origin working class or lower-middle class and a much more specific force, being predomi-nantly the mirror of a certain age group (i.e. youth) and representing, not coincidentally, a form of protest against the older traditions; although, to confuse matters, 'pop music' is a term used sweepingly to describe any music designed for large commercial popularity.

Moreover, whereas popular culture works by a process of absorption, pop is conceived at its most fundamental to frame the instant, *but with initial reference to the social convolutions of adolescence.* It was when pop began in the mid-1960s to have higher aspirations towards seeing itself as a fresh, rejuvenated form of high art that the phrase 'progressive pop' or 'rock' came to be deployed. Rock, a hard, bright, word lopped off, with a degree of inverted snobbery, from the older fifties phrase 'rock n' roll' (meaning the synthesis of Negro blues and white, Southern 'hillbilly' music), is thus *of* pop music while standing apart from it as a form much less compromising and yielding to the demands of the teenage audience. Pop, in effect, changes course through a series of palace revolutions

— the insurrection, for instance, of rock n' roll against crooning and the sixties counterblast of British against American pop — at the same time that it broadly revolts against its cultural surroundings. Also, it needs to be stated now that unlike jazz, which is essentially an instrumental form, the vocal tradition integral to pop has meant that with little exception pop has only been musically reproductive in English language countries. Continental pop has invariably been slavishly imitative and unremarkable.

These definitions once established, the aim of this essay is to show how pop has been a propulsive movement within the European social and musical situation, imposing a new order upon traditional values and narrowing the gap between everyday life and art in a mass-communication society. And the impetus for this rebellion has come not from Europe itself, whose roots were deep in a nineteenth century way of life until the advent of World War Two, but from America, symbol of the technological age and therefore better-equipped to express the artistic ambitions of a post-Victorian social schema. The irony is, however, that the seeds of pop music, later to cross-pollinate with Negro strains, had already been planted in the soil of inner America by European immigrants, principally from the Celtic countries.

It is important to consider the early musical interrelationships between Europe and America up to the Second World War since they illustrate how the ground was cleared for the great pop explosion of the fifties.

Throughout the eighteenth and nineteenth centuries, of course, there had been European entertainers — fiddlers, yodellers, pianists, trombonists and all sorts of musical and variety acts from every country — traversing America with material generally embedded in traditional European music. But by the 1850s their popularity was overshadowed by that of the nigger minstrel shows, a hotchpotch of song, dance and verbal patter dominated by the theme of white impersonation of blacks, a form which, however amiable, indicated early on the expanding pattern of black cultural exploitation by whites which perseveres to this day in the British television programme, the 'Black and White Minstrel Show'.

The musical background to minstrelsy was the European song experience, but as the minstrel shows were slicked into the rough-and-tumble of variety, or vaudeville, the French euphemism it employed, a need became apparent for cheap, home-grown music, and soon song publishers moved onto the scene. It was at this juncture, around the turn of the century, that the pop song was given some shape as a commercial response to public demand. This was the acknowledged birth of showbusiness, with publishers and songwriters operating from a couple of blocks in New York around 28th Street and Broadway known idiomatically as 'Tin Pan Alley', the dominating influence within this claque of the Jewish immigrant thereby sustaining the link with old Europe.

It was natural, in view of America's burgeoning influence, especially on Europe, that Britain should import the more successful of these songs for its own music halls, whose native stars and songs tended to be too insular to succeed in America, and that British publishers should consequently form their own Tin Pan Alley. (This developed around Charing Cross Road towards the end of the First World War.) Britain was patently receptive since the biggest-selling songs, however Anglicised — like 'Nellie Dean' and 'If You Were The Only Girl In The World' — were usually American in-origin. Thus a ready market existed for the craze of ragtime, the first authentically American music, precursor of jazz and a distant relative of the pop song.

Ragtime, designed essentially for the piano, was a rhythmic innovation significant for its use of syncopation, though it leant on European harmonies and the marching signatures of Sousa. A style spawned amidst the jumbled geography of American low-life and stamped with the imprimatur of the Afro-American, in 1912 it came to Britain as a flourishing form via the American Ragtime Octette, and the young J.B. Priestley percipiently noted 'the menace to old Europe, the domination of America, the emergence of Africa'. Rupert Brooke went several times to see the show 'Hello Ragtime' in London, while T.S. Eliot quoted from a ragtime song of the day, 'That Shakespearian Rag' ('Is there nothing in your head but "O O O O that Shakespeherian Rag — It's so elegant, So intelligent"?'). The French called it *'les temps du chiffon'*, and 'serious' composers were entranced by its new musical possibilities. Debussy wrote 'Golliwog's Cakewalk' as a pastiche of the 'cakewalk', a ragtime dance described as a 'stiff-backed, high-stepping prance', which supposedly sprang from the plantation negroes' ambulatory imitation of their white masters. In 1920 Darius Milhaud composed 'Le Boeuf Sur Le Toit' as an *hommage* to this new improvisation, while Stravinsky, the most enraptured of them all, wrote several works incorporating ragtime and was long an admirer of jazz.

Scott Joplin, a black Texan and self-styled 'King of the Ragtime Composers', was, however, the artist who most clearly appreciated ragtime for itself rather than as a novel device, and his self-conscious strivings for academic respectability, expressed through a series of operas which he wrote, can be compared with the 'legitimising' process that occurred in pop music in the late sixties, initiated by the highbrow critics' espousal of the Beatles and the Beatles' own subsequent belief in the devolvement upon them of a grand artistic role. But certainly ragtime was significant from a European point of view: its rhythms, considered quite extreme for that period, and its associated dance, the cakewalk, quickened the interest of a new, young audience anxious to discard Victorian formality as it entered the twentieth century; and simultaneously it alerted the emerging British music business to the musical upheavals across the Atlantic and the financial lessons to be learned from them. Thus the recurring twin elements of pop — youth and commerce — were early revealed.

Jazz, which hit Britain in 1919, when the Original Dixieland Jazz Band played at the Hammersmith Palais, confirmed America as the source of a new popular music in the developing Urban Age and emphasised the appeal to youth. The ODJB was white, but its style had been taken from black musicians, who were now spiriting ragtime along the line of collective improvisation. But jazz, though it made a sharp musical and social impact for a decade, proved increasingly to be too technical and aesthetic to participate in the mainstream of popular music. Tin Pan Alley was disturbed by the jazz bands' growing inclination to use their own material, which lay outside its control, or else to reinterpret in an unfamiliar way songs that were copyrighted. Jazz quickly began to split up in reaction. There was the more commercial, 'sweet' music of the (usually) white-controlled big bands with their singers, like the crooner Bing Crosby, a style which, simplified and reliant on the repetition of melodic lines, was known as Swing; and then the more abstract less accessible modes, more usually played by Negroes and pungently described as 'hot', whose most complete rebellion against current tastes and commercialism resulted in bebop.

After 1930 innovations invariably stemmed from this latter school and jazz has correspondingly become a minority music. In Europe, though, it was initially welcomed as a novelty by the masses. George Formby Jr's amusement at jazz, reflected in his song 'John Willie's Jazz Band', which related the jazz situation to 'Wigan-Land', was widely echoed. Its most sympathetic audience in Britain, besides the community of discerning musicians, tended to be 'underground' among the young and educated, often those from Oxbridge, who associated its liberated rhythms with an easing of social inhibition in the aftermath of the Great War. Jazz, therefore, like pop later on, acted somewhat as a focus for dissent, or rather it satisfied a youthful need to be 'different', though its audience was of a more élitist kind.

Popular music was now beginning to fragment and diversify at some speed, hastened by the development of communications. Radio became a national institution both in America and Europe, though the British Broadcasting Company, under the Directorship of Lord Reith, tried hard to protect the British way of life from excessive American influence — which involved, in his view, amusement for its own sake. The technical advances on the flat disc, invented by Emile Berliner in 1887, ensured that the very moment of creation could be perfectly reproduced for a mass audience, while the installation in places of entertainment of the 'juke box', descendant of the nickelodeon, an early type of pay-as-it-plays machine, inculcated even further in European audiences a desire to ape the American lifestyle. Microphones, too, whose development paralleled that of radio in the twenties, were seen to be increasingly necessary if the singer was to compete with the volume of his backing band (although for a while economics dictated the use of a megaphone by European vocalists). And, most significantly, there came the phenomenal expansion of the motion picture industry, whose glossy packages of dreams with their promises of an alternative lifestyle heavily influenced all classes in Europe, but especially the working classes, whose own existence, disjointed by the effects of war, bore scant indication of 'the Good Life'. It is also worth noting that the old American Tin Pan Alley was almost entirely controlled by Hollywood by the mid-1930s. It harnessed songwriters and publishing companies to the production of musicals, which vied with the Western as the most popular talking pictures. Thus there grew up a new, more sophisticated type of songwriter, a craftsman who wrote for the cinema sound track as well as the Broadway show. It was as a protest, too, against this species of urbanity and good taste that pop, in its most contemporary form, arose.

These events comprised the broad background to the dissemination of American popular music up to 1939. World War Two, however, precipitated a much closer contact between Europe and America, and one which socially and musically was to have a deep effect on Europe.

The presence of US soldiers in Europe had already had some significance in the Great War in that the Allies had got a close look at the American lifestyle. In fact, the American Tin Pan Alley had had something of a history of exporting war songs. 'Goodbye Dolly Gray', American in origin, had been popular during the Boer War, and throughout the 1914-18 conflict there had been a spate of 'moral attention' songs designed for the boys in the trenches. Between the Wars there had also been attempts at propaganda by the Jewish-dominated body of publishers; the hit song of 1923 'Yes, We Have No Bananas', had assumed an anti-Teutonic interpretation in its translation 'Ja, Wir Haben Keine Bananen Heute'. But the situation in the Second World War was intensified by the fact that not only did the American forces arrive, they also stayed on once the war had ended, surrounding themselves with the artifacts of American domesticity, including records scarcely available in Europe. Furthermore, they were witness to all the rapid changes that had occurred within a technological society since the previous war.

The existence of radio programmes, designed for American soldiers and containing a high percentage of American popular music, gave the local populations a chance to hear music that, in Britain at least, was often inaccessible under the traditional auspices of the BBC. All over Europe the American Forces Network (AFN) beamed swing music and the language of bebop and the modernist jazzmen. And in general it emphasised the very latest crazes in America *as they happened*, the immediacy being an integral factor in pop; but more broadly it helped to popularise, in association, of course, with the ubiquitous Hollywood movie, American speech patterns. Although Britain largely clung to her traditional way of singing and writing, as personified by the sturdy purity of the 'Forces' sweetheart' Vera Lynn, the process of Americanisation had already taken firm hold and most of the newer popular singers felt the necessity to round out their regional accents. Even George Orwell gave a kindly nod to this linguistic borrowing. Writing in 1945 he commented: 'American has gained a footing in England partly because of the vivid, almost poetic quality of its slang, partly because certain American usages (for instance, the formation of verbs by adding *ize* to a noun) save time, and most of all because one can adopt an American word without crossing a class barrier.' The language and accent of American pop thus began to germinate within the British vocal tradition to the point where nowadays it is an automatic reflex, and the basis of pop slang is still the Afro-American sub-culture as filtered by white musicians. (This was particularly so in the fifties when the Beat movement was in yearning imitation of the tastes and mores of the 'modernist' musicians, and in the sixties when the 'hippies' mixed negro slang with the sub-cultural language of hallucinogen worship.)

So as Europe gradually compromised her own traditions and began to assume a 'mid-Atlantic' accent, an immense underlying desire arose for new pleasures, for a modernity that symbolised a different post-War Europe. In Britain the music halls seemed tired and tattered – above all, old-fashioned – when set beside the spruce, gleaming music-machine pulsating from the United States, whose principal and most popular figure was Frank Sinatra, a ballad singer with a style more angular than the usual crooner, who captured the mass imagination to an extent hitherto unknown in popular music. Sinatra's public and private personae were represented as synonymous in a way that increasingly reflected the inability and/or unwillingness of the pop artist to be separated from his performance. Sinatra was always 'involved' — a key pop word — in whatever he did. And most importantly, he was backed by a great publicity machine, which focused upon him the fierce attentions of young girls, a group whose age, sex and romantic inclinations have always figured prominently in the calculations of the pop industry. Commerce and youth again, plus another word, 'image', which was gaining in general currency.

In the ration-book conditions of the late forties and early fifties Sinatra and other American balladeers (notably Frankie Laine and Johnnie Ray, whose styles were more melodramatic) set the fashion for European youth, who associated the smooth, easy style with a more liberated life which they believed existed in America. They imitated the drape clothes and the crew-cut hairstyle, later to be ousted by the DA, a polite acrostic for back hair fashioned into a 'duck's arse'. Apart from this, and most fundamental to this story, young people in Europe were finding themselves in a relatively sound financial position, certainly in Britain, where unemployment was comparatively low. With this economic leverage they could command a measure of independence from their parents that would have been impossible before the Second World War. They were, therefore, uniquely receptive to rock 'n' roll, the next American trend, and the beginning of modern pop in that it was aimed exclusively at the teenager.

Rock *and* roll — the term most commonly used in classification — sprang up in the early fifties out of an interest expressed by a young, white American minority in rhythm and blues, a harsher, more explicit form of popular music, a modernisation of the blues designed specifically for the urban negro market. Inevitably, as the minority expanded and the commercial potential was realised, white-owned record companies began to release records of white groups, featuring rhythm and blues-orientated material, and not long afterwards the music of the black musicians, loud and driving, was playing on white radio stations too. It was sufficiently radical enough to be the 'different' thing for which youth was searching.

British audiences became aware of it with the release in late 1954 of 'Shake, Rattle And Roll' by Bill Haley and His Comets. But in the personification of Elvis Presley, its first really charismatic and ultimately most potent figure, rock and roll brought fully to the surface those half-submerged instincts which had been apparent in Sinatra's heyday. This is to say that its appeal was founded on the straight proposal of sex from the singer to the audience, and initially, in Presley's case, to a male audience — not in any overt homosexual sense — but with a view to general incitement. At the same time it bore the seeds of ritualistic violence, which made it intensely exciting for an audience hell-bent on emancipation from social responsibilities in the depressed and depressing aftermath of the War. Europe as a whole experienced this feeling of incoherent revolt, but in Britain the most disaffected young crystallised into a group known as the Teddy Boys. They dressed in clothes vaguely Edwardian but quite possibly inspired by 'gambler types' in Western B-pictures, just as the Rockers of the sixties, with their motorbikes and black leather gear, imitated the Hell's Angels motorcycle gangs of California as depicted in cheap literature. The Teds swiftly acquired a reputation for vandalism as a dramatisation of the new music.

But by now, in the mid-1950s, Britain was making tentative efforts to create its own brand of music with a form called skiffle, a do-it-yourself sound often incorporating home-made instruments and spiritually related to the homelier aspects of the old music halls, although in reality it was an off-shoot of British traditional jazz (a purist movement harking back to the early forms of jazz). Much more significant in the long-term was that British imitators of American rock and roll were being turned out, virtually on an assembly-line, with such elemental names as Marty Wilde, Billy Fury, Johnny Gentle and Adam Faith. Similar enthusiasm was provoked on the Continent, but only in France with any substantial, indigenous result. The French had their own Elvis Presley, a blond imitation, Americanised down to his name, Johnny Halliday, but although he appeared several times in Britain and America he was never convincing or 'different' enough to be successful outside the Continental countries, where he continued to prosper even after the Beatles swept Europe.

The British Presleys, however, were rapidly projected to audiences who wanted direct contact with the phenomenon, through a rapid succession of pop television shows, many of them produced by a university graduate named Jack Good and given frantic titles such as '6.5 Special', 'Oh Boy!' and 'Wham', which reflected the new emphasis on speed and the celebration of the instant. It was Good who secured a national breakthrough, on 'Oh Boy!', for Cliff Richard, the best of these ersatz artists, although Richard, like Tommy Steele, Britain's first rock and roll singer, progressively softened his material in a way that typified the weak, diluted nature of British pop until the Beatles' arrival in 1962 signified another internal revolt.

Television, however, proved to be a crucial factor, like the 'pirate' radio stations of the mid-sixties (principally Radios Caroline and London, which played the more experimentally-inclined records never heard on the BBC and helped to expose to the public music

New York in 1924 from Brooklyn Bridge.

Redesign of Mobil filling stations by Eliot Noyes.

The Las Vegas Strip in 1970.

The Original Dixieland Jazz Band, c. 1919.

Ken Colyer's Jazzmen in early years.

The Beatles leave London for a tour of America, August 1966, to a warm send-off by fans.

Bardney, Lincolnshire, May 1972: pop festival fans settle down for a night under polythene.

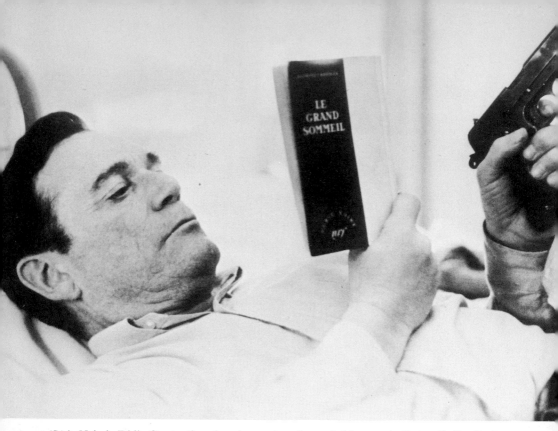

'Série Noire': Eddie Constantine, American actor who made his name in Franco-Italian B-pictures, as Lemmy Caution in *Alphaville* (1965). His leisure reading: Raymond Chandler's *The Big Sleep*.

Billy the Kid in the Paris suburbs: a pair of petty criminals who botch the job because they have seen too many movies. Sami Frey and Claude Brasseur in *Bande A Part* (1964).

Cross-cultural fantasy projections: New York Herald Tribune ingénue looking for Existentialism meets Paris crook looking for Humphrey Bogart. Jean Paul Belmondo and Jean Seberg in *A Bout de Souffle* (1959).

Hollywood in Cinecitta: Jack Palance (left), Hollywood heavy par excellence plays the producer of European sex-idol Brigitte Bardot (centre). Scriptwriter-husband Michel Piccoli (right) wears his hat 'like Dean Martin in *Some Came Running*'. On the wall: John Wayne of Hawks's *Hatari* faces Anna Karina of Godard's own *Vivre Sa Vie* (*Le Mépris*, 1963).

'Walt Disney with plenty of blood': that is how Godard described *Made in USA* (1966). The 'real' Donald—Siegel, not Duck—(Jean-Pierre Léaud) among the cardboard cut-outs in a film-poster workshop.

Cast-offs of Imperialism: Ford Galaxy, sneakers and the US Army Combat Jacket. Anna Karina and Jean Paul Belmondo as the thriller couple on the run in *Pierrot Le Fou* (1965).

that would never reach the pop charts). TV's potential as a mass medium was properly recognised in 1954 with the advent of the commercial channel, ITV. Shows like Good's proclaimed the identity of pop in a way that couldn't be ignored by any section of the community. In effect, youth was placed squarely on the map, which in retrospect appears to have been an inevitable end-product of the forces of American popular music. The cult of youth, which in Germany during the late thirties engendered the Hitler Youth Movement, and in Britain led to Canadian Ralph Reader's Gangshow for scouts, was animated less sinisterly but most tellingly by the mid-sixties when a British pop lyric by the Who included the line, 'hope I die before I get old'. Even the powerful Lucean organ, *Time* magazine, nodded its assent when in 1967 it named youth the 'Man of the Year'.

By 1967, however, what had been the trend of popular music since the turn of the century had been reversed. Ironically, the sixties belonged less to American than to British pop, which by the time the Beatles surfaced had been quietly shaping its own identity in clubs and second-rate halls the length of Britain, but also in Germany, among the clubs of Hamburg in particular. In Hamburg, the headquarters of Polydor records, one of the largest recording companies in the world, the Beatles cut their earliest tracks for the label. Here also several English groups tried to formulate a style without inhibition, before half-comprehending Germans and American GIs. It is also a port city, like Liverpool, and therefore open to a wide variety of linguistic and cultural influences (San Francisco, another port, styled itself the 'Liverpool of the West' and claimed its own distinctive kind of music in the eruption of West Coast pop in 1966 and 1967).

The formative style of the Beatles was contained in their exploration of various forms of Afro-American music, notably hard rock and roll and the softer rhythm and blues of the gospel-influenced black groups, but rendered through their own songs and delivery, which had a fresh, cocky quality with a specifically Liverpudlian humour and accent. The enormous significance of the Beatles was that they represented a successful counterblast to the music they began aping, so that attitudes to pop *everywhere* were subsequently and irrevocably transformed. Within Britain, their emphasis on their Liverpudlian origins — quickly encompassed as 'the Mersey Sound' — showed rare candour in an idiom which until then despised provincialism. But in addition to this, it served to relax the constricting monopoly which London held on the British entertainment industry, in that record companies were consequently much more willing to audition provincial talent, hitherto largely ignored unless it conformed to the slick professionalism of accepted showbusiness standards.

Furthermore, the Beatles wrote most of their own songs, and as this example was followed by successive waves of pop musicians, the dominance of Tin Pan Alley, that centralised pool of all-purpose songwriters, inevitably faded: a culture based upon sheet music was basically anachronistic in an age of giant electronic media with its built-in necessity for instantaneous feedback.

And there were other innovations. The increasing supremacy of long-playing records over singles increased the scope for popular music and paved the way for the experiments of progressive pop. Harmony, which had been lacking in the British pop scene returned and shifted the emphasis from the solo singer to the group vocal.

Yet the Beatles were rightly celebrated, not only for their impact on music and the structure of the music industry but because they offered authentic evidence of what it was like to be young, British and working class. Sinatra had dared to tamper with the showbiz stereotype of artists by his public pronouncements on racism and other issues of the day; the Beatles' critique of society, initially at least, lay in their collective, freebooting personality, contemptuous of pretension and dismissive of convention. They were irreverent, conforming neither to the liberal establishment's paternalistic idea of the working class as earthy proles, nor to showbusiness' demands for tinselled caricatures. They encouraged amongst the public an acceptance of realism from entertainment figures; but they also focused in themselves the media's attention on a new social upheaval within the young working and lower-middle class 'war babies', the products of the art and drama schools who had found it difficult to gain a public hearing in fifties Britain, when class structures were still fairly rigidly observed. By the mid-sixties, however, Britain had seen her Empire break up and the framework of society which supported it weakened; it seemed the fulfilment of Hoggart's prophecy of 'cultural classlessness', a Britain which the young of all classes, fuelled by peacetime affluence, had turned into a supermarket decked with fashion and sex boutiques, Mods and Rockers, drugs and the 'New Wave' theatre and films, all bearing pop's brand name. And the Beatles had acted as catalysts for all this social change, just as they were felt to be its embodiment.

In this assault on traditional values they were complemented by the Rolling Stones, whose music and social style were, however, much more uncompromising. Though their music expanded to take in synthesised forms of Indian ragas, musique concrète and almost every kind of American idiom, the Beatles nevertheless retained an emotional sense of the old music hall tradition and therefore re-asserted to a degree an essential spirit of *Englishness* on the British pop scene. Other rock bands, particularly in the South of England, which had been the stronghold of British traditional jazz, adopted more positively a harsher rhythm and blues style, containg few soft gospel harmonies. This music, which often had a heavy sexual content, was well-suited to the Stones, a group much less sentimental than the Beatles, who strongly emphasised their phallic stance in a deliberate, nihilistic rebellion against convention.

The paradox was that such music, performed by white British males and re-introduced to America as part of the British counter-blast, almost as a by-product gave its negro originators a new lease of life, both in America, where youthful audiences had never heard of them, and in Europe too, where their material was known almost entirely in the British rhythm and blues context. Soon there were tours of Europe by these musicians, often including old negro bluesmen who had been 're-discovered' in the revival. And in their wake have come ever-increasing numbers of 'soul' musicians with modern black music primarily intended to express the contemporary black experience for a black *and* white audience (and often within a commercial structure controlled by blacks).

However, the 'invasion' of America by British groups was a good deal more total than this. American audiences were convulsed for the same reasons as everyone else, only more so. The flippancy towards convention, the eccentricity of the long-haired fashions and the unexpectedness of the Liverpudlian accent came as a cultural shock, then a source of delight, to Americans, who traditionally conceived of the British as either aristocrats or Cockneys. But the success of the counterblast in establishing a new American musical culture, stylistically imitative of Britain while contextually dependent on its own traditions, doesn't seem too unexpected in view of the fact that in America, as elsewhere, pop in the early sixties had lost impact and momentum after its initial explosion, while the increasing universality of youth culture was strong enough to transcend geographical barriers. The Beatles, arriving in America in February 1964, fulfilled and old pop dictum of 'being in the right place at the right time'. For the first time in the twentieth century Britain was fully able to make an original contribution to pop music as a medium for self-expression and in the process revitalise the sources from whence it sprang. Since 1963 American pop has never been able to re-establish its old dominance over European music, although in the years since there have been major American factors within pop: the music and personality of Bob Dylan, the overall effects of West Coast 'acid rock', and the somewhat lesser influence in Europe of Country and Western music.

Dylan's early career was spent in the folk clubs of New York's Greenwich Village, under the radicalising influence of current socio-political thought and conversation, but the extent of his talent forced him to embrace new styles and contexts, the most dramatic being the ·substitution for his acoustic guitar, at the height of his popularity as a folksinger, of electrified accompaniment. His reputation for uncompromising social comment, together with his involved, unsentimental approach to the usual Tin Pan Alley love song, had already established a following among a substantial minority of young Europeans at the outset of the sixties; his ability to articulate complex feelings touched nerves no popular singer working in the English language was capable of.

But in deliberately entering the pop arena, and with conspicuous commercial success, his sphere of influence widened enormously: as a personality whose iconoclasm served as a model for musicians and audiences who wished to thumb their noses at the System, but more specifically as a lyricist who warranted real poetic and intellectual appreciation. To pop composers everywhere he opened up possibilities of much deeper lyric interpretation, while expanding the public's range of appreciation, so that henceforth pop had a broader vocabulary to express complicated emotions. It's arguable that his assumption of the electric guitar was prompted by his exposure to the Beatles' music, but it's undeniable that his thematic freedom was quickly grasped by, amongst others, John Lennon, the most sensitive lyricist of the Beatles, and by the Rolling Stones, who harnessed Dylan's angry style to their own anti-social sloganising. Moreover, as an influential folksinger who had seized the tools of commercialism, his example was soon followed in folk circles everywhere; there were many young folk musicians who, as children of the rock revolution, could not long resist the electric idiom with the wider audiences it promised, but were waiting for someone to make the crucial breakthrough. In Brittany, for instance, the harpist Alan Stivell had been intrigued by the possibilities of combining Celtic material with rock instrumentation since hearing the British instrumental group the Shadows, and using this approach he went on to revive the Breton folk song as music independent of French and American influence; his success, therefore, can be construed as firstly an imitation of, then a reaction against, the Americanisation of Breton culture, which Dylan's influence had helped to promote. Dylan's influence, in fact, was so acute that when, in the late sixties, he made an album of Country and Western-orientated music — the white, 'hillbilly' descendant of the American rural South — he set off a whole new pop movement, tagged, appropriately enough, 'country rock'.

Country itself, however, a music of simple, polarised statements and closely related to the folksy white American lifestyle, has remained only a strong minority attraction in Europe, although its growing appeal has been marked since 1969 by an annual tour of Europe by the International Festival of Country Music, a revue of prominent American singers and musicians. Outside Britain the European strongholds of Country and Western are those countries where English is generally the second language, notably Scandinavia and Switzerland, which are trying to create an indigenous approach to the form, albeit based on a translation of the original songs. But in Britain it enjoys a specialist popularity: records of its big stars, like Johnny Cash and Jim Reeves sell in hundreds of thousands, yet as a whole it's largely ignored by the mass media, particularly television, perhaps because its acceptance tends to be outside London in suburbia and the provinces. Its attraction stems partly from its association with an alien lifestyle, romanticised by Hollywood, partly from its reliance on solid, identifiable values and emotions: the appeal is less to youth, as is invariably the case with minorities in pop, than to a family audience, who apparently share a sense of conservatism with their American counterparts.

Encouraged by the personal appearances in the late sixties of American performers, previously known only from their records, British country gained confidence to the point where British musicians now regularly record in Nashville, Tennessee, the industry centre of American Country and Western. Country, though, has been accepted more idiosyncratically in Ireland — unsurprising, perhaps, since many American rural ballads have their origins in Celtic musical traditions ('Bluegrass', for instance, a fiddle-orientated style, has been shaped by the droning tones of the Scottish bagpipes). The Irish showband, an entirely indigenous phenomenon, dating back to the late fifties, developed from large fifteen or sixteen-piece orchestras playing light ballroom music, but as rock and roll seeped through the popular music scene in Ireland smaller economic units emerged, using brass sections at first, which were then largely dropped in favour of the American country influence of fiddles.

A greater overall influence in Europe was 'acid rock', a form gestated and conceived in San Francisco, and described at its narrowest as the aural evocation of effects produced on the human senses by the drug LSD, lysergic acid diethylamide (effects known as 'psychedelic'), although the *notion* of a drug culture posited by acid has simply served as a common frame of reference for musicians and audiences everywhere.

San Francisco had peculiarly appropriate qualifications as the centre for this activity in that its insistent air of nineteenth century gentility symbolised, more than other American cities, the traditional values that young people sought to overthrow in the sixties, while the potentially radical presence of Berkeley University created an environment for rock bands to experiment. San Francisco marked the end of the road for those 'going West', the climax of the American Dream, and it magnetised unsettled youthful elements, often of an extreme nature, throughout America.

Spearheaded by the Jefferson Airplane and the Grateful Dead, the 'West Coast Sound' attempted in 1967 a simulation and/or enhancement of the acid experience, using multi-media collages of stroboscopic lights, experimental films and oil paints swimming in saucers of water as accompaniment to music devised with no particular beginning or end, in an effort to capture the feeling of hallucinogenic timelessness. Musically, it was a departure in its lack of obvious negro influence; it assumed the overall guitar sound of British rock and Dylan's electric style, although strong characteristics of West Coast music were gentle harmonies and Blakean-derived lyrics intended to reflect the transcendental nature of drug consciousness.

In Britain the experimental ideas of acid rock had a strong impact on rock groups struggling themselves to find a style outside white imitation of the blues — like Pink Floyd, the chief exponent of the new 'Underground' music, as it was called (because it wasn't publicised through the usual mass media, but by the pirate stations, posters and newspapers sold on the streets). This 'Underground' music, emerging as recognisably British, was expressed on albums rather than singles and owed debts to the American West Coast groups as well as the British blues revival. In the period 1967-69 Cream was the most innovative new British band, leaning strongly on blues rhythms but adapting freely from Dylan's folk/rock mode. Another innovator was Jimi Hendrix, an American negro guitarist who came to Britain in 1966 and applied Dylan's apocalyptic imagery to the blues tradition, but transfigured it by electronic effects.

Yet, like previous pop music trends, acid rock signified more than just the music. It contained at the outset an anti-authoritarian attitude, but the difference this time lay in its explicitness. There was a deliberate search among the West Coast communities and disaffected groups in Europe for an alternative lifestyle to that offered by traditional culture and power structures, and this encouraged an impulse to radicalism and to 'drop out' of the established system; 'love' was most frequently invoked to express this curious mixture of passivism and revolt. In an America where draft induction for the Vietnam War was a constant threat, the new ethic was fervently embraced, and European anti-Vietnam sympathisers sparked a wave of dissidence, often student-controlled, throughout Europe in the mid-sixties. In Amsterdam, for instance, where there was no such major issue confronting youth, the Provotariat movement (Provo = to provoke) embraced Vietnam as a cause, but its essential impulse was anarchic and directed against *the idea* of an established order.

This kind of youthful sedition existed in Britain too, but amongst British youth, who were later than their American counterparts in enjoying the fruits of affluence and liberation from parental control, the political message was gradually emasculated in a more superficial quest for a new youthful style — the sensationalism of fashion and drugs, and the generally frantic atmosphere of 'Swinging London'. 'Flower power', as it was dubbed — a phrase which had originally seemed to promise a return to innocence — was gradually absorbed and mass-marketed by the financial brain of pop. Certainly the Revolution did not happen in Britain, nor were there any incidents as violent as those which occurred at the Democratic Convention in Chicago in August 1968, the student-worker demonstrations in Paris in May of the same year, or the riots in Berlin during Easter, 1968, which followed the shooting of Rudi Dutschke, a prominent figure in the S.D.S. (German Socialist Students' Federation). Still, once and for all the collective identity of youth had been established, and pop was the common language in which it expressed itself.

We come now to music on the Continent which, as I have said, underwent influences similar to those seen in Britain, although nowhere near as intrinsically productive. Of course, pop is essentially an English lyric medium and there exists the obvious difficulty of composing in a foreign language a rhythmically Afro-American song for an audience that's really more interested in American and English pop, as is the young European public in general. Closely allied to this is the fact that such a song is unlikely to have any commercial potential outside the country of origin, and the express desire of European pop musicians is for acceptance in the English-speaking world, where lie the rewards of money and prestige. For these reasons jazz had always found Europe a more fertile ground, while the most interesting pop produced in Europe is invariably reliant upon instrumental ability alone, even though a French group, Magma, have made a virtue of the language difficulty by inventing their own, *kobayan*, which has the attraction of universality at least, if not comprehensibility.

From their side, English and American musicians have tended to see Europe as a further source of employment, rather than of creation to be fed back into their music, and several English groups are either permanently based there or spend most of their time in Europe, where there is less competition. Moreover, the business structure enforces this secondary role upon European pop since the majority of record companies there are merely adjuncts of those in Britain and America; thus local autonomy is not encouraged. However, Holland, because its inhabitants speak English more widely than any other European country, and because it is in turn more sympathetic to Anglo-American culture, now produces commercially successful pop of an essentially instrumental kind whose musical identity is indistinguishable from that of its English mentors (the groups Focus and Golden Earring, both of whom are popular in Britain).

But the Germans who, together with the English, comprise the third largest market for pop in the world, have been much more individualistic and adventurous, though not much of this indigenous experiment has survived outside Germany. If there is a unifying characteristic to their music it's a generalised feeling for Expressionism and a delight in the application of abstract ideas; the most original German music is marked by its single-minded intelligence and is light years away from the loose rhythms of the blues. It's most closely related in fact to the more experimental work of the British Underground bands: the visual, cinematic music of Pink Floyd and the Free Jazz-inclined pieces of Soft Machine. In fact German music began to find its own voice in 1968, the year of the student revolutions. But it's hard to talk of 'a German situation' because the music industry there is decentralised, with key cities supporting their own music, so that the stigma which has been attached to provincialism in Britain simply doesn't exist.

Berlin is the headquarters of the Ohr label, Germany's only independent avant-garde pop company, while the country's one big TV pop show, 'Beat Club', is produced in Bremen. Amon Duul 11 — a more successful offshoot of the original Amon Duul — operates from Munich, a city with a Bavarian levity that finds few echoes in the band's music. Amon Duul 11, however, have been a decisive influence within German rock: their Wagnerian use of electronics has been widely imitated, as has their communal lifestyle. They have been a guiding light for German rock, although with their increasing assimilation of the Transatlantic musical vocabulary originality has worn thin.

Since 1972 the true leaders of German pop music have been Can, a group from Cologne who have toured several times in Britain, where they are regarded as a surviving outpost of the old Underground. They exhibit a fascination with sound *per se* — Stockhausen's belief in sublimation through sound — and a preoccupation with uncompromising rhythms: a peculiarly Teutonic rhythmic propulsion, inflexible and inexorable, that has no equivalent outside Germany.

In the late sixties and early seventies too there existed a nucleus of German rock bands with political motivation, such as Ton Steine Scherben, with its extreme Left stance, and the Marxist Floh de Cologne. Their interest was in lyrics rather than music, and their subject matter frequently a diatribe against the capitalist system. This polit-rock in fact, was symptomatic of a refusal amongst the more radical young Germans to be bound by the language of Anglo-American pop. The background to this refusal was that after the Second World War the Germans had become so disillusioned with their own culture that they had turned to America, in particular, for ideas in popular culture — a rejection so complete that it wasn't until the native hippie revolutions of 1967 and 68 that self-confidence began to return.

In Europe as a whole the effect of American pop has been that popular music now has little use for its traditional rhythmic patterns, represented by the waltz, say, which offered brief scope for self-expression both on the dance-floor and on the bandstand. Just as Priestley prophesied, Europe, like America, has absorbed and utilised the negro inflections whose history stretches back to Africa, rhythms with an obvious emphasis on percussion and the percussive use of other instruments. Even British folk music, that most traditional of forms, has had to witness in the last decade a certain re-interpretation in the light of this changed rhythmic emphasis. The desire of young folk musicians for contemporary validity has led them to embrace amplified sounds, but this has signified, too, a move away from tradition towards individual creation.

Not only music, however, but social conventions have been irrevocably shaken up, and pop has both prompted and reflected this in its role as a mirror held to the changing face of society. And because the speed of its response is an integral factor, the history of pop can serve as a chronicle of the twentieth century's rapidly changing lifestyles, with an increasing emphasis over the decades on youth and sex, those two particular watchwords of contemporary pop. In all, the youthful eroticism of popular music might well be said to have helped liberate social restraints in Europe: a casting-off of the nineteenth century strait-jacket. Young people now dance not 'with' their partner, but 'to' the music. Self-expression and improvisation have infiltrated the European classical order.

Jazz is Where you Find it:
the European experience of jazz

PAUL OLIVER

> *'The Original Dixieland Jazz Band has arrived in London',*
> *says an evening paper. We are grateful for the warning.*
> *Punch*, April 1919

> *I can't help thinking Mr Punch left the sentence unfinished; it should have continued, surely, 'for the warning to go to the Palladium early and book seats'.*
> *Pall Mall*, April 1919

Pall Mall's rejoinder on the first appearance of the 'ODJB' in Europe recognised the tremendous excitement that the brash, raucous music of the five white jazzmen from New Orleans aroused. The reactions of the two papers were the forerunner of all European views on jazz from then on: cynicism and dislike on the one hand, enthusiasm and admiration on the other.

That jazz was welcomed as widely as it was on the Continent was a reflection of the euphoria at the end of World War One, and an aspect of the desire for the modern and the novel which marked the dramatic social changes of the nineteen twenties. If jazz was often contemptuously dismissed by the musical establishment as 'jungle music', it represented for a young generation the discarding of Edwardian values and a future of freedom and emancipation. The very quality of improvisation epitomised the spirit of exploration in the arts, and the wave of interest in black culture that followed the discovery of African sculpture by the artists of Die Brücke, Cubism and Fauvism, opened doors for black musicians, in Paris in particular, that would have been closed to them in the United States.

Not that the Original Dixieland Jazz Band was a black orchestra, but its music of strident, braying horns, and wild rhythms on drums, 'traps' and woodblocks, thumbed a nose to accepted standards in musical taste. The young Marquess of Donegal took the Prince of Wales to see the band and there was even a Royal Command

Performance which received applause from King George V, a royal accolade which did more than anything else to gain acceptance for the new music in Britain. The ODJB returned triumphant to New York and a few brave spirits tried to emulate them in England.

In fact they were not the first jazz musicians to perform in Europe. There were many in the regimental band of the all-Negro 369th Infantry Regiment, the 'Hell-Fighters', which toured the allied countries during the War under the direction of Lieutenant Jim Reese Europe. (He was later murdered by his drummer in Boston while the ODJB were rocking the Hammersmith Palais de Danse.) As early as 1914 black drummer Louis Mitchell led a band at Ciro's Restaurant and after playing a season in Belfast with his Syncopated Band took his 'Jazz Kings' to Paris in 1917. Will Marion Cook, another black leader, also brought a large, partly improvising orchestra which even *The Times* welcomed as 'an entertainment that all would feel better for seeing and hearing'. But it was the ODJB that brought the full blast of uninhibited collective improvisation to Europe, and a 'fat black boy with white teeth and narrow forehead' who gave Europeans the first taste of the jazz genius for solo improvisation.

"There is in the Southern Syncopated Orchestra an extraordinary clarinet virtuoso who is, so it seems, the first of his race to have composed perfectly formed blues on the clarinet', wrote the Swiss conductor, Ernst Ansermet in the *Revue Romande*. 'I wish to set down the name of this artist of genius, as for myself I shall never forget it — it is Sidney Bechet.' The New Orleans musician with his straight soprano saxophone bought in London thrilled Europe with his sweeping *glissandi*, his soaring improvisations. But he 'can say nothing of his art, except that he follows his own way' Ansermet noted, adding prophetically, 'and then one considers that perhaps his "own way" is the highway along which the whole world will swing tomorrow.'

It was. But decades were to pass before European jazz could be said to have a life independent of American jazz. To discuss jazz in Europe one must acknowledge the overriding importance of the work of American musicians who toured, worked and in many cases lived across the Atlantic from where the music came. They provided contact with the well-springs of jazz and it was the music of the visitors which shaped jazz in Europe. To a large extent it was the members of the earliest bands to visit Europe who made the most enduring contacts, and as they played to ecstatic crowds in one capital after another they often felt more at home and welcome in Europe than in a road band doing one-night stands in the Mid-West. Sam Wooding's Jazz Symphonic Orchestra, for example, included many musicians who stayed on in Europe after their sensational 1925/6 tour through Germany, Sweden, Denmark, Spain, Russia, Czechoslovakia, Hungary, Austria, France and England. When the band went on to South America several members stayed behind, or returned to Paris, like the trombonist Herb Flemming who formed his own International Rhythm Aces in France before taking jazz to Calcutta, Shanghai and Ceylon. Another member, the outstanding New Orleans trumpeter Tommy Ladnier, a master of the muted horn on the blues, was a sensation in Russia. Later he worked in Poland and after a brief spell in New York was back in Europe with Bennie Payton. Payton himself came over with Will Marion Cook's Southern Syncopated Orchestra, formed his own band at the Hammersmith Palais de Danse, and for more than a dozen years led bands from Hungary and Switzerland to the Netherlands. Similar careers were followed by Willie Lewis, who played several reed instruments, and Sam Wooding's pianist, Freddie Johnson. They were both still working in the Netherlands when the Germans invaded in 1940.

For a long time Freddie Johnson had been regular pianist at the Paris restaurant-cabaret run by the negro entertainer Ada 'Bricktop' Smith. Her cabaret was important as a natural focus for visiting black musicians who met old friends, made contacts and got new engagements there. In this way famous musicians, on brief visits to Europe, were secured as star performers with resident bands, and the jazzmen with long experience in Europe were able to fill out their club and restaurant dates. So multi-instrumentalist Benny Carter was able to work with Willie Lewis in Paris, with Freddie Johnson in Amsterdam and even act for a period as staff arranger for Henry Hall's Orchestra in London. Similarly, the great saxophone player Coleman Hawkins could leave Fletcher Henderson in New York in 1934 to work with both Johnson and Carter as well as keep recording dates with Jack Hylton in England.

This catalogue of names and places is not meaningless, for it reveals the web of links and associations that these musicians established. In general black musicians were less happy in England than in France; several white bands and individual musicians from the Chicago and New York schools also came to Europe and, following the success of the ODJB which did not go to France, were welcome in England. As early as 1924 the Mound City Blue Blowers with the brilliant guitarist Eddie Lang were playing in Britain and the classically-trained English band-leader Fred Elizalde brought Adrian Rollini to London straight from his sessions with Bix Beiderbecke. Chicagoan Danny Polo was also a long-term resident in England, playing clarinet for Ambrose and his Orchestra. Until 1930 there was little recognition of black jazz in Britain but the visits of Louis

Armstrong in 1932 and 1933 on tours which also took in Denmark, Sweden, Norway, Holland, Belgium, Switzerland and Italy, made enthusiasts aware of the melodic originality of improvisation and the daring, unorthodox use of the full potential of instruments in black jazz. 1933 was in fact a sensational year in England, for Duke Ellington, debonair and loving everyone madly, brought his Orchestra to the London Palladium.

Nevertheless, it was Paris that was the strongest draw for visiting Americans and it acted as a jumping-off point for tours throughout Europe. There wasn't a country in Europe that hadn't heard lots of jazz by the early nineteen thirties, and most of them were selling jazz records. As the centre of the world of art and the home of numerous American ex-patriate writers, as a city with a liberalism on the Left Bank comparable to that of New Orleans and safer than that of Prohibition Chicago, Paris provided a milieu in which jazz thrived. Not only American jazz though. In 1932 the Hot Club of France was formed and two years later the twenty-four year old gipsy guitarist with a crippled hand, Django Reinhardt, created a sensation with his startling improvisations, his use of diminished and augmented chords and his playing of solos in octaves. Reinhardt was the most original jazz musician that Europe produced before World War Two and one of the few of any period. The Quintet of the Hot Club of France featured his guitar and the unexpectedly swinging violin of the conservatoire-trained Stefan Grappelli. Against a rhythm of two guitars and bass the lead soloists created, and at their best inspired, original music that was indisputably jazz but which owed little directly to the United States. Duke Ellington was greatly impressed. Another French musician of the period was the alto player André Ekyan, who worked with Reinhardt on occasion, and with the tenor player Alix Combelle. Both men attracted good local talent around them with the capacity to swing and to improvise, though none had the unique flair of Reinhardt.

Elsewhere in Europe the tours of the American musicians inspired local jazz bands and orchestras. In Belgium, Charles Remue led bands from the early 1920s, playing clarinet and alto himself, and in 1927 he began to make recordings with his New Stompers Orchestra. Later he joined Bernard Ette in Germany where the Ette Orchestra was one of several jazz groups — the Marek Wever Orchestra, the John Muzzi Heliopolis Band, the Friedrich Hollander Syncopators among them. There was even a jazz band at the Bauhaus, in which Lux Feininger played, but this, like most other jazz in Germany, was a casualty of the rise of the Hitler régime. Even so, Herb Flemming managed to hold down a job in Berlin during the late thirties, but generally in the fascist countries of the period, first Italy, then Germany and finally

Spain, there was little jazz to be heard. Before the Spanish Civil War, however, Pedro Casadevals formed the Hot Club of Barcelona only a year after the French organisation.

Scandinavia played a better host to jazz in these years; a black American banjo player, Russell Jones, had his own group of Swedish musicians in Stockholm as early as 1921 and a few years later Helge Lindberg was leading a good band. In spite of the advantages of language Great Britain came low in the jazz field before World War Two, with a few notable exceptions. Of these quite the most remarkable was the classically trained composer and bass player, Spike Hughes. Early in the 1930s he was influenced by the records of Duke Ellington and, forming his own band, made many interesting recordings with orchestras with various players, including trumpet players Norman Payne and Max Goldberg, and the tenor player Buddy Featherstonehaugh. With the trombonists Ted Heath and George Chisholm, Featherstonehaugh contributed some of the best British jazz of the nineteen thirties. As for Spike Hughes, he achieved his ambition in 1933 when he went to New York to record fourteen titles with his 'Negro Orchestra'. This was in fact Benny Carter's, which included Henry 'Red' Allen and Dicky Wells. 'With my last desire fulfilled there remains little to say, for with it my ambitions in jazz reached their logical end', wrote Hughes many years later.

Live jazz in Europe did not come to an end with the onslaught of the Second World War, but it was severely curtailed. There were many visiting orchestras entertaining American troops in the United Services Organization but unless there were combined operations European servicemen did not often hear them (though Marian Page, an English pianist on an ENSA show met Jimmy McPartland, jazz trumpeter at this time, and later emigrated to the United States). Civilians would strain at their radios to catch the programmes of Willis Connover and the occasional jazz on the American Forces Network. What they heard was largely 'swing' — the music of big bands with a strong emphasis on music for dancing. The more purist jazz enthusiasts deplored this sinking of soloists in 'riffing' brass sections. Until now there had been few factions in European jazz, although there were disputes as to the relative merits of black and white jazz, or the superiority of small group improvisation and 'jamming' over lofty aspirations to 'symphonic jazz'. The new sounds in swing indicated something of the dramatic changes taking place in the United States during and immediately after the War.

A long dispute between the respective Musicians' Unions of the United States and United Kingdom denied British enthusiasts the chance of hearing live jazz bands for more than a decade after the end of hostilities; only the American demand for British rock groups in the late nineteen fifties ended the deadlock. Records therefore became extremely important and the 'jazz collector' sought the company and the music of those with similar interests. Jazz societies and 'rhythm clubs' proliferated even though jazz was still a minority interest, disapproved of by every establishment body. Imported records revealed a major division in American jazz which was reflected in the mutual contempt of the 'revivalists' and the 'boppers' in Britain. The rediscovery of Willie 'Bunk' Johnson, legendary trumpet player and alleged teacher of Louis Armstrong, had led during the nineteen forties to the finding of many other veteran New Orleans jazz musicians. 78 rpm recordings of George Lewis or Wooden Joe Nicholas made for such labels as American Music or Jazzman fetched extraordinarily high prices in Britain and were treasured as Holy Writ. They revealed that an unsophisticated, uncompromising music of collective improvisation still existed in New Orleans; all subsequent jazz had been, it seemed, a corruption of its authenticity. The admirers of the 'New Orleans Revival' learned them note for note.

At much the same time a very different form of jazz was winning converts just as passionate. Charlie Parker, Dizzy Gillespie, Fats Navarro were producing a music as cerebral as New Orleans was emotional, as 'cool' as the other was 'hot'. Fans of the new music marvelled at the 'changes', the unorthodox chord sequences, the virtuosity of the instrumentalists and the brilliance of their extended solo improvisations. Like the 'revivalists', the 'boppers' wanted to hear live music, but in jazz-starved Britain the problem was how. Ken Colyer joined the merchant navy and jumped ship at New Orleans so that he could play with the veteran black musicians he had so admired on record. His exploit, including a spell in prison, was evidence of his 'authenticity' and 'sincerity', important criteria in the New Orleans following, and took on the character of an epic. Sax players Johnny Dankworth and Ronnie Scott were two of many young musicians who joined 'Geraldo's navy' — the Cunard liner orchestras — so that they could hear their bebop idols in New York.

Back in England Ken Colyer formed the Crane River Jazz Band, modelled on the music he had heard. George Webb's Dixielanders played at the Challenge Jazz Club organised by the Young Communist league who recognised, or hoped for, a genuine working-class movement in the growing Revival. But it was Graeme Bell's Dixieland Band from Australia which showed London in 1947 what live New Orleans-style jazz could really sound like. Among the modernists Dankworth became an exceptional musician and composer of international calibre following the success of the Dankworth Seven, while Ronnie Scott teamed up with the late

Tubby Hayes (he died in 1973), a tenor sax and vibraphone player considered by many critics to be one of the few European jazz musicians of a stature equal to American contemporaries.

There were a few others: among them Stan Hasselgard from Sweden, with Reinhardt the only other jazz player from Europe to make a significant change of direction for jazz in the States. Tragically, he was killed in a car accident there when he was only 26 and his full potential remained unrealised. Sweden produced several musicians who leaned easily to the new music, among them, until he fell victim to drug addiction, Lars Gullin, a sax player. He is now working again with another saxophonist in the modern vein, Bernt Rosengren. Bernt sits in with SEVDA, an unlikely combination of two Swedes and three Turkish musicians resident in Sweden, led by Maffy Talay whose playing excited Dizzy Gillespie on tour in Stockholm as early as 1956.

Musicians of the new school were visiting the rest of Europe regularly: Gillespie toured Scandinavia in 1948 and the following year Charlie Parker and Miles Davis both played the Paris Jazz Festival. But jazz in France was split by factionalism. In Britain this led to bantering writing; in France it led to acrimony which ended on occasion in physical violence. The Hot Club of France broke up with Hugues Panassié, representing the traditionalists, retreating metaphorically to his chateau in Montauban while Charles Delaunay and *Jazz Hot* supported the moderns in Paris. Contemptuously the opposing camps of 'montaubanais' and 'zazzoteurs' taunted each other and, with memories of the Occupation in mind, made political capital out of their respective positions. But the passions aroused were also expressed in much good post-war French jazz, from the New Orleans inspired bands of Maxim Saury or Claude Luter to the technically better and more original music of Henri Renaud, Claude Bolling or Bernard Peiffer — all pianists. Renaud worked with the brilliant Belgian flautist and tenor player Bobby Jasper, considered one of Europe's best soloists until his death in 1964. Peiffer eventually settled in the United States: America offers both a magnet and a challenge to European musicians and some of the best of them, including Britain's George Shearing, Marion McPartland, Dill Jones (piano players) and Victor Feldman, drummer, have long been resident there. But European jazz has been impoverished as a result. European jazz musicians have undoubtedly made their contribution to the music but the greatest benefit that jazz has gained from Europe has been in criticism and appreciation itself. It is this that makes the Panassié/Delaunay split so much more sad in European eyes.

'Jazz is where you find it', enthusiasts in Europe used to say, hearing American musicians whenever they could and by whatever means possible. After the visitors had left, for all the thrill of their live performances, nothing remained: there was no way to check the points of their solos, no way of examining their ability to work together or to improvise individually — except, that is, through recordings. For the jazz fan in Europe records were a way of gaining an insight into the music, augmented when possible by attendance at live concerts.

The Belgian writer Robert Goffin can lay claim to have been not only the first European jazz critic, but the first in the world. His reviews and articles were appearing in *Disque Vert* in 1920 and the following year he founded the first jazz magazine, *Music*. His book, *Aux Frontières de Jazz*, was the first to be written on jazz and for its times, extremely percipient. With the added advantage of a few more years' listening, Hugues Panassié published in 1934 the first major work on the subject, *Le Jazz Hot* which introduced both European and American supporters of jazz to basic criteria in the music.

With the increasing number of records being issued in Britain and France the need for regular jazz comment became apparent: the English *Melody Maker* began to review jazz records and cover jazz events, while in Sweden the oldest and longest-running jazz magazine in the world, *Orkester Journalen*, started publication: it is still published today. Three years later, in Paris, *Jazz Hot* appeared and has now been in existence for nearly forty years. Early contributors included Jean Cocteau and Max Jacob, and an editor for a long period was Charles Delaunay, a relative of the cubist painters Robert and Sonia Delaunay. Later, the surrealist writer and excellent jazz musician in his own right, Boris Vian, wrote regularly for *Jazz Hot*, which has remained among the most erudite and well-produced of jazz publications.

In the United States few jazz periodicals have lasted for long, but in Britain *Jazz Journal*, edited by Sinclair Traill, has been running since 1949. It was preceded by war-time publications of the 'Jazz Sociological Society', the 'Jazz Anthropological Society' and the superior *Jazz Music* edited by Max Jones. These frequently took shades of political colour: communist and anarchist alike have found in jazz the musical evidence of social reform and integration — off-setting perhaps the impression drawn from the very real interest in the music of Baron Timme Rosencrantz, Count Carlos de Radsiztky, Lord Montague of Beaulieu and the Hon. Gerald Lascelles, all of whom have written about, or promoted, jazz in Europe.

Jazz magazines and books have appeared in virtually every European country, including those of Eastern Europe where there is a small but dedicated following. But Britain, with magazines like *Jazz Monthly* (now *Jazz and Blues Monthly*) and *Storyville*, circulating for many years, has also produced more books on jazz than any other country. The Jazz Book Club, a branch of Readers' Union, alone published well over three-score books. But not all of them were of high quality and few books of jazz criticism have paralleled the often irritating but always stimulating *Jazz: Its Evolution and Essence* by the French writer, and also past editor of *Jazz Hot*, André Hodeir.

Many of these publications were remarkable, if not for their writing, at least for the wealth of information which their contributors uncovered through interviews, record listening, and patient sifting of trade publications: visiting jazz musicians were always astonished at the knowledge of their music which European enthusiasts displayed. The jazz fan likes to know all he can about the music, its musicians and records, and this led to another major contribution of the Continent — 'discography'. The accurate logging of all details of jazz recordings is seldom undertaken by the record companies, or their files are soon destroyed, so that the discographer's task has been extremely difficult. In 1936 Hilton Schleman published *Rhythm on Record* in England and later the same year Charles Delaunay produced *Hot Discography* in Paris — a completely revised edition was somehow compiled during the Occupation and ran to 558 pages. Since then discography has grown at such a rate that the Belgian, Walter Bruynicx, is currently publishing a loose-leaf *Fifty Years of Recorded Jazz* which runs to two thousand pages for the section A-D alone.

All this activity has exerted its own fascination and has also brought jazz collectors closer together; a tradition of mutual help exists to a remarkable degree among them, only occasionally affected by partisan views of the music itself. Typically, jazz enthusiasts both delight in its minority appeal, and complain bitterly of lack of representation on say, radio programmes. Undoubtedly its appeal has not always been purely musical; it has also symbolised revolt, progressive ideas, commitment to individual expression or to racial integration. And it is interesting to note how many innovatory, creative people in other fields have been attracted to it: Cocteau, Picabia and Robert Graves have sat in with jazz bands; Samuel Beckett's first published writing was a review of Duke Ellington; Matisse produced a series of paper-cuts inspired by jazz. In post-war Britain alone jazz enthusiasts included poets like Philip Larkin and Jim Burns (both prolific writers on the subject), Kingsley Amis, John Wain, Kenneth Allsop and Eric Hobsbawm (who published an excellent study, *The Jazz Scene*, in 1959 under his pseudonym of

Francis Newton). Jazz also appealed strongly to artists and nearly every art school in the country had a jazz band at one time or another, and nearly every jazz orchestra has had its artist members. Notable were Wally Fawkes, clarinettist, who has drawn the *Flook* cartoon since its inception, and Humphrey Lyttelton and George Melly who both wrote its captions and eventually became noted as critics and commentators; many others could be cited. But it is not the members of the intelligentsia who matter in the jazz audience, although in Europe they have played an important part in the propagation of the music. Above all it is the considerable international body of people who found aesthetic fulfilment as dancers, listeners or performers from one form or other of jazz, who matter. For them jazz has provided a focus, an experience, an enrichment of intellectual and sensual life appropriate to the times, expressive of the mood after the wars and exploratory in terms of individual and group expression.

Today there is less popular jazz than there was in the period of 'trad' enthusiasms when the bands of Chris Barber, Acker Bilk or Kenny Ball hit the charts. Jazz has remained something of a minority interest, though it is a large minority, but it has its supporters in every part of Europe, including those formerly largely deprived of the music. Partly influenced by the American Jazz Ensemble in Rome, Italy has heard the New Jazz Quintet in Turin, the group of Gianni Safred in Trieste and Antonello Vannuchi's quartet in Lucca with the leader on vibraphone. The Orchestra of the Dutch Swing College with its musicianly but traditionalist policy has been challenged in more modern vein by the groups of Louis van Dijk or Pim Jacobs; Albert Magelsdorff's Quintet and the quartet led by the tenor player with a style reminiscent of Sonny Rollins, Klaus Doldinger, have been important in Germany. Even Spain has seen native jazz played by Tete Montouliú, a pianist blind from birth, and by the saxophonist Pedro Iturralde, while Pedro Casadevals after four decades is still promoting visits by leading jazz men from other countries. Jazz also has a following in Eastern Europe. In East Germany the Eberhard Weise Orchestra has been under some political pressure, but has pursued a jazz policy close to that of the West Coast modernists, while the Manfred Ludwig Sextet and the Werner Pfuller Quintet in East Berlin have been well reported. Such groups tend to have a somewhat academic approach since they hear little live jazz and this is reflected in the work of Jazz Studio Prague and a most interesting band, the Study Group of Traditional Jazz (Czechoslovakia), which uses the New Orleans form for new compositions by its members. In Poland, Ian Wroblewski models himself on Wardell Gray while trumpet player Andrej Trajaskowski is in the forefront as a soloist. There are big bands in Zagreb and Lublijana – in fact, the big band which has become economically almost impossible in the United States, still has a strong following in Europe, especially in Britain where Mike Gibbs's, and outstandingly, Mike Westbrook's orchestras have produced original compositions and arrangements of great quality by any standards.

Such a list of names gives only a hint of the styles and abilities of the personalities and bands concerned, but if it does injustice to them and to the scores of musicians overlooked it does give some indication of the widespread distribution of creative jazz on the Continent. Yet jazz musicians still have problems in obtaining regular employment and though there are clubs in most cities using jazz musicians they have either to concentrate upon building a faithful and local following for a few groups only, or provide the attractions of visiting bands and soloists. To make the latter possible loose links have existed between clubs in most European countries while in Britain the National Jazz Federation performed a booking service for several years. In 1969 the European Jazz Federation was formed in Vienna with Jan Byrczek as its Secretary-General. One of its services is to provide an annual calendar of jazz festivals. These are important for they enable musicians to play together, to hear new sounds and to experience the music of visiting 'name' soloists or orchestras. The festivals at Antibes and Nice on the Riviera, the Comblain-la-Tour festival in Belgium, the Jazz Week in Budapest, the Stockholm Jazz and Pop Festival, the festival at Pori, Finland and other important ones in Montreux, Warsaw and even Richmond have been regular events.

Jazz in Europe then, can now stand on its own. Unlike the progression through blues, skiffle, rhythm and blues to rock and roll and progressive pop, it has not made an irreversible impact on the popular music of Europe. Nor has it had a profound effect upon American music in the way that the rock music of the Beatles, the Animals, the Who or the Rolling Stones did in the nineteen fifties and sixties. Nor has there been a vast 'underground' following as there was for the progressive rock groups like Cream, T. Rex or Slade. Jazz symbolised a spirit of healthy revolt among a sector of the community but it did not speak as the music of a whole teenage culture, as did rock. The jazz experience in Europe was on a smaller scale and its achievements were not as dramatic nor as universal. This is partly a matter of timing, and of media, but it is also to do with the language of the music itself.

The achievement of Europe in the history of jazz was that of comprehending the language and providing it with criteria. European jazz writers have undoubtedly shaped the nature of criticism and appreciation in its literary forms. But perhaps the most rewarding aspect of jazz in Europe was intangible and unseen, to be witnessed only in the astonishment, delight and ultimately, self-respect of the American jazz musicians themselves. To them, and particularly to the black jazzmen, the knowledge of their music and their recordings, the unbounded appreciation of their audiences and the esteem in which they were held, visibly restored their dignity and pride in their own music. Many were induced to settle in Europe then, and now, while others returned to the United States with a new confidence in themselves. It may not be too much to claim that ultimately the most important aspect of jazz in Europe was the contribution it made to international and inter-racial understanding through the language of a twentieth-century art form.

The Mean Streets of Europe:
the influence of the American 'hard-boiled school' on European detective fiction

JENS PETER BECKER

In his famous essay 'The Simple Art of Murder' Raymond Chandler discussed the difference between English and American detective fiction and even if many of his polemical observations must be viewed with some reservation, the essay nevertheless is still of great relevance. For Chandler, the English detective novel of the so-called Golden Age of Detective Fiction is a highly artificial product, devoid of convincing characters, and depicting social life as little more than the anachronistic idyll described by Graves and Hodge in *Long Week-end*. That the English detective novel seemed so artificial to Chandler in no way destroys the English concept of the genre, for (as Graves and Hodge remark):

> 'Detective novels ... were no more intended to be judged by realistic standards than one would judge Watteau's shepherds and shepherdesses in terms of contemporary sheep-farming'.[1]

Chandler contrasts the decadent,[2] artificial English detective novel with its 'realistic' American counterpart and at this point of 'The Simple Art of Murder' the argument becomes relevant to our concern, for he points out that:

> 'Graves and Hodge decided that during this whole period only one first-class writer had written detective stories at all. An American, Dashiell Hammett. Traditional or not, Graves and Hodge were no fuddy-duddy connoisseurs of the second-rate; they could see what went on in the world and that the detective story of their time didn't; and they were aware that writers who have the vision and

the ability to produce real fiction do not produce unreal fiction.'[3]

This is one of the first aesthetic assessments of Hammett as an American detective novelist and it is significant that the American Chandler — whose education (of course) was that of an Englishman — should quote two European authorities in order to justify Hammett's importance to his countrymen.

For a long time America has had difficulty in assessing the value of the hard-boiled school. Even as late as 1960, Leslie Fiedler in *Love and Death in the American Novel* labelled André Gide's positive judgement of Hammett as 'a symptom of European cultural malaise',[4] and while it was not until 1970 that a large-scale attempt was made, in the form of David Madden's anthology *Tough Guy Writers of the Thirties*, to do justice to the authors of the hard-boiled school, European authors and critics of note have always shown a certain weakness for this form of the American detective novel. Horace McCoy and James M. Cain were judged more important by the French existentialists than Faulkner or Hemingway. Albert Camus observed in a footnote to his penetrating survey of the American novel in *L'Homme Révolté*, that what he meant by the 'American novel' was, '*of course* the tough novel of the Thirties and Forties'. At most, the American critics regarded these novels as social documents, whereas European intellectuals were ready, perhaps too ready, to assign to these authors an aesthetic importance. Indeed, most of their remarks hardly go beyond enthusiastic demands, such as made by Auden, for example, that 'Chandler's powerful but extremely depressing books should be read and judged, not as escape literature, but as works of art.'[5] Here, after all, Leslie Fiedler's view must be considered just.

Apart from the constant admiration for the hard-boiled school expressed by European critics and reading public alike, there was also a direct influence on European detective fiction. It should, however, be noted that the term 'hard-boiled school' encompasses disparate elements: the prim realism of Dashiell Hammett is different from the symbolic art of Chandler, yet both tend to be put into the same category by critics. Likewise, the gangster film of the 1930s is (as Robert Warshow has shown) in essence different from those films which glorify the figure of the tough guy detective.[6]

In the following analysis I have deliberately ignored the work of such authors as Edgar Allan Poe, Anna Katherine Green, Jacques Futrelle, 'S.S. Van Dine' *et al.* for two reasons. Firstly, the influence of Poe on Doyle, and thus on English detective fiction, has been sufficiently researched,[7] secondly, the novels of these authors are essentially only imitations of European models as A.E. Murch has shown in the case of A.K. Green. The specifically *American* detective fiction which concerns us here are the short stories of the 1920s and 30s, which appeared with such success in *Black Mask* under Joseph T. Shaw's editorship, the novels of Raymond Chandler, and then the work of Kenneth Millar (Ross Macdonald) and the *romans policiers* of Pike and McBain which, although written much later, essentially re-developed themes popular in the 1930s. They are American in that characters and setting are uniquely American. However, as we shall see, this by no means precluded European authors from seizing, sometimes gracelessly, on material which seemed at first blush unexportable.

The earliest influence of the pulp magazines on Europe was described by George Orwell in his essay 'Raffles and Miss Blandish' (rightly included by Rosenberg and White in *Mass Culture*, the first great attempt to classify popular culture):

> 'There exists in America an enormous literature of more or less the same stamp as *No Orchids*. Quite apart from books, there is the huge array of 'pulp magazines', graded so as to cater for different kinds of fantasy, but nearly all having much the same mental atmosphere. A few of them go in for straight pornography, but the great majority are quite plainly aimed at Sadists and masochists.'[8]

Orwell deplores this process of 'Americanisation' as a cultural decline:

> '... the career of Mr Chase shows how deep the American influence has already gone. Not only is he himself living a continuous fantasy-life in the Chicago underworld, but he can count on hundreds of thousands of readers who know what is meant by a "clipshop" or the "hotsquat", do not have to do mental arithmetic when confronted by "fifty grand", and understand at sight a sentence like "Johnnie was a rummy and only two jumps ahead of the nut-factory". Evidently there are great numbers of English people who are partly Americanised in language and, one ought to add, in moral outlook.'[9]

While in English sensational fiction there has always been a sharp contrast between 'right and wrong and a general agreement that virtue must triumph in the last chapter', there is obviously in 'America, both in life and fiction, the tendency to tolerate crime, even to admire the criminal so long as he is successful'.[10] In this example from Orwell, criticism of a popular literary form becomes criticism of American culture; it is an ironic twist of fate that this distorted image of American culture, characterised by brutality and violence in Orwell's eyes, is provided by a European, James Hadley Chase, who, at the time of writing *No Orchids for Miss Blandish*, had never seen America. It not infrequently seems to be the fate of America in the realm of popular culture that a large audience receives its image of America from non-American authors. The adventure novels of Karl May, for example, which present a myth similar to Cooper's Leatherstocking tales, have been for a long time (and are perhaps even today) the only source of information on the history of the American West and the American Indian for a large German audience.

In Europe the popularity of this imported detective literature has hardly diminished, in no way fulfilling Orwell's expressed hope that 'it is possible that it is an isolated phenomenon, brought about by the mingled boredom and brutality of war'. Orwell had further lamented, ' . . . if such books should definitely acclimatise themselves in England, instead of merely being a half-understood import from America, there would be good grounds for dismay'.[11] He would presumably, therefore have been considerably disturbed to discover the millions of Jerry Cotton novels which appear in Germany every week. Just like the adventures of Nick Carter (undoubtedly a forerunner of Jerry Cotton) these stories are written by an anonymous group of writers and are presented as the true reports of G-man Jerry Cotton. The German writers try to give the reader as realistic a picture of New York as possible for, as the head of the publishing firm explained, only America can be the scene of action:

> We still believe that in the USA gangsters and policemen battle amidst a hail of machine-gun bullets. We still believe that there are organised gangs of criminals, and policemen ready to give their lives in fighting them. The range of descriptive possibilities is much broader. Besides, the action must take place if possible in the city. Such graphic phrases as 'streets like canyons', 'seas of houses', 'skyscrapers' and 'basements' create an impressive dark silhouette against which the action takes place. Detective novels set in Germany are mostly boring — and if not boring, then incredible. The neighbouring countries around us have been shown to be commonplace by streams of tourists. Even England, home of the classic detective novel, is no longer a suitable background. Today the belief in the omniscient powers of Scotland Yard has been completely destroyed. Only America is left for us. It is the only place where the reality of things cannot be checked personally by most European readers. American crime is still credible.[12]

Shifting the scene of action to another country was a favourite device in the German detective novel of the Third Reich, when it was ideologically impossible that any crime should take place in the perfect world of the German People. (Similar examples can also be seen in the detective fiction of the GDR.) The menace of disorder, disturbing the ideology of this period, is transposed in the world of escape literature all too readily to countries abroad, preferably to America.

Even though the Jerry Cotton novels (whose influence must not be underestimated) try to imitate certain elements of the hard-boiled school and pretend to be American in their background description and the use of Americanisms and 'tall talk' in the dialogue, there is nevertheless in the figure of the hero a fundamental difference between the German and the American version of the hard-boiled school. The Continental Op and Philip Marlowe are private detectives who restore law and order on their own. They are heroes in a long American tradition. The German counterpart, on the other hand, is not surprisingly an official FBI agent — servants of the state being held in great esteem in Germany.

In 'The Simple Art of Murder' Chandler describes his hero as a kind of superman and assigns to him the role of a knight in a troubled world: 'if there were enough like him, I think the world would be a very safe place to live in'. Philip Marlowe and his type were the only figures of fantasy who, in the eyes of the dissatisfied citizens, could successfully put an end to the chaos of the times, just as all hope rests on the honest sheriff in the Western. But this solution to the problem of evil is still only a temporary one in popular fiction: the gallant Philip Marlowe has to take the field against evil in the American city year after year and even if at the end of each Western the world seems to be safe for a while, Wyatt Earp and others have to demonstrate again and again their quickness on the draw and their accuracy of shooting. In contrast to these loners in whose adventures order is re-established almost coincidentally and certainly only through their intervention, law and order in the German variations of the American detective novel are never seriously questioned because of the activities of the officials of the all-powerful FBI.

In this respect all the German imitations and also the Lemmy Caution novels, by the Englishman Peter Cheyney, which are very popular in Germany, do not match up to the hard-boiled school. It is not enough, as is common practice in Germany, for authors merely to assume the most American-sounding pseudonyms possible, to try to evoke an American atmosphere by giving places and streets suitable names and then to put their heroes into a world of sex and violence. (Sex incidentally, is missing from the prudish Jerry Cotton novels although recent attempts to bring him into the permissive society may be observed.) The heroes of all these synthetic, 'American-type' novels are only imitations and are never the archetypal American folk-heroes, descendants of the Westerners, as Durham and Fiedler have described them. Only this type of hero makes the novels of the hard-boiled school so typically American.

Thus, in most cases German crime fiction writers have been able to see themselves only as imitators of American novels, although at present in such authors as H.J. Martin, Wittenbourg and '-ky', a movement away from the American type of detective novel is discernible.

In France Marcel Duhamel brought out a series of detective novels for Gallimard called *Série Noire* in 1947 (the name was coined by Jacques Prévert who in the thirties wrote the film scripts for Marcel Carné's versions of the hard-boiled film, featuring Jean Gabin as tough guy) which soon became the most important influence in the 'Americanization' of the French detective novel. Duhamel (who asked Chester Himes to write his first detective novel) favoured American authors, especially the tough guy writers of the thirties, and in the first years of the *Série Noire* French authors were forced to write 'American' detective novels under American pseudonyms (e.g. Serge Laforest who wrote as 'Terry Stewart'). But whereas the German detective novel continued in a state of mere imitation, the French (with authors like Boileau-Narcejac, Monteilhet and Japrisot, to name only a few) soon found their own style again, returning to the tradition of Georges Simenon.

The English detective novel, like the French, has maintained its independence. The idyllic country-house scenes which Chandler described so accurately and which Agatha Christie and Michael Innes perfected, are still there and even the English detective novel and psychological crime novel preserve their English independence (or European independence, if Simenon's influence is taken into account). Freeling, Innes, Bingham and Symons, or whoever may be designated the leading crime authors of the sixties and seventies, similarly owe hardly anything to the hard-boiled school.

In contrast, however, Hammett and Chandler have had great influence on the modern English spy-novel.[13] Ian Fleming, who in a letter to Chandler once ironically called his novels 'straight pillow fantasies of the bang-bang, kiss-kiss variety' modelled himself on these two writers. Even if James Bond is after all only a distant relation of Philip Marlowe's, Fleming still possessed Chandler's gift for making the poetic setting and the exotic atmosphere work in his novels. In some sense only Len Deighton can really be called the legitimate European heir of Chandler and Hammett. In his novels, from *The Ipcress File* to *An Expensive Place to Die*, he succeeds splendidly in synthesising Hammett's nameless tough-guy and Chandler's poetical depiction of setting and society.

The hard-boiled school as a reaction to social reality is limited to a certain period of time; in *Playback* Chandler was already looking back nostalgically rather than writing hard-boiled fiction. In America the genre deteriorated into the sex-and-crime novel in the hands of James Hadley Chase, Mickey Spillane and Richard S. Prather, and only Ross Macdonald has been able to re-awaken interest in this field by his realistic description of Californian life. As Raymond A. Sokolov said, in a *Newsweek* article, 'Macdonald has survived into the 70s and filled his story with today's new truths and problems'.[14] Macdonald also succeeds, with his Lew Archer, in transforming the tough guy hero into a modern Everyman. Macdonald's definition of his hero:

> '[Archer] represents modern man in a technological society, who is, in effect, homeless, virtually friendless, and who tries to behave as if there is some hope in society, which there is. He's a transitional figure between a world that is breaking up and one that is coming into being in which relationships and people will be important.'[15]

is a modern variation of the Chandler formula, and is incidentally of immense importance for the early work of the Swedish writers Sjöwall and Wahlöö, whose detective novels criticise Swedish life and Swedish society. It was one of the achievements of the American hard-boiled school to fill the melodramatic form of the detective story with social criticism, and at this point Sjöwall and Wahlöö are true followers of the Hammett/Chandler/Macdonald tradition. They show (as the hard-boiled school did) that crime is a product of society and not just an intellectual puzzle. Simenon and Freeling, it is true, show the sordid side of life and society, but they are more interested in the psychology of the criminal than in a critical depiction of society .or an investigation into the causes of crime. Sjöwall and Wahlöö are more radical in their outlook than any other detective novelist — with the exception of Chester Himes.

Hammett and Chandler criticised American society of the 1920s and 30s; Hammett was a left-wing realist who never lived up to the promise of *Red Harvest*, Chandler was a melodramatic traditionalist who seems to have believed in the equation, rich=evil. But both authors offered a way out; their heroes were saviours of society (perhaps the eternal function of detective fiction, for even Sherlock

Holmes was assigned that role). For Sjöwall and Wahlöö, two intellectuals who have their own personal grudge against the Swedish welfare state,[16] there is no hope for society (at least not Swedish society, though Denmark is sometimes spoken of as a sort of paradise), and while it sometimes seemed that they subscribed to the sentimental optimistic outlook of Chandler and Macdonald in their early novels, they have become more and more radical over the years.

Taking up the melodramatic form of the detective novel and trying to fill it with a message obviously leads to frustration for the serious novelist. Chandler and Hammett gave up. 'If you are tired you ought to rest, I think, and not try to fool yourself and your customers with coloured bubbles,' Hammett wrote.[17] Chester Himes and the Europeans Sjöwall and Wahlöö became radical nihilists. Their last novels *Blind Man With A Pistol* and *Den merkvärdige mannen från Säffle* (The Remarkable Man from Säffle) show with painstaking realism the effects of blind violence untempered by the melodramatic triumph of law and order. Himes planned to kill off his detectives Grave Digger Jones and Coffin Ed Johnson;[18] Sjöwall's and Wahlöö's Martin Beck is killed off (together with half of the police force) at the end of *Den merkvärdige mannen från Säffle*. This is the end of the hard-boiled school.

It seems to be the fate of America in the history of detective fiction to invent new forms of literature which are later exploited by European writers. Poe invented the detective short story and Conan Doyle became famous for it, American authors of the 1930s propagated the hard-boiled formula and two Swedish authors brought it to unprecedented perfection.

Translated by Ian E. Oliver

The Impact of American Science Fiction on Europe

GÉRARD CORDESSE

After the Second World War, American science fiction burst upon the European scene and carried it by storm: in Italy, Germany, Spain, Belgium and France, science fiction magazines first became available in English; then came scattered translations of short stories and novels, and finally the best American magazines were regularly published in most European languages. Their reign was long unchallenged, except in Great Britain. It was not an isolated phenomenon of course; it came along with American cigarettes, G.I.s, the Marshall Plan, thrillers, blue-jeans, Western movies and chewing gum. Chewing gum was a genuine American invention and deserved its hegemony, but American science fiction should not have had such an easy conquest, for European science fiction looked like a formidable competitor.

In fact Europe was in no mood for fighting: Italy and Germany had been crushed and all the illusions of fascism shattered. As for France, the elation of the Resistance and the Liberation could not obliterate the slur of Vichy. The collapse of the economy and of morale left a near-vacuum which was to be filled by the steam-roller of American culture — boosted by victory, affluence, and the messianism of the New World which had come to redeem corrupt Old Europe. Although the Europeans, made cynical by history, were wary of such ideological simplification, the success of the American system was dazzling: science, with systematic research and development programmes, had insured progress and confidence in the future. Europe, particularly France and Great Britain, had practically stagnated since the First World War; these countries were prone to conservatism and bourgeois caution, whereas the United States represented movement, innovation and adventure. As the future seemed to belong to the United States, it was logical to grant her a monopoly on anticipation literature. This link between science fiction and American success based on science explains partly why American influence was more sweeping in this field than elsewhere. In 1880 the citizens of France could well be imagined to be pioneering moon exploration; in 1950 such a thing would have seemed ludicrous or merely pathetic.

The proof of this European abdication lies in the universally-shared belief that science fiction is uniquely American. This misconception, coming from the American public, is understandable, but held by the generality in Europe, indicates a sad lack of information. A rich outcrop had flourished in Europe long before Hugo Gernsback founded *Amazing Stories* in 1926. A recent, massive work compiled by Pierre Versins[1] makes a point of rehabilitating the European precursors of Sturgeon and Heinlein. With considerable humour, Pierre Versins sets the record straight by tracing the development of most of the major themes. Let us take parallel history or 'uchronia', a sophisticated theme that we have learnt to associate with Sprague de Camp's *Lest Darkness Fall*, (1949) (about how to keep the declining Roman empire from falling), Ward Moore's *Bring the Jubilee* (1952) (how the North was defeated at Gettysburg), or Philip K. Dick's *The Man In The High Castle* (1962) (in which Japan and Germany have won the last war and now occupy the United States). Louis Geoffroy, as early as 1836, published *Napoléon et la Conquête du Monde, 1812 à 1832: Histoire de la Monarchie Universelle*, in which Napoleon carries the battle of Waterloo and goes on to conquer the world. Following this, in 1876 an academic French philosopher, Charles Renouvier, published *Uchronie (l'utopie dans l'histoire), Esquisse historique apocryphe du développement de la civilisation européenne tel qu'il n'a pas été, tel qu'il aurait pu être*. After these works Pierre Versins unearths a steady stream of similar inspiration, including an essay by Winston Churchill, 'If Lee had not Won the Battle of Gettysburg' (1931).

In a similar way, nearly all the American themes and even technological inventions have been foreshadowed by European writers. It would be tedious to call the roll of honour but it is impossible to assess the impact of American science fiction if we do not keep in mind this rich heritage. Martians, space exploration, time-travel, mutants and robots were already familiar. Besides, the literary reputation of some specialists puts to shame the American field. In Great Britain alone one might mention Samuel Butler, Sir George Chesney and his prophetic *Battle of Dorking* (1871), Sir

Bulwer Lytton, R.L. Stevenson, Rider Haggard, William Morris, H.G. Wells, Rudyard Kipling, G.K. Chesterton, Sir Arthur Conan Doyle, Olaf Stapledon, Aldous Huxley, J.B.S. Haldane and C.S. Lewis. It is impossible to imagine English literature without these names. Anticipation was for them a respectable form of expression which could carry, besides, entertainment, commitment, satire, poetry and even philosophy.

In France the list is less distinguished but just as long. Many American readers assume that Jules Verne was American. As a matter of fact, he shared with them a passionate interest in technique, inventions and also figures. Except in his last works, he evinces the same enthusiasm for science and the same childish wonder in the face of its promises. Like many Americans, he also was writing for a young audience, and during forty years, published little else but anticipation fiction, from 1863 to 1910. Surprisingly, he is a rather isolated figure in as much as few writers shared his optimism. His contemporary, Antoine Robida, used his effervescent imagination to burlesque the contemporary vision of progress. Even at the height of the scientific revolution a very sceptical vein was prominent in France. New inventions were caricatured as ludicrous rather than uplifting by professional deadpan humourists like Alphonse Allais. Even the earnest successors of Jules Verne: Maurice Renard, who wrote from 1900 to 1930, and Jacques Spitz from 1935 to 1945, were gradually to lose Verne's naive optimism. Disillusionment, irony and satire crept in over the years and the last great French specialist before the American influence, René Barjavel, describes the collapse of scientific civilisation, chaos, and a return to an archaic, agricultural utopia.

In Britain we find a similar tradition of warning against the future, from Wells's *A Dream of Armageddon* to Ballard's apocalypses. This mounting pessimism is rarely absent from European science fiction and stands in striking contrast to America's triumphant paean to science which lasted from 1900 to 1950. It is tempting to ascribe this difference to the very diverse socio-historical situations, contrasting European stagnation with American expansion, but this is unsatisfactory: even in the thirties the cult of science remained unshaken by the Depression.

American magazine science fiction proved impervious to outside change because it was a self-sufficient, closed system. European science fiction, on the contrary, was only one of the many forms of expression at any writer's disposal. Many mainstream writers felt science fiction to be more flexible than realism, in that it contributed distance, perspective and drama. Writers like Henri Barbusse, André Maurois and Aldous Huxley used science fiction as a vehicle to deliver a message. The first Goncourt Prize was awarded in 1903 to a science fiction novel, *Force Ennemie,* by John Antoine Nau.[2] This contact with the rest of literature made European science fiction more adult: when American science fiction became blinded by the progress of science, Europeans began to look with strong misgiving at man's unchanging nature.

The Founding Father of popular science fiction is Hugo Gernsback, the creator of *Amazing Stories,* referred to earlier. Although he invoked Jules Verne, H.G. Wells and Edgar Allan Poe in his first editorial, it is impossible to trace an imitation or even an influence in the trashy production of *Amazing.* The pulp magazines were simply not 'in the same league' as their European or American predecessors.[3] The difference may be made explicit through a brief analysis of Gernsback's still famous novel *Ralph 124C41+* (1911). The book is made up of three elements: first, a love story, whose function is presumably to provide what is characteristically called 'human interest'; it also gives birth to the plot since everybody wants to kidnap the heroine; secondly, space opera, when the good scientist and the bad Martian chase each other in space-ships — the best trick of the scientist being to camouflage his ship as a comet in order to approach his rival undetected! Thirdly, a remarkably ingenious prophecy of gadgets and inventions of the year 2660, coupled with an absolute faith in science and the United States. Among the highlights we find a parade of 6,000 planes over New York, representing the Star-Spangled Banner, which leaves the British spectator appropriately dazzled: 'You Americans still lead the world. Upon my word, the old saying that Nothing is impossible in America still holds good.'[4] The only part of the book which has any merit is the technological forecast, i.e. the only subject Gernsback and his peers were interested in. The narrative frame is mere sugar-coating.

Ralph is not irrelevant, since its awfulness has not shaken the allegiance of later writers. In his introduction to the book's republication in 1958 Fletcher Pratt lavishes praise on it, and equates it with the genre: 'In a very proper sense, *Ralph 124C41+* may be called the first science fiction story ever written'.[5] Besides, Gernsback's ancestry has been institutionalised through the 'Hugos' awarded every year by the fans.

It would be absurd to condemn magazine science fiction on the grounds that it is unliterary for it has very few literary pretensions. In effect, its worship of science implies a deliberate scorn of literature. As late as 1953 Sprague de Camp, when giving advice to young writers, quoted R.A. Heinlein with approval: 'Heinlein is right in saying that you must not simply write and rewrite in search for perfection. Every time you rewrite you diminish your effective word rate, because you have written more words for the same-sized check'.[6] At the same time Heinlein would excommunicate any writer who neglected his scientific information.

This superb indifference to form is not unique in popular literature but it is enhanced by the militant, almost messianic interest in science. When Gernsback founded his magazine, exclusively devoted to science fiction, it was to avoid the promiscuity of other impure sub-genres, which had no message to give. By so doing, science fiction isolated itself into a narrow impassioned world of fans, editors and specialised writers. Whereas the popular media often tend to diversify their range in order to provide everybody with something (e.g. the politics, sports, astrology and women's pages of any newspaper), science fiction chose concentration, exclusion of the non-connoisseur, specialisation, passion.

The production of these stories was not an individual effort but the result of collaboration. The editor of each magazine gave suggestions, advice, imposed changes, selected the kind of material that was supposed to fit his public. The public itself was far from passive: in letters to the editor the stories would be analysed, and criticized in terms of scientific accuracy or plausibility. Since the space devoted to letters was limited, the fans got together to develop a parlour game of error-hunting; they formed clubs, exchanged judgements and published 'fanzines'. Both editors and writers were anxious to listen to this continuing criticism, and to the frequent praise. In the culture of mass-media only too often it is only sales which give an indication of public response; in science fiction, however, the public was uniquely vocal.

The threefold collaboration had both advantages and drawbacks. This particular form of direct democracy limited the freedom of the writer. The sacrosanct literary values of inspiration, self-expression and independence were given no consideration, but rejected as intolerably élitist. A writer could only be original in his scientific extrapolation. According to Sprague de Camp: 'There is an old rule of magazine writing that if you are writing with a particular magazine in mind, your best textbook is a file of copies of that magazine.'[7] This necessity for the writer to have a chameleon-like adaptability is revealed by the incredible number of pseudonyms used by science fiction writers: almost one for each magazine.

Yet according to classical aesthetics rules and obstacles are fecund; in this field where the message, or the idea were of the essence, the communication of that idea had to be efficient. Embellishment, verbosity were accordingly out, so were digressions, abstractions and comments by the author. What was needed was clarity and a fast-moving narrative; these were after all the demands of good American journalese, which influenced much modern writing. The spare, economic style was very different from the European one. The dominant magazine form was of course the short story, which called for concentration and impact. In Europe science fiction existed almost exclusively in novels. The literary, ornamental style, the didacticism of frequent moral, social and political digressions, and above all the use of irony, made for a slowing-down of the narrative.

R.A. Heinlein is a typical product of the system we have described; he has been fandom's favourite for more than thirty years, getting four Hugos and placing almost all his books as runners-up, year after year. He reflects the mood and prejudices of his public like a mirror. His heroes are engineers and inventors rather than egghead scientists (Edison versus Einstein), aggressive men of action, dynamic businessmen (*The Man Who Sold the Moon*, 1951). His values were authoritarian, verging on the fascist during the Cold War, (*Starship Trooper*, 1951), they became almost hippie-like in the nervous sixties (*Stranger In A Strange Land*, 1961), then softly pornographic in the swinging seventies (*I Will Fear No Evil*, 1971). So it would in theory be relatively easy to make an ideological analysis of American science fiction, reflecting the values, concerns and prejudices of its public, projected into the future in thin disguise. In fact, however, I do not believe this aspect has had much impact on Europe, which had enough prejudices already: European science fiction had been through a particularly rabid phase around 1900, with the writings of the racist and bloodthirsty Capitaine Danrit and many others. Fu Manchu himself was after all a French creation exported to the United States in 1917, and I do not think it added significantly to American racism. Ideologies, values and prejudices are difficult to transplant unless they fall on fertile ground. At any rate, if Heinlein's values could fluctuate so easily over the years they were rather secondary than essential to his science fiction.

Much more basic is the formal side of American science fiction, elaborated by a kind of collective creation. Original ideas are scarce, so most writers, urged on by demanding fans, exploit the variations of a given theme. Each theme is thus projected and endlessly refined by different imaginations. A common body of themes, situations, characters, motifs, gadgets, theories, key-words and tricks has been accumulated in American science fiction over the years. So that, whereas an isolated writer (or — previous to the American influence — a European writer) would have to elaborate on his concepts or inventions in order to ensure the suspension of disbelief, a contemporary writer may simply allude to the accepted formulae. So this was America's contribution to European science fiction: a new streamlined quality, a sense of belonging to a well-oiled system of conventions and references. To the newcomer this was a world of perfect consistency, a self-sufficient system in which the suspension of disbelief was not founded on one man's talent but on a collective creation: hence this tremendous assurance. How did the literary European tradition react to this challenge?

Britain was the only European country which was not swept off its feet by the American wave. To all appearances the British had held their own in the Second World War and national pride ran high. American influence did not find the attitude of resignation it had met elsewhere on the Continent. More importantly, the British had been exposed to American culture for a longer period (both through the shared language and historical links) so the resistance to American culture was more efficient.

During the thirties several British writers, lacking a market at home, wrote regularly for American magazines; the list includes Vargo Statten, Eric Frank Russell and John Beynon Harris (later John Wyndham). They had of course adopted American standards but remained familiar with the European field. As far as the public was concerned, American magazines sometimes reached the British market; while a few British magazines (*Scoops*, 1934, *Fantasy*, 1938) were visibly American-inspired. One magazine, *Tales of Wonder*, even published mainly American stories. Similarly, a few fan-clubs and fanzines duplicated the American system while even the British Science Fiction Association, founded in the early thirties, had significantly adopted the American label.

Yet, for the most part, the British withstood American influence. *New Worlds*, founded in 1946 by John Carnell, just back from his commando duty, became a stronghold of British science fiction. In the introduction to the first anthology of *The Best From 'New Worlds Science Fiction'*[8] John Wyndham, who ironically had been first published and trained in American magazines, rejoiced that:

'*New Worlds* foiled the prospective American inundation of the British market, threatened as one of the blessings of peace. No great exercise of the imagination is required to perceive what would have happened to a large part of the straitened and severely rationed British press under a transatlantic deluge of well-fed glossies and bulky pulps. . . . We think there can be something in this science fiction if it is handled intelligently. Why should the Americans have a stranglehold on it?'[9]

In his turn, John Carnell protested against American self-complacency:

'Long before the phrase science fiction was coined (by an astute New York publisher looking for a publicity phrase), there were book-length novels and romances with their plots centered somewhere in the future. And it was primarily British authors and publishers who pioneered them . . . (it is) a cult which is not new but merely re-dressed in modern style.'[10]

Incidentally this 'modern style' made all the difference. The shrill national note is surprisingly absent elsewhere in Europe, possibly because the other nations knew they were not ready to emulate the new American formula; probably also because Great Britain was more severely hit by the American deluge whereas non English-speaking countries only had translations to cope with.

Paradoxically, *New Worlds* fought the American invasion by using the same weapons, i.e. largely by imitating the new formula. *New Worlds* was founded on a typically American fanzine basis, with forty-seven small shareholders, all of them devoted fans. New British writers started publishing in the United States: Arthur C. Clarke, Peter Phillips, William F. Temple, A. Bertram Chandler. Their familiarity with the American magazines was an important tactical advantage that other countries lacked. But imitation took its toll: of the young writers published by *New Worlds* (E.C. Tubb, James White, Alan Barclay, Peter Hawkins, Ian Wright, E.R. James) not one left an original mark on science fiction. Only John Beynon, uninspired when writing for American magazines, suddenly blossomed as John Wyndham in the British climate, by uniting American drive with the literary distinction of British science fiction.

In his introduction to *The Best Of New Worlds* John Wyndham tries to delineate a national character for British science fiction:

'We become aware of limitations which prevent us taking a whole-hearted interest in a never-never universe where anything goes — anything, that is, but inaction and probability. . . . *New Worlds* was founded upon the theory that science fiction is capable of dealing with matters of more general interest than cosmic cowboys and galactic gunmen, and one hopes that the present selection from its stories may not only bring the reader some fascinating, novel ideas, but also prompt him to murmur: "You know, there are some interesting possibilities in this kind of thing".'[11]

The blast at cosmic cowboys is visibly aimed at American space opera, but in 1955 this was not new. Since the creation of *Galaxy* and *The Magazine of Fantasy And Science Fiction* in 1950, the never-never universes of space opera had fallen into disrepute. Campbell's *Astounding* in 1939 has superseded galactic cowboys. So, in spite of this manifesto, when we examine the production of *New Worlds*, we fail to see the difference between it and a good American magazine. American penetration can even be insidious: in A.B. Chandler's *Jetsam* which describes the first landing on the moon, the characters have suspicious Americanisms: 'Come on, kid . . . Like I said'. This homage confirms that British independence was achieved at the price of originality — certainly for a number of years.

The breakthrough for science fiction, which jerked it away from the low-brow, closed-circuit American pattern, came in 1955. Established literary critics (American fans would call them main-stream critics, that is, intruders), like Angus Wilson, Edmund Crispin, Marghanita Laski, Kingsley Amis and C.S. Lewis, drew attention to science fiction, giving it self-respect, respectability and its own identity. This in turn attracted a more demanding public. It was a crucial step in encouraging new talent, particularly in the person of Brian Aldiss who started exploring the mysteries of consciousness in a poetic, personal manner, (Sturgeon at the same time was tapping the same vein but in a much more pedestrian manner). In 1954 William Golding, a mainstream star, had made use of science fiction in *Lord of the Flies*; by then publishing *Envoy Extraordinary*, in the company of John Wyndham in *Sometime Never*,[12] he proved that the science fiction ghetto was over.

In the United States, on the other hand, the very system which had nurtured science fiction was now blocking its further evolution. Ray Bradbury, after being rejected by *Astounding*, was offending many fans both by his literary style and his anti-scientific, pessimistic views. He was the first writer to break out of the science fiction world to attain general recognition. This was resented as a betrayal and a threat to the cosy security of the group.

In Britain it was easier to try to combine the best of both worlds: together with Brian Aldiss, the great innovator was J.G. Ballard. With *The Drowned World*,[13] *The Voices of Time*[14] and *Terminal Beach*,[15] popular science fiction was no longer opening wide, childlike eyes at technology but was exploring man's inner self. When, in 1963, Michael Moorcock took over *New Worlds*, the magazine quickly became a laboratory for a group of young writers, admirers of Ballard, to start experimenting with science fiction. 'Now writers assume increasingly the responsibilities of the poet — they seek to match their techniques to their vision.'[16] Thus *New Worlds* became more and more avant-garde, abandoning the low-brow level of popular literature. One of the first casualties was the worship of science. The break was manifested by its assertion that science fiction was merely a sub-genre of 'speculative fiction' and that as such it was not necessarily linked to science, but was defined in terms of its distance from present reality.

Nor was the central change simply related to new subject-matter (the pessimistic, chaotic vision of the future, a nightmarish post-atomic world where all values have collapsed and counter-culture Superman Jerry Cornelius is creating new ones), the form itself was frequently revolutionary: down with the logical, deductive, rational sequence of narrative, down with the well-rounded characters, the notions of climax, dénouement and plot. These writers experiment with suggestion, association, circular patterns, mosaics and flashes, perhaps owing something to the influence of Marshall McLuhan. They produce cryptic, dense, compressed novels of three pages; making for unusually difficult reading. No wonder that the traditional science fiction public is nonplussed. Moreover, in true Dadaïst style, these writers are out to shock the bourgeois reader, for example in *The Assassination of John Fitzgerald Kennedy Considered as a Downhill Motor Race*,[17] borrowed from Alfred Jarry's piece on Christ's Passion. The price to pay was a change of public, and commercial censorship (no news-stand distribution), so that in 1966 both *New Worlds* and *Science Fantasy* went bankrupt. Their importance was recognised by a £1,800 annual grant from the Arts Council, pressed for by such celebrities as Kenneth Allsop, Anthony Burgess, Angus Wilson and J.B. Priestley.

British science fiction may still be insecure financially, (*New Worlds* after going quarterly, is still floundering) but it has now been recognized as one of the most dynamic and promising art forms. There is no doubt that *New Worlds'* experiments will have been crucial in shaping the future of science fiction the world over.

Science fiction in Britain has long been a special case. Its community of language with the States has allowed a two-way relationship which has proved extremely fruitful. As far as the Continent is concerned, the relationship has been one-way, since very few European SF writers have been translated into English. On the other hand, Europe has been to a large extent spared the more trashy American productions; only the best works have been translated into French, German or Italian. (Comics are an exception since they require little or no translation.) Whereas British writers had an ambiguous relationship with America, rebelling against the stereotypes and limitations of pulp science fiction, while depending to a large extent on their American sales for subsistence, (Ballard, Aldiss, Keith Roberts are popular in the States, while John Brunner got the 1969 Hugo Award from American fans), European SF writers have suffered from American supremacy, without deriving any economic benefit.

A first paradox is this: how could such a product, so perfectly tailored to a specialised American public have any relevance for Europeans? Surprisingly, American popular science fiction was launched in France by the Paris left bank avant-garde: Raymond Queneau, Jacques Audiberti, Boris Vian, Michel Butor. And this support did not derive from any kind of misapprehension. These writers were attracted to American science fiction precisely because of its non-literary quality. It was a perfect weapon in their war on traditional literature, much as *'l'art nègre'* had been against academic art. Generally speaking they used what was alien in American popular culture to explode the stuffy traditions of a stagnant society. The pataphysicist (post-dada) Boris Vian, for example, was also an excellent jazz musician, and wrote imitations of Mickey Spillane-type thrillers. Besides, science fiction was specially privileged in that it was concerned with the future and with change — implying a certain disregard for, or distance from, the present. Its aesthetic was then a denial of the bourgeois realism that had plagued European literature for so long. This element had been obscured in French science fiction by its inter-penetration with highbrow literature, its concerns and style. The closed system of US science fiction, which to outsiders even had a cryptic, disquieting quality, represented, on the contrary, the ultimate in the way of non-realism; it was almost a parallel world in which the rules of creation were not hidden by the mimetic illusion.

The irony of this is that the Americans were of course unaware of the extra dimension: on the contrary, Robert Heinlein, establishing his Future Chart, prided himself on his realism and even paid homage to Sinclair Lewis, in his preface to *The Man Who Sold The Moon*. For European intellectuals the formal contribution far outweighed the naive content[18] — the mystique of science or the American middle-class ideology. In this model formula for international trade, one side bought what the other side never suspected it was selling.

In spite of this warm welcome, the emergence of the French writers was not an easy one. The market was monopolised by Americans. Only occasionally could a French story steal into *Galaxy* or *Fiction*[19] or into the series of books (*Le Rayon Fantastique* from 1951 and *Présence Du Futur* from 1954). The only opening for French writers was a low-brow juvenile series, *Anticipation (Fleuve Noir)* which published 466 novels from 1951 to 1971, two out of three being French. Rather than having American works translated, it was cheaper to hire French writers to grind out cheap pot-boilers under merciful pseudonyms. It is a miracle that some few writers (for example Stefan Wul) could produce good work under such a handicap.

In Germany the native tradition of science fiction was annihilated first by the War, and then by the floods of American stories. Since then, Germany has produced an impressive quantity of popular and young science fiction. One distinctive feature is the relative neglect of the short story form (and correlatively of magazines) in favour of the novel and novel sequence. The most famous one is the Perry Rhodan series, relentlessly churned out by Scheer and Darlton. Out of this prolific mass production, few first-class writers have emerged, with the single exception of H.W. Franke. (The great literary tradition of Ernst Jünger and Herman Hesse has suffered interruption.) The emphasis on the young market is reflected by the strength of German fandom, organized American-style, often under the influence of G.I. clubs. Their activity was crowned by the occasion in Heidelberg in 1970 of the first World Science Fiction Convention to be held in a non English-speaking country.

Italian fandom is less widespread but no less dynamic, since its organisation in 1972 of the first Eurocon in Trieste. This is proof of the lasting influence of US science fiction at the teenage and adult level which, however, remains quite independent of the major mainstream writers: Dino Buzzati, Giuseppe Tomaso di Lampedusa, Italo Calvino, who still keep alive the literary tradition.

After a somewhat gloomy period, the last five years have seen a renaissance in publishing, with several new series, directed by competent connoisseurs, mostly writers. These new collections boast better translations, critical introductions, and bibliographies, which indicates that they are aimed at the highbrow public. Thanks to this new wave of publishing, more French writers have been given a chance. Jacques Sternberg, Gérard Klein, Daniel Drode have not yet made a real breakthrough but the best stories so far are true to the national vein of irony and complicity with the reader rather than to the positivist tone of American science fiction. So there is a natural attraction to the experimental trend initiated by the British.

An original feature of French science fiction has been the creation of sophisticated adult comics, generally of an erotic kind, such as Jean-Claude Forest's *Barbarella*,[20] or more recently the emergence of the baroque, Philippe Druillet, whose wild drawings recapture the poetry of delirious space operas. These expensive, luxury comics reveal how far SF has moved from the popular ghetto; it may even be in danger of running into an élitist one.

The most promising development in the matter of contact between science fiction and experimental literature is coming from less frivolous circles. Since its discovery by rebellious intellectuals, the non-realistic potentialities of SF have continued to fascinate those French writers who seek to avoid the dead-ends of realism. The 'Nouveau Roman', modern linguistics and structuralism point to the conventional, code-like, self-generative quality of meaning and writing; under this influence several remarkable books have combined the freedom of SF with a highly formalised approach. Typical of these is Jean Ricardou's *La Prise* (or *La Prose*) *De Constantinople*,[21] which generates itself out of combinations of the elements of the title page: it includes a future galactic conspiracy which uses the book as its secret code. Jean Ricardou is a well-known critic and writer who has long been associated with the experimental *Tel Quel* magazine. For the Nouveau Roman writer Claude Ollier too, the near-impossibility of writing a contemporary realist novel prompts the use of a science fiction framework, much as Alain Robbe-Grillet used the conventions of the detective novel in *La Maison De Rendez-Vous*.

For obvious political and historical reasons Russian science fiction has remained free from outside influences. The only foreign writers translated into Russian were those deemed compatible with communist ideology: Jules Verne for his faith in science, H.G. Wells for his criticism of the capitalist system and his socialist allegiance.

After the nineteenth century flowering, Russian science fiction cannot be separated from revolutionary fervour. For Maïakovsky, Khlebnikov, Bulgakov, Ehrenburg, Adamov and even Zamiatin, the vision of the future included as a matter of course the utopian ambitions of the Revolution. Revolutionary ideology was committed to modern science and industrialisation. Anticipation was the order of the day: according to the expert in the field, Darko Suvin, 155 anticipation novels were published between 1920 and 1927.

The social and utopian commitment of those feverish years is in sharp contrast to the lightweight sense-of-wonder and space opera stories of the contemporary American magazines. If any influence is to be traced it is a movement from Soviet science fiction to America rather than the other way round. In the years of the New Deal, in accordance with the militancy of the Proletarian Novelists, a splinter group of the New York fandom movement led by one John B. Mitchell, advocated more social relevance and commitment in science fiction. After a bout of polemics they were denounced as fellow-travellers (cf. Sam Moskovitz in *The Immortal Storm*) and social relevance was buried with them.

At the same time in the USSR, social relevance was being buried too. Stalinism and Jdanovism had spread their cloak over Russian science fiction. Freedom to speculate had become suspicious: fear of deviation and heresy imposed the so-called theory of limits. Writers had to limit themselves to the solution of technological problems or the popularisation of science — hence the reign of stereotyped situations, characters and 'safe' themes.

While Europe was busy discovering American science fiction, all writing in the USSR was determined by party policy. The rebirth of Soviet science fiction was accordingly prompted by purely domestic factors: Stalin's death and the liberalisation that followed. In 1957 the publication of *Andromeda* by Yefremov and the passionate debate that ensued rekindled the great utopian tradition. But far from moving in the American direction Russian SF was, according to Darko Suvin, 'in complete contrast to American science fiction' — with which Yefremov is obviously in a polemical dialogue — 'in its optimistic faith, its enthusiasm for the future, its linking of science with human creativity and harmonious self-realisation'.

Either from personal belief, or ideological pressure, this contrast has persisted. In the last few years when a cold wind has blown again on Soviet literature, science fiction has come under particular suspicion because of its capacity for masked satire. Yet even the alienated writers derive their inspiration from the domestic scene rather than from abroad. The talented new writers: Arkadi and Boris Strugatski, Abramov, Gorbovski, Mirer, Smagin, Varshafski do not seem to be attracted by the anti-scientific, irrational attitude of the Western New Science Fiction: 'the salvation of the creative imagination cannot be found in mythical, existential, surrealistic writings'.[22]

The massive introduction of popular American science fiction into post-war Western Europe has had striking, and somewhat unexpected results. American science fiction did not triumph because of new themes or motifs, and its optimistic values (partly modified after 1950) were not generally fitted to the mood of Europe. In view of this, its complete take-over of the strong European traditions of science fiction seems paradoxical. The reason for its impact was its highly 'conventional' quality, its specialisation on the short story, with established vocabulary, situations, characters, narrative technique, symbols and mythology: it drew its strength from this collective elaboration. This new high-powered way of writing met with success because the literary European tradition had not developed an equal concentration.

Yet, once adopted, the formula could evolve more easily in

Europe (and especially in Great Britain) precisely because it was cut off from its sociological basis, which could have kept it too rigid. Fertilisation from intellectual sources, always strong in European science fiction, was thus quicker and, in turn, had a liberating influence on the American ghetto, which had outlived its usefulness. This is how Tom Disch acknowledged his debt to British SF:

> 'as to what I'm so pleased about here — I think ... it's the seriousness of what goes on here, or at least the fact that seriousness can be admitted, that it's not an embarrassment, that people just take the whole business of writing seriously ... in the States I simply would have felt, "Well, it can't be done." I would have resigned myself to what I thought were certain facts of the market-place.'[23]

Since 1967, impatient new American writers have been emboldened to challenge the self-complacent conservatism of the American field, mainly through provocative 'original' anthologies. The ambitious 'seriousness' growing out of the field has coincided with (or called forth) fresh interest by outside writers: Anthony Burgess, Jean Ricardou, Claude Ollier, William Burroughs, Thomas Pynchon, John Barth, John Hawkes and many others. This parallel emergence inside and outside the field proper shows that the walls are crumbling down. The America ghetto period was a very useful but not necessarily an eternal avatar of speculative literature.

Captain America Meets the Bash Street Kids: *the comic form in Britain and the United States*

ROGER LEWIS

All comic characters, from Dagwood to Ming of Mongo, are socially significant in the sense that they propagate images that play up to our prejudices.

Jules Feiffer

Anyone can be a cartoonist! It's so simple, a child can do it!! 'ART' is just a racket! A HOAX perpetrated on the public by so-called 'artists' who set themselves up on a pedestal and promoted by pantywaist ivory-tower intellectuals and sob-sister 'critics' who think the world owes them a living . . . IT'S ONLY LINES ON PAPER FOLKS!

Robert Crumb

It has taken a long time for the comic form to gain any kind of recognition. The quality papers in Britain resisted the incursion of pictorial illustrations for many years. Middle-class Victorians preferred to keep pictures and prose distinctly separate. Publications other than *Punch* and the *Illustrated London News* were regarded with suspicion as a potential threat to literacy and a tidy mind. In fact story-telling through a series of graphic illustrations has a history far older than printing. Palaeolithic cave paintings, Egyptian hieroglyphics, friezes on Greek vases, Trajan's column and the Bayeux tapestry were all intended to communicate the social and cultural concerns of their time.

In Britain there is a popular misconception that comic books originated in America. Comic books were established in Britain long before they came to prominence in the United States. Nor was

America the sole progenitor of the comic strip, although popular newspapers in the United States carried strips some twenty years before they were introduced in Britain. British comics have always been directed primarily at a juvenile audience, whilst in the United States the content of comic books frequently reflect the interests of a higher age group. Initially, however, British comic books were read by young clerks, white-collar workers and others who had benefited from the late-nineteenth century advances in popular education. The first American newspaper strips were a central factor in the circulation battles between popular dailies and were devised to attract new readers and sell papers. Consequently, they were limited by the need to collect the widest possible audience.

Given the immense popularity of American comics throughout the world, one would expect misgivings to be expressed about their effect on other cultures. Mussolini made a point of banning American comics in fascist Italy, although the outcry at the suspension of *Popeye* was so great that he was forced to tolerate the continuing presence of the spinach-addicted sailor.

The American comic industry has never directly influenced its British counterpart to any great degree. There are few American strips in the British press compared to newspapers abroad. The British seem to prefer their own products. Likewise, the Americans do not find British strips particularly stimulating, although there are exceptions on both sides of the Atlantic. Reg Smythe's *Andy Capp* has a considerable following in the United States and *Peanuts* is widely read in England. A number of American comic books are imported into Britain but their sales are vastly outweighed by those of British children's comics. The relationship between Britain and America might be described as a fairly subtle interchange of techniques and ideas rather than the dominance of one national industry over another.

The early days of the industry in both countries were characterised by a vigorous form of slapstick humour, epitomised by the Yellow Kid and the Katzenjammer Kids in the United States and by Ally Sloper, Weary Willie and Tired Tim in Great Britain. In America the riotous behaviour of these early characters gradually diminished as their readers began to ascend the social scale. The rough, tough humour of immigrant New York became domesticated. Existing strips were toned down whilst the more recent Gasoline Alley, Little Orphan Annie, and Dagwood Bumstead reflected the familiar concerns of small-town America. This development may be observed in the constant tension between Jiggs and Maggie in *Bringing Up Father*, the nostalgic husband looking fondly back at his social and ethnic origins and the socially-aspiring wife desperately attempting to integrate herself into the upper middle-class. George Macmanus, who created *Bringing Up Father*, was a fine artist with an acute eye for the kind of decors that would appeal to the fashion-conscious Maggie and irritate the down-to-earth Jiggs.

The adventure and detective strips of the thirties illustrated the need for escape from the insecurities of the Depression. The comic story provided a fantasy outlet from the frustrations of the day. For despite the overtly moral attitude of comics to gangsterism, the reader could vicariously identify with those who defied the restrictions of society yet virtuously endorse the retribution that fell upon them in the final frame. The introduction of Superman in 1938 was a watershed for the American comic. The hero was no longer limited by the frailties of the human body and the acclaim with which Superman was received established the comic book as an integral part of American life. In 1937 D.C. Thomson of Dundee, Scotland, launched the *Beano* and the *Dandy* upon the unsuspecting British public. They have dominated British comics ever since. However, by the turn of the century, English comic books were aimed primarily at children and, consequently, have been far less responsive to changing social conditions than American newspaper strips. British editors refused to treat newspaper strips seriously until at least the thirties, and there have never been Sunday comic supplements in Britain. Instead, comic books are published weekly rather than monthly.

Reitberger and Fuchs have suggested that comics may mirror the American collective subconscious more faithfully than any other medium.[1] American archetypes, like Dagwood Bumstead and Lil' Abner, are compelled to perform in all kinds of complicated situations, and the average reader recognizes in their behaviour the responses of his neighbour if not of himself. Given the changes that American comic books have gone through in the last ten years, it seems entirely fitting that the chief protagonist in the film *Easy Rider* should have been called Captain America. During World War Two the Captain in his stars-and-stripes uniform beat off the Axis powers almost single-handed and, with his wasp good-looks, was the personification of the American ideal. Today, in company with his black colleague, the Falcon, he ponders on slum conditions, racism and the inadequacy of his old moral code. He is a less invincible but far more human figure. The drastic changes in style, presentation and content pioneered by Marvel in the sixties show how an intense social and cultural reassessment within a society influences all forms of media. In 1965 the adventures of Marvel creations, like Spiderman, Hulk, Doctor Strange and the Silver Surfer, were being followed by that section of society — students and the radicalized young — that was most critical of old-established values. The letters pages of Marvel Comics contained frequent arguments about Vietnam, ecology, racism and so on. Stan Lee, editorial director of Marvel, encouraged the correspondence although he never backed one side against another. A letters column has always been a part of the basic format of most British comics. They remain, however, determinedly non-controversial. Whilst Marvel were changing the face of the American comic scene, the form was undergoing a favourable critical reappraisal in Europe. Adult British fans tend to concentrate on American comic books, due to the juvenile orientation of their own national products, and they were aware of the Marvel renaissance. The Academy of Comic Book Art was founded in America in late 1970, establishing annual awards for outstanding contributions to the comics field. Stan Lee was its co-founder and first president.

There are many fanzines, or comic fan magazines, throughout America, Britain and Europe and journals, like *Linus* in Italy, have contributed considerably in establishing the credentials of the comic as an art form. The distinctions between fanzines, prozines and adzines are often blurred. Prozines usually contain heavyweight critical articles, as well as original contributions from professionals, who may wish to publish material that their employers will not handle. A Jim Steranko drawing of a bare-bottomed Wonder Woman, for instance, could only appear in a fanzine or a prozine. Fanzines also encourage amateur contributions and successful underground artists, like Skip Williamson and Jay Lynch, have sometimes started out in this way. Adzines are commonly published by specialist bookstores and are viewed with suspicion by the average fanzine reader. The quality of fanzines can vary enormously and they are often full of in-jokes, parodies, and acrimonious debates involving points of fact and opinion. It can seem a weird and arcane world to the uninitiated outsider. The enthusiasts see the comic world as their world, just as it was during their childhood, when it offered a refuge from adult interference. Comics provided them with characters, a frame of reference, and a vocabulary with which they could play, and this is especially so of British comics directed entirely at a school and pre-school audience.

The most popular series in England consist of characters like the Bash Street Kids, who totally reject the adult world. Symbols of authority — teachers and policemen — are their natural enemies and they battle against them with a cheerful nihilism that is rarely seen in American comics. Ironically, although the quality of American comic books has improved remarkably, there has been a drastic decline in sales in the past twenty years. Television has taken its inevitable toll. The British industry, which has seen few breakthroughs over a similar period, has suffered likewise. Underground comics in Britain and America have not been affected in quite the same way. They have only been in existence since around 1967 and are not dependent upon distributors in the same way as conventional comics are. They have a specialized and enthusiastic audience and are less susceptible to the vagaries of the market. Along with younger comic enthusiasts, underground comic readers resent uninformed criticism and the carping of more 'mature' minds.

'I'll bet this happened when you were a kid! Did you ever receive warnings about how comic books were going to RUIN your MIND? Were you given lectures about how comics were CHEAP TRASH put out by evil men? Let ZAP comics whisk away all such foolish notions!'[2]

Dime novels and 'penny dreadfuls' were the direct forebears of comics in prose form. They declined in popularity in Britain during the 1890s as their audience turned to comic publications. Although *Ally Sloper's Half-Holiday* first appeared in 1884, the turning point came in 1890 when Alfred Harmsworth published *Comic Cuts* and *Chips* with the specific intention of breaking into the penny dreadful market. Tramps and other cheerful layabouts were the most popular characters, defying as they did the stuffiness and class-consciousness of late-nineteenth century England. This anarchic tradition persists in the best contemporary British comics. The irrepressible wise-cracking tramp, like the romanticised freight-jumping hobo and the lone cowboy drifter, is the free spirit with whom the entrapped reader identifies as he continually adjusts to the pressures of industrial society. As was the case with the penny dreadfuls, there was a great deal of transatlantic borrowing. American material would be adapted for a British audience, just as American businessmen would raid Europe for short stories for their own publications. Plagiarism and theft seem to have been so rife that comic strips in the *San Francisco Examiner* in 1905 were clearly marked 'All Britain Rights Reserved'.

Within a short time *Comic Cuts* and *Chips* had a joint circulation of over half a million. Other publishers were not slow in trying to imitate their success. The appearance of *Rainbow* in 1914, for a younger age group, helped to confirm British comics as primarily children's reading. It was a comfortable, brightly-coloured paper, with attractively mischievous characters like Tiger Tim and the Bruin Boys. Although its values were essentially middle-class, it recognized that children were frequently capable of aberrant behaviour, unlike the later Rupert Bear strip in the *Daily Express*. Rupert has never erred from the path of Home Counties virtue. In 1916 *Funny*

Wonder featured Charlie Chaplin in his own strip, setting a precedent that was to result in *Film Fun, Radio Fun* and, finally, *TV Fun*. *Film Fun* characters outwitted rent collectors, unscrupulous landlords, pawnbrokers and policemen with the same regularity as their counterparts in *Chips* and *Comic Cuts*. Today, Andy Capp, unemployed by choice, continues this tradition in the *Daily Mirror*. Billy Bunter of Greyfriars School is another perennial shirker, who munches his way through mountains of food, albeit with the disapproval of his classmates. Because British comics are directed at children, food, rather than sex, is a prime motivation. Heaven consists of a feast of sausages, mashed potato, jelly, fish, chips, soda pop and cream cakes. Like Snoopy, Bunter was originally a minor character, who came to prominence through sheer force of personality. School stories are quite popular in British comics, particularly if they involve an exclusive upper-class establishment. Their appeal has faded recently except in girls' comics where their fantasies of asexual comradeship are still in demand. Football, cricket, the Wild West, war stories, and the Mounties have been staple fare since the twenties, as adventure tales transferred from prose to picture form. The British army is still the bravest in the world and British sportsmen always win in the end. Now that Britain no longer has an empire, her nationalism is far more muted. However, something remains of that jingoistic spirit that George Orwell described so well in 1939.

> 'The King is on his throne and the pound is worth a pound. Over in Europe the comic foreigners are jabbering and gesticulating, but the grim, grey battleships of the British fleet are steaming up the Channel and at the outposts of the Empire the monocled Englishmen are holding the niggers at bay. . . . Everything is safe, solid and unquestionable. Everything will be the same for ever and ever. That approximately is the atmosphere.'[3]

And, broadly speaking, that is how it was, until D.C. Thomson unleashed the *Beano* and the *Dandy* upon us.

American newspaper strips reach two hundred million people in sixty countries every day. R.F. Outcault's *Yellow Kid* first appeared in 1896 and is widely regarded as the first American example of the strip form, although *Little Bears and Little Tigers* appeared in the *San Francisco Examiner* in 1892. The association of the Yellow Kid's particular form of scabrous wit with Hearst's circulation war resulted in the phrase 'yellow journalism'. *The Katzenjammer Kids* arrived in 1897 with a distinctly immigrant flavour to their behaviour and accent. However, the trend towards an increasing conformism was well under way by the turn of the century to be countered only by Winsor McKay's *Little Nemo in Slumberland* and George Herriman's *Krazy Kat*. Both strips had a dreamlike, surreal quality heightened by McKay's exquisite use of perspective and Herriman's weird landscapes and bizarre dialogue. *Krazy Kat* was a particular favourite of Hearst's and both strips acquired a sizeable intellectual following.

The first American comic books were reprints of popular newspaper strips and original comic book material did not develop until the late thirties. The appearance of *Little Orphan Annie* in 1924 paved the way for direct social commentary in the strip form. Previously the artist had never been directly propagandist, but Harold Gray had no scruples about advocating his particular brand of conservatism. Daddy *Warbucks*, a patriotic munitions manufacturer and Annie's guardian, represents all that the Left loathes and the Right holds dear. Annie's adventures prepared the public for the melodramatic themes of the thirties — *Tarzan, Buck Rogers, Dick Tracy, Terry and the Pirates* and the *Phantom*. These, in turn, created the climate out of which *Superman, Batman* and the super-heroes emerged.

The first British newspaper strip occurred as *Teddy Tail* in the *Daily Mail* in 1915. *Pip, Squeak and Wilfred* followed in 1919, and *Rupert Bear* in 1920. *Pop* arrived in 1921 and was the first British newspaper strip to seek an adult audience. During the thirties, the *Daily Mirror* was the only newspaper to carry a number of strips, including *Belinda Blue Eyes*, modelled closely on *Little Orphan Annie*. It launched *Jane, Diary of a Bright Young Thing* in 1932. Unlike Blondie, Jane did not find her Dagwood until 1959, when the strip terminated. She was a forces' sweetheart throughout the war, spending most of her time slipping in and out of her skimpy underclothes. One day in 1943 she appeared completely naked and an American forces paper reported heavy British advances during the following week. British newspaper strips have always carried more nudity than their American counterparts.

British newspapers contain family strips, adventure stories, and specifically indigenous forms of humour, such as *Andy Capp, Flook* and *The Perishers*. The only British creation who ever remotely resembled a super-hero is the muscular *Garth*. Unfortunately, he is none too bright, although he possesses a humility that American super-heroes have only recently acquired. Flook, Andy Capp and the Perishers, like the Bash Street Kids in the *Beano*, are the Yellow Kid's spiritual descendants, if in a very British kind of way. They have few illusions. They know the score. Flook is a likeable, funny little animal with a very short trunk, who continually seems to bump into public figures thinly disguised as comic characters. Like Walt Kelly's

Pogo, the strip provides a continuous and perceptive commentary on current events. Only the *Adventures of Grocer Heath*, in the satirical magazine *Private Eye*, is more direct in its portrayal of the ludicrous in public life. Andy Capp, on the other hand, lives in a restricted world of pubs, dole queues, football pitches and factory chimneys. His origins lie in the unemployment and desolation of the pre-war industrial North-east. Through Andy, the British working class manages to laugh at itself, although the laughter sometimes has a bitter ring. Andy may be work-shy, but his voluntary unemployment was once an unavoidable fact of life for millions.

The Perishers and the Bash Street Kids possess the limited freedom of childhood. Their lives are dominated by school, waste ground, the gas works and occasional trips to the seaside. Whilst the Bash Street Kids are bent solely on the disruption of the structured adult universe, the Perishers are more subtle in their approach. Wellington, the deer-stalkered thinker, shares a precarious existence with his Old English sheepdog, Boot. Maisie and Marlon treat him with grudging respect, although they are never entirely sure what he is talking about. A Nazi tortoise, sporting a Hitler moustache, a Communist caterpillar, and a baby called Grumpling occasionally make an appearance. The tortoise, like the Reverend in *Pogo*, talks in gothic script. Leo Baxendale created the Bash Street Kids for the *Beano* in the fifties. They consist of a gang of children gathered together under the supervision of a long-suffering teacher. They are entirely grotesque. The ringleader, Danny, is a tough little thug clad in a vivid, red sweater, emblazoned with a black skull-and-crossbones. Plug, a child of outstanding ugliness, has teeth that protrude six inches from his mouth and the blankest expression that you have ever seen. Smiffy's roll-neck sweater covers his face as far as the bridge of his nose. The only parts of him that are visible are a pair of beady eyes and a bald pate. Each week they rip through school and town like the advance guard of Genghis Khan's army, and their audience love it.

Occasionally, British children indulge in American imports, but Thomson's *Beano* and *Dandy* are their staple diet. *Beano*, alone, is reputed to sell over 600,000 copies per week. The supply of American comic books depends upon shipping, customs and the whims of the distributor and retailer, and it is usually only adults who are prepared to tolerate the delays. Some British comics reprint original American material but this rarely comes out satisfactorily in black-and-white. Only the Disney productions have managed to corner a reasonable share of the market just as they have done everywhere. There was parliamentary legislation to counter the alleged effects of imported American 'horror' comics, which was quite unnecessary, for horror comics had been blocked at their source by the introduction of the American Comics Code.

Contemporary British comics are almost entirely visual. The appearance of *Beano* and *Dandy* without prose content in the late thirties spelt the end of the pulp heritage in British comics. Story themes remained much the same, but their structure was to be determined by pictures, not words. The middle class attempted to stem what they viewed as a potential tide of illiteracy by producing *Eagle* in 1951. It was a well-intentioned attempt at a 'quality' comic devised for the children of 'worried' parents. For a while it was accompanied by *Girl, Swift* and *Robin*, all equally respectable productions. *Eagle* made the mistake of believing that kids want to read what adults think is good for them. It was this most elementary error that killed it. American parents tend to have a slightly better idea of what their children are reading because there is less of a distinction between children's and adults' comics in the United States. This partly explains the rapid elimination of 'horror' comics in the fifties and also the blandness of American comic book humour. The American *Dennis the Menace* is a mere tow-haired, freckle-faced child with a high energy quotient, compared to his British counterpart. The British *Dennis*, with his tousled, unruly mop, his raggedy, black and red sweater, and his ferocious mongrel, Gnasher, who looks more like a predatory ink blot than a dog, wreaks havoc wherever he goes. He is a malign demon whose only fear is the beating that his father will administer if he is ever caught. *Minnie the Minx, Beryl the Peril* and *Roger the Dodger* are almost equally anti-social, although Dennis surpasses all of them in the sheer perversity of his behaviour. It seems fairly certain that such a disreputable bunch would never have passed the unrevised American Comics Code. Even the comparatively well-behaved *Lord Snooty and his Pals* and *Desperate Dan*, who shaves with a blow torch and whose environment contains a strange mixture of British bobbies, cacti, stagecoaches, chimney sweeps, soccer matches and cow pies, would probably have received short shrift from the comics panel. Their raison d'être is to thwart officialdom and the Code clearly stated that 'policemen, judges, government officials, and respected institutions shall never be presented in such a way as to create disrespect for established authority'. Oddly enough, D.C. Thomson are probably the most implacably right-wing publishers in the United Kingdom. Dudley Watkins, 'a comic artist of genius', set the style for both the *Beano* and the *Dandy*, but it took years before Thomsons allowed him the privilege of signing his work. Signed work is rarely permitted in British comics. Later Thomson characters, like *Dennis the Menace* and the *Bash Street Kids* are as abrasive as the inhabitants of many

underground comics, although they lack the sexual pubescence of
Honey Bunch Kaminski and other Robert Crumb creations.
Baxendale's Bash Street monsters have had an all-pervasive influence
on British comics since the fifties, to the extent that contemporary
British comics seem to be peopled solely by their offspring.

Whereas British comics tend to be about kids, for kids, and
starring kids, American comic books usually have adult heroes.
Adults are expected to set examples and behave responsibly. British
comics are not only more anarchic but more working class in their
orientation. American comic heroes tend to be good-looking,
successful and middle class. In Britain their background and their
vocabulary, like their audience, is essentially proletarian. American
popular culture prefers not to admit to class divisions, but in Britain
these divisions are as familiar as the face of the reigning monarch.
British humour can afford to be more violent, splenetic and
disruptive, because the stability of the society can contain it. Thus
in the past British comics have been more juvenile but, uninten-
tionally, more honest. However, the changes initiated at Marvel, and
taken up by National D.C., have altered the entire outlook of
American comics in the last ten years.

Comic book enthusiasts commonly refer to the years between
Superman and the Comics Code as the 'Golden Age of American
comics'. A vast industry developed in the early days of the war as
Flash, the *Sub-Mariner, Captain America*, the *Human Torch* and a
host of other super-heroes moved against America's enemies.
Contrary to George Orwell's expectations, the super-heroes never
revealed the fascist tendencies of which he suspected them. They
were the creations of a society short on mythical heroes. The Flash
has his origins in Mercury, Green Arrow in Robin Hood, Namor in
Neptune, and Thor in Thor. It is not a coincidence that National
D.C. called one of their recent titles, *New Gods* — a case of old gods
in new bottles. Super-heroes were usually limited by their puny alter
egos until the sixties. Their human form enabled the average reader
to identify with their activities. National D.C. so valued their
Superman idea that they sued Fawcett for infringement of copyright
when the latter introduced Captain Marvel. The courts upheld
National's plea and the 'big red cheese' was consigned to oblivion
until National chose to revive him in the 1970s. However, the
well-tried formulas have recently been stood on their heads. Marvel
and National have humanised their super-heroes and reduced the
need for dual identities. Super-villains, too, are no longer all-bad.
Reasons are given for their anti-social behaviour. Moleman hates the
world because of his social and sexual rejection and Dr Doom just
'thinks of himself as a guy who wants to rule the world 'cause he can do

a better job than anyone else. And he is amazed that people try to stop him.'[4] Before Marvel's innovations, super-heroes were only interested in fighting crime; now they are beginning to consider its causes.

The Comics Code, which almost destroyed the comics industry in the United States, resulted from the public outcry against 'horror' comics. Dr Frederic Wertham's book *Seduction of the Innocent*[5] was the hook upon which the anti-comics lobby hung its arguments. Around 1950 Bill Gaines of E.C. Comics had switched from crime and war comics, which had a largely adult and late-adolescent audience, to titles such as *Crypt of Terror, Vault of Horror* and *Haunt of Fear*. Literature and the cinema had catered to this taste for the supernatural, the mysterious and the ghostly in the past, as had the penny dreadfuls and the pulps. The comics quite naturally drew on themes from Edgar Allan Poe, H.P. Lovecraft, Bram Stoker and others. Artists and editors felt less restricted and produced some remarkably scary and beautifully organised stories. Unfortunately, less scrupulous publishers decided that the financial success of the comic corresponded directly to the size of the body count. Their excesses provided Wertham's supporters with a considerable amount of ammunition. Wertham himself saw psychotic and sexual imagery wherever he looked and comics were blamed for the kind of delinquency that was to be later attributed to rock'n'roll, television, marijuana and sex education. Their critics never seemed to realise that their readers came from a far higher age group than they suspected. The Comics Code was established as an act of self-censorship by the industry itself. The controversy had been affecting sales, so once again comics adjusted to the social pressures of the time as the effects of McCarthyism penetrated almost every aspect of national life.

Warren Comics revived the 'horror' story in 1965 with *Creepy*, using a slightly different format to avoid the restrictions of the Code. *Eerie* soon followed, and *Vampirella*, a particularly alluring vampire lady, appeared in 1969. The artwork in the Warrens was exceptionally good and the inking, subtle and balanced. The Code's seal of approval was refused to *Spiderman*, 96, in 1971. Spidey had given a warning against hard drugs and the Code specifically forbade the mention of drugs. Marvel, nevertheless, released the comic and the Code's administrators were forced to reconsider their regulations. Criminal behaviour resulting from oppressive social conditions may now be treated sympathetically and official corruption may be portrayed provided that the guilty are punished. In this, at least, comics appear to be ahead of real life. Captain America himself underwent some protracted soul-searching in 1969.

'I'm like a dinosaur. . . . An anachronism . . . who's outlived his time. . . . It isn't hip to defend the establishment! only to tear it down. And in a world rife with injustice, greed and endless war — who's to say the rebels are wrong? . . . I've spent a lifetime defending the flag and the law! Perhaps I should have battled less, and questioned more!'[6]

By the early seventies even the reformed super-heroes had begun to lose their popularity to stores loosely referred to as 'tales of sword and sorcery'. Obscure yarns from the old pulps were revived or entirely new characters were created. They lived in a post-apocalyptic world, determined by tribal loyalties and vague super-stitions, where time and space no longer has meaning. As comic sales continue to decline, the industry is making increasingly frantic attempts to devise new formulae. Humanised vampires and were-wolves have recently appeared, although their sympathetic treatment tends to detract from their basic appeal. Dracula in *Dracula Lives!* has had a particularly rough time since he mistakenly drank the blood of a New York junkie.

Underground comics originated in the United States in the latter half of the sixties. Many of their finest artists are comic fans of long standing, who created their own comics as children and were deeply influenced by *Mad* magazine's attacks on the respectable mass media. *Mad* specialised in parodying conventional comic characters, as did the older pornographic 'eight-pagers' or 'Tijuana bibles', which delighted in placing Popeye and his friends in various sexual predicaments. The undergrounds combine the sexual license of the eight-pagers, *Mad*'s iconoclastic approach, and the political and social attitudes that developed out of the youth culture of the 1960s. Sex is represented as it is, not as it should be. One of the reasons that *Oz* magazine was taken to court in Britain was because the head of Rupert Bear had been superimposed on the body of a Crumb character, preparing to penetrate a female with his erect member. Micky Mouse has also been observed doing nasty things to Minnie, in Paul Krassner's *Realist* and elsewhere.

The Rip Off Press, the Print Mint and Last Gasp Eco Comics were started as publishing co-operatives so that underground artists could have total editorial freedom. In recent years Marvel and National have encouraged greater artistic license, but only the fanzines and the undergrounds can permit an entirely free hand. Robert Crumb is one of the acknowledged masters of the underground form. Mr Natural, Leonore Goldberg, Girl Commando, Honey Bunch Kaminski the Drug-Crazed Runaway and Fritz the Cat are all products of his fertile imagination, although he maintains that he does not invent anything.

'It's like all there — all there to pick up on. It's a rich culture.'[7] Rick Griffin, Victor Moscoso, Gilbert Shelton and S. Clay Wilson have worked with him in the past, concentrating on abstract shapes and symbols that mutate as they progress in an underground artists' jam session. The visual effects of hallucinogenic drugs are quite obvious in the drawings as well as in the subject matter of many underground comics. Gilbert Shelton's *Fabulous Furry Freak Brothers* has been serialised in Britain and the United States, and a large number of American strips have been reprinted in the United Kingdom. The influence of American comics on British comics is nowhere more evident than in the underground press. Unlike the overground comic industry, the undergrounds reflect the state of the counter culture as well as that of straight society. The vulgarity of the comics is, in turn, a reflection of the vulgarity and commercialism of American society.

'Hey Grown-ups! Ever wonder why those old-timey horror stories don't chill you and thrill you like they used to? You know, the ones about vampires, ghouls, werewolves, and all that crap? I'll tell you why — because now all those creeps have been replaced with a *reality* scarier than any bogeyman.'[8]

The resurgence of 'horror' comics since 1970 has been mirrored in the undergrounds and, because there are no limits, the products of artists like Richard 'Gore' Corben can be both sick and terrifying. Other artists feel that underground comics devoted to death and destruction no longer merit the name. Occasionally, the mutilation and blood seems justified. Greg Irons' story 'The Legion of Charlie' draws some disturbing parallels between the treatment of Charles Manson and Lt Rusty Calley. Ecological disaster is another constant theme.

British underground comics were almost totally derivative until a couple of years ago. Talented individuals, like Edward Barker, emerged fairly early on but Britain produced little until *Cyclops* appeared in 1970. William Burroughs contributed a script and Martin Sharp and Barker provided drawings. It folded, however, after four issues. *Nasty Tales*, another underground comic, consisted at first almost entirely of American reprints. Gradually, native artists made themselves evident. By 1973 *Cozmic Comics, Zip, Edward's Heave, Rock'n'Roll Madness* and *View from the Void* had appeared. The material is quite noticeably British, although there are fewer references to British overground comics than one might expect.

In 1969 a federal court declared the comic to be an art form. It was a fair indication of the direction in which informed opinion had been moving. It took time for the novel, the silent picture, the moving picture, and the newspaper strip to be accepted. It would appear that the turn of the comic book had finally come. Many professionals, like Jules Feiffer and Roy Thomas, work in the field because they have a vocation. They started drawing as children and have never looked back. Marie Severin, of Marvel, has affirmed that the comic industry is 'one of the few businesses where individuals will take a cut and stay in the business'.[9] However, the limitations of the comic form can be discouraging; Russ Manning finally gave up his Tarzan strip because he grew 'tired of doing artwork on a postage stamp'. It is interesting that the names of illustrators, like Arthur Rackham, Gustav Doré and Aubrey Beardsley, became well-known soon after their work was recognised. As far as comics are concerned, it is the characters rather than their creators who become household names.

Comic books are usually a joint production, in the same way as films. The first annual comic book awards included categories for colouring, writing, inking and pencil artistry. Fellini, like Tashlin, began his career in comics and has referred to Stan Lee as the 'maestro', while Truffaut, Resnais, Godard, and Dick Lester have all been influenced by the style of comic strips. *Citizen Kane* had a marked effect on some comic artists, and Resnais, at one point, asked Stan Lee to script his first English film. The comic and the film are both visual forms sharing similar techniques in their use of narrative, cutting, close-ups, long-shots, back-tracking, and pictorial sequences. The two forms meet in the animated cartoon, although the comic, unlike the film, can be collected and looked at again and again.

The comic can be a hard taskmaster. Many writers find it hard to be succinct and compact enough in their scripts, and a lot of artists have trouble keeping up with deadlines. Only a few panels can be spared to express many ideas, and one wrong decision can ruin a whole comic. Marvel have sometimes used photo-montage to achieve deliberately weird effects. Sometimes a number of small panels are used for closely observed detail or huge splash panels for major confrontations. Exceptional comic artists like Jack Kirby are beginning to have portfolios of their past and present work published as collector's items.

What the fans did for American comics at one level, Lichtenstein and Warhol did at another. Pop art made it possible for critics to look at comics as something more than a peculiar social phenomenon. They were more entertaining than Campbell's soup cans and, although ephemeral, entailed decidedly more craftsmanship. The avant-garde, unlike the middle-aged collector or the Berkeley student, may not have known what the *Silver Surfer* was about, but they knew that the graphics were brilliant and that he was fashionable. The Silver Surfer, like the Seafarer and the Wanderer, had been exiled from his liege-lord to roam an alien planet, earth, until the end of time. The Surfer was a truly tragic hero but, because the circulation was never high, his creators were forced to kill him. The monetary priorities of a mass medium make allowances for no one.

The commodity nature of the comic means that it either has to cater for the aspirations and desires of its readers or else it fails. British society is more static than that of America and its old comic formulae have lasted longer. They have, also, stagnated. The most successful British comics have shown little real development in the past twenty years, and the transient nature of their childhood audience has not encouraged change. The inflammatory activities of the Bash Street Kids have been isolated behind school desks and within playgrounds. The Kids are the last incitement to rebellion that many of their readers will see before entering the factory gate and the adult world. British comics are launched, merged and folded every year, whilst their publishers urgently search for fresh gimmicks and ideas to sustain the old formulae. As in America, it is only the undergrounds that seem to be expanding. There was a general depression throughout the industry in 1973 and the erosion of the market shows no sign of abating. A number of people think that the comic will eventually cease to be a mass medium, whilst quality comics continue to serve a specialised minority demand. It would be a strange twist of fate if economic necessity, combined with the elevation of comics to an art form, finally killed them in their present form.

The Television Series as Folk Epic

MARTIN ESSLIN

The most revolutionary aspect of the electronic mass media of communication is their continuous availability, even more so than their ubiquitousness. Never before in the history of mankind has there been a continuous stream of collective consciousness into which — in the advanced Western societies — every member of the community can at will at any time of the day or night plug himself in, thus filling his individual consciousness with the thought and emotional content shared at that instant by several million of his fellow citizens. In considering the sociology and aesthetics of the electronic mass media this is the principal and paramount factor to be kept in mind. Television critics tend to treat single programmes in isolation as though they were individual works of art. In some sense they may be that, yet many other and more decisive aspects of their impact and indeed aesthetic ground-rules will be lost by such a consideration.

For example, as the programme-builders are intent on stopping people switching off when one item ends, the opening minutes, even seconds of the next item are of crucial importance; for it is through these that the viewer's decision whether to switch off, or over to another channel, will be determined. If the first few seconds of the new item arouse expectation of something really good or thrilling to come, he may stay with the transmission; if not, he is irrevocably lost. Hence, no consideration of the structure of a television broadcast, whether dramatic or documentary, can dispense with a consideration of this iron law of programme building. In American television, where commercials are bound to intrude all too frequently, the same consideration applies every few minutes. Before each commercial break the viewer must be left hooked and expectant as to how the programme will continue. Hence the dramaturgy of most American television plays or series will inevitably have to consist of a series of short-term cliff-hangers and climaxes.

But the consequences of this continual electronic media flow go even deeper. With the loss of a sense of occasion which accompanies a visit to the theatre, and even cinema-going and the ease with which one can enter and leave the continuous stream of mass consciousness, one of the prime objectives of the programme-builder who wants to attract the maximum audience for the maximum length of time, must be to shape that amorphous continuity, to create fixed points which stick in the mind of the audience, to condition the audience into regular habits of viewing. Fixed points which articulate the time-flow each day (e.g. fixed times for news, weather reports etc.), and for each day of the week (sports on Saturday or Sunday, a certain star's variety show each Thursday etc.) are essential to enable the audience to build up expectations, to make them turn to this channel or that with some regularity. This is one of the prime reasons why the electronic mass media thrive on repetition and recurrence.

Another reason, no less potent, is the all-devouring nature of a medium which has to churn out material without interruption, practically for ever. A stage playwright may labour over a single work for years; if he gets it performed and it is successful it will remain accessible for years, in its first long run, then on tour, then perhaps in revivals. The material of the mass media is instantly consumed. A piece of dramatic writing, once performed and seen by millions may get perhaps one or two repeats much later, but once broadcast it is, to all intents and purposes, finished. The programme-planner sees an endless expanse of hours, days, months, years in front of him which must, relentlessly, be filled. It is clearly quite impossible (as was still possible in the theatre or even the cinema) to wait for good material to turn up and then to plan on the basis of what one has found. What if nothing good, or good enough, does turn up? Here too the regular fixed item is the answer to the planner's nightmare. A regular series every Monday followed by a regular series every Tuesday, Wednesday and on through the week, assuages his *horror vacui.* Television planning is planning in strips: a fixed sequence vertically through the hours of the day: news, parlour game, chat-show, dramatic series, variety series etc., and horizontally through the week – the same show every Monday at eight, another every Tuesday at eight and so on through the days of the week, month and year. Only thus can the amorphousness of an unending timeflow be structured into a fixed roster of predictable items – which can then be varied to allow the once-off prestige show or classical play.

The planner's needs coincide with the viewer's urge. Anyone who has worked in mass communications knows that familiarity is not a handicap; the masses delight in the pleasures of recognition — of the familiar face, the familiar character, the familiar tune. Once they have found a hero in a play, they would like him to return and appear in a different adventure, different enough in detail from the last to have the suspense of the unknown, yet familiar enough in pattern to recapture the pleasure of the previous one. When faced with a completely new dramatic work the viewer has to undergo the difficult and intellectually demanding process of de-coding a new exposition: who are the characters? how related? in what period of history? where do they live? All these questions have to be answered anew for each new play. The television series relieves the viewer of this recurring intellectual burden. He already knows the principal characters and their situation. Thus the exposition can be confined to presenting the particulars of just that one episode; and here too most of the work has been done beforehand: knowing the hero to be, let us say, a detective working in Los Angeles, and knowing the pattern of the series in question, everything falls instantly into place.

That is why television drama, properly speaking, has practically disappeared from the commercial television screen in the United States, and why it has to fight an embittered rearguard action in the more fortunate European countries which have public service networks.

It is important to remember that there is not merely a difference in degree between television drama in the sense of a 'single play' (as the TV jargon in England has it: there is a flavour of oddity in the term which sets the exception apart from the rule which is the series) and the television series. The latter is a new genre, different in *kind* and obeying different aesthetic laws. If the single play is a product of *craftsmanship*, the series is an *industrial product*, mass produced.

Series are planned in multiples of thirteen (thirteen weeks are a quarter of the calendar year and television planning is done in quarters). Thus, even the least extensive series will need at least thirteen scripts; but it is far more likely that twenty six, thirty nine, fifty two, or if the series manages to run for years, one hundred and four, two hundred and eight, three hundred and six scripts will be needed. No author can write thirteen plays about the same character within a reasonable time (and series must go out at weekly intervals), let alone three hundred and six or four hundred and eight. Hence the necessity for series to be mass-produced by teams of writers.

Teams of writers must be centrally briefed and directed. (We are here in an industrial mass production process with high initial investment.) An idea is mooted, a pilot programme written, discussed, produced and market researched. The result is a *format*, i.e. a number of recurring characters in a recurring pattern of situations: the lawyer who is also a detective; the sheriff in a Western town and his sidekick; the spy; the spaceship with its autronauts; the silly ass husband and his resourceful wife in the situation comedy. The characters have descriptions which can be handed to the scriptwriters of different episodes; the structural pattern is mapped out once and for all. It remains only to decide on the nature of individual episodes in the series — there must be sufficient variation: the spy, for example, cannot operate in South American countries two or three weeks running, so an episode in South America must be followed by one in Eastern Europe or the Arctic and that, to get maximum variation, by one in the Far East; a very gruesome episode must be followed by a more light-hearted one; and there must be one with a lot of love-interest after one which was confined to conflict between hard-faced men. All the permutations of such variation must be gone through before a viable sequence is centrally determined — it is only after this that the writers can be commissioned and briefed and supplied with their do-it-yourself kits: 'Here are your characters; here is your basic structural pattern (e.g. there must be a chase, or suspense sequence toward the end of each episode); and here your basic situation. Now go away and write your episode!' There may be variations on this model of the production process, but basically this is how it must be set up.

Is this then the point at which we throw up our hands in horror at the death of individual creativeness, the degradation of art, the cynical manipulation of the masses by commercial interests and greedy exploiters? Possibly. Yet we should perhaps also pause and see the matter in perspective. From the point of view of nineteenth-century aesthetics (largely romantic in origin and basic viewpoint) this situation is indeed horrifying — the death of individuality, the end of art as a means of individual expression of individual emotion and experience. Yet there are possible standpoints which differ from the nineteenth-century romantic and individualist one. Elizabethan drama was written rapidly by teams of collaborators hurrying to supply material that was needed to vary the programme. Here too the entrepreneurs farmed out predigested material to teams of hack writers (and yet many masterpieces resulted from this production process). And if we go back into the period of purely oral literature (and McLuhan is right in postulating a return to a period of electronically disseminated pre-literate literature) we find very similar situations: bards spontaneously making up episodes in the lives of stereotyped heroes by using stereotyped elements (lines, situations, villains) for purely mercenary motives (to please the ruler who had summoned them to entertain his guests, to flatter his family, etc.). The literature of the folk epic is anonymous, does not express the author's individual emotions, uses prefabricated material — and yet it has produced some of the greatest works known to man.

How could this come about? The advocates of romantic aesthetics have their romantic answer: these works were not written by individuals, true enough, but they are the products of the soul of a whole people. Each individual bard has improved one or two lines as he repeated them, has adapted his material to the sensibility of his audience, so that ultimately the works in question were written by the nations which produced them, retaining the passages and episodes that pleased, forgetting those that proved unpopular.

How could we compare the products of calculating businessmen with the sacred distillation of a great nation's storehouse of folk myth? The answer, paradoxically, lies in the commercial motivation of the producers. As Kracauer has rightly pointed out in his study of the German film before Hitler,[1] the cinema, by being responsive, for commercial motives, to public demand, can actually be regarded as the collective dream material of a given culture and can be psychoanalysed like an individual's dreams. The same, but even more so, is true of television, which is much more sensitive to the psychological needs or cravings of a much wider public (namely virtually the whole nation) simply because its products are consumed more frequently, in larger quantities, than any cinema films produced for showing in movie houses could ever be.

Once the format of a series is worked out, once it is running, the producers are subject to a constant stream of feedback: audience ratings, market research, correspondence etc. If they want to keep a series going they have to adapt the characters, the situations, the basic pattern to the demands of the public. Unsuccessful series die. But the survivors, as they progress, are ultimately shaped — indeed written — by the audience's subconscious. In my own very practical involvement with radio soap opera I have experienced this process at first hand. A series is launched with a given set of characters. An audience survey is made about the popularity of the main characters. Surprisingly, one of the more secondary characters proves the most popular. Gradually he is pushed into the centre. And in the same way a series, once started, responds to the currents of public demand. It is *because* the makers of the series are motivated by their desire to succeed that the series, the longer they run, become more and more the product of the imagination, desires, fears and dreams of their audience.

This, after all, and to establish the historical continuity, was equally true of pulp fiction before the advent of the electronic mass media, of the early cinema, which met similar requirements from a mass audience. (One has not only to think of the recurring character personified by Chaplin's Little Man, by Buster Keaton, the Marx Brothers, Laurel and Hardy, but also heroes and heroines like Douglas Fairbanks, Lillian Gish and Mary Pickford, who, although they appeared in different situations, always portrayed themselves.) Or going back even further in time we recall the folk theatre (Harlequinade, pantomime, *commedia dell'arte*) and earlier still the vast oral literature of folk tales (Robin Hood, King Arthur, knights errant) until we finally link up with the oral literature of the epic poetry of ancient Greece or Scandinavia.

This folk literature is the very opposite of individual creativeness: it represents a common meeting-ground of the imagination of a people or civilisation where its preoccupations and interests are focussed. It is no coincidence, for example, that in American popular culture, long before the electronic mass media, the Western theme dominated pulp fiction and popular entertainment like the circus (cf. the Wild West shows). The Western is a genuine folk myth: in vastly exaggerated and overdramatised terms it recounts the creation of a new country. The basic themes revolve round the introduction of law and order, the conflict of cattle men versus cereal growers, the conquest of the original inhabitants of the country, and so on. In this way the Western myth is thematically analogous to the cycle of stories about the Trojan War which focussed on a very similar subject, the conquest of Asia Minor by the Greeks. Similarly, the gangster cycle represents a preoccupation with the problems of the new urban society; and the spy and secret agent cycles show the fears of the cold war period. On the comedy level, innumerable situation comedies highlight the ever-recurring problems and anxieties of family life: the clumsy spouse ruining the party for the boss on whom promotion depends, the unruly children, and so on.

Folk art of this type, springing as it does, directly from the collective subconscious of simple people (including, of course, the vulgar and uneducated entrepreneurs who promote it) will inevitably be mostly crude, vulgar, repetitive, unoriginal, poorly characterized and sentimental. What we must remember, however, is that the analogous productions of previous ages were probably equally crude and without merit. Of these, after all, only the very greatest have survived. The *Iliad* and the *Odyssey* are distillations of hundreds and thousands of crude episodes that were not worth preserving. And there are whole centuries of such popular products which have not survived at all, because they brought forth nothing worthy of survival.

In the cinema the Western, the Gangster, and the Private Eye cycle have already produced a few masterpieces. In a thousand years' time, if they survive at all, these may be the only examples out of many thousands of worthless products of the same thematic cycle which will be known and admired. There is no reason why the television serial should not also produce a few lasting masterpieces out of its many hundreds of thousands of worthless, crudely manufactured episodes.

Viewed in a purely American context therefore, the television series appears as true folk art, however vulgar or crude it may be. The impact of this folk art on Europe — and the rest of the world — is far more problematical.

The size of America as a market for this folk art, which enables its products to be sold cheaply, as a kind of bonus to their producers, to other parts of the world, means that the products of the collective subconscious of one nation are inundating the consciousness of other nations, whose problems may be completely different. One of the many revolutionary aspects of the continuous nature of the electronic media, particularly television, is that small nations are simply unable to mobilise the talent that would enable them to fill the endless hours of transmission time with indigenously produced material. Hence the inevitable invasion of the television screens of the world by material from those cultural units which are numerically strong enough to produce sufficient material. The United States and, to a lesser degree Great Britain, are the prime source of such material in the Western world. As far as the English-speaking countries are concerned, their screens are even more easily inundated by American television material. But all the other countries of Western Europe also import vast quantities, which they show dubbed or with subtitles.

We thus have the paradoxical situation of the folk art of one, very specialised and particular culture, invading the consciousness of the members of very different cultures; or, to put it at a different level of impact, the subconscious preoccupations and problems of one, highly neurotic, part of the world, being used to meet the perhaps very different subconscious needs of other areas and cultures.

The result, in the first instance, is bound to be misunderstanding and confusion. On the conscious plane, there is confusion about the true nature of American society: the country appears to many of the more simple-minded European consumers of mass entertainment as a land of gangsters and cowboys — primitive, lawless and aggressive. On a deeper level, there is the spread of basic American attitudes and lifestyles. There may also be subconscious revulsion and rejection of these lifestyles. The anti-Americanism of many of the less sophisticated Europeans may be an outcome of such subconscious rejection of the American attitudes which are constantly dangled before them.

In the long run all this may turn out to be just one aspect of a global process of cultural unification, levelling, or ironing-out of cultural differences, a reflection in the superstructure of consciousness of what is already taking place in the economic and social infrastructure. As vast multi-national companies divide the markets of the world among them, as the politics of the atomic deterrent erode the autonomy of smaller units, so the iron laws of the technology of electronic entertainment will tend to abolish the cultural and psychological differentiation between the countries of the Western world. It is one of the ironies of this process that Western Europe, which numerically and in economic potential might be the equal of the United States, cannot reciprocate this process in the field of mass entertainment, simply because of its cultural and linguistic divisions. If the import of American popular art could be matched by a corresponding export of European folk art to America, the situation would be far healthier. But with the exception of Britain, which does export a large amount of television material, as well as writers, actors, musicians (one only has to think of the Beatles or Rolling Stones) to America, Western Europe seems practically excluded from making an impact on the United States. The traffic here is strictly one-way. No wonder that this creates unease among European intellectuals, and a certain amount of revulsion among the masses.

The process thus seems inevitable. As American breakfast cereals, American soft drinks, American pop music and American industrial practices spread in Europe, the American folk heroes also, inevitably, take over the fantasy world of Europeans. The conquest of the American West becomes one of the folk myths on which Italian peasants and German steelworkers are reared; Dr Kildare and the inhabitants of Peyton Place; Ironside and the secret agents of UNCLE, Lucy and Dick Vandyke become their own folk heroes. One may regret this development, but short of totalitarian suppression (and this would leave large and painful gaps in the material needed by the mass media in Europe) there seems to be no remedy. What is particularly unfortunate in this situation is that by a historical accident the electronic mass media fell from the very beginning into the hands of the advertising industry in America, while in Europe the concept of public service broadcasting mitigated some of the more deplorable aspects which distort popular entertainment in the United States. Perhaps the success of some of the efforts to correct this imbalance in America by promoting at least one public service television network there provides some hope for the future. That programmes like 'Sesame Street' are now among those American television series which begin to have an impact on Europe may be a sign of better things to come. For, while there is nothing wrong with popular entertainment consisting of folk art, what is needed more than anything in the cultural impasse of our time is a bridge between the world of crude folk art and that of consciously cultivated high art. The deep division between the two spheres, which is so painfully manifest in the United States, is unhealthy and dangerous. Only conscious control of the electronic mass media, not in a totalitarian sense, but to provide a better admixture of material for the important culturally conscious minority and a chance for the masses to sample such material and to develop their tastes towards it, can counteract the dangerous tendencies towards a polarisation of masses and élites which is only too apparent in the United States today.

Two Decades in Another Country:
Hollywood and the Cinéphiles

THOMAS ELSASSER

In a 'history' of the impact on Europe of American popular culture, the systematic elevation of Hollywood movies to the ranks of great art would make an intriguing chapter. Legend has it that the feat was accomplished almost single-handed by motivated and volatile intellectuals from Paris sticking their heads together and pulling off a brilliant public relations stunt that came to be known as *Cahiers du Cinéma* and *Nouvelle Vague*.[1]

The legend bears some relation to the facts, but only insofar as it has allowed a very crude version of a very complicated cultural phenomenon to gain widespread or at least topical currency. Today, at a time when film criticism is again increasingly oriented towards theory, the more controversial sides of the episode seem to have been put to rest.[2] Nonetheless, two implications deserve to be studied more closely. One is the feedback which Hollywood's European fame has produced in the United States, and the value now attributed by Americans to their indigenous cultural assets in this field. It is noticeable, for instance, that after a very fitful start, when news from France was greeted with derision and incredulity in New York and Los Angeles, the Hollywood cinema, especially the films of the 1930s, '40s and '50s, has come to be recognized and often nostalgically celebrated as a (if not *the*) truly original contribution of the United States to art and aesthetics in this century.[3] The fact that there exists an American Film Institute,[4] and that courses are being taught on the American cinema at countless universities, indicates a change of attitude quite as decisively as do the antiquarian labours and pastiche work of Peter Bogdanovitch (cf. *The Last Picture Show, What's Up Doc?*, and *Paper Moon*), and the many New York movie houses which are taking notice of the 'director's cinema' when billing their re-run double features, while even five years ago only the stars would have been the attraction.

The other question is prompted by a more general reflection: what does enthusiasm for Hollywood tell us about intellectual or scholarly interest in popular culture, and particularly American culture? There is little doubt that this enthusiasm is, within Europe, predominantly and characteristically French. Critics in Italy, Spain and even Poland have subsequently taken their cue from the Paris line, but as an example of highbrow interest in lowbrow culture the phenomenon only makes sense if one concentrates on France. This is not to deny that Britain produced the most important pro-Hollywood journal outside France,[5] or that as a consequence an ideologically significant, though brief debate flared up in the early 1960s between the 'aesthetic Left', the 'Left' and the 'liberal Right' in England. But historically, the important piece of evidence to keep before one's eyes is that after the Second World War, a number of French cinéphile intellectuals (some of whom — but by no means all — went on to found an eventually very influential platform for their views, the said *Cahiers du Cinéma*)[6] began to apply a highly literate sensibility and a sophisticated appreciation of aesthetic problems to a body of films (roughly the Hollywood output from 1940 onwards) which on the face of it appeared impressive mainly by its quantity. This output had previously existed in 'serious' writing, with the exception of a handful of films by Welles and possibly Ford, only in the wide-meshed grid of sociological generalisation, the more so, since on another level the promotional activities of the film industry were deemed to speak for themselves: the star-system, gossip-columnists, fan-clubs and other accessories of the show-biz machinery proliferated the image of crass commercialism, unspeakably vulgar, sensationalist, and turning out on celluloid and in newsprint a never-ending flood of cut-price fantasies. Or so it seemed to the educated European. And it rendered the products of such efforts beneath contempt — until, that is, rumour got round of how in France they thought differently.

To understand the change, we need a brief historical flashback: in the 1920s the cinema, including the American cinema (Griffith, Stroheim, Chaplin), enjoyed an enormous intellectual prestige, condensed in many a weighty volume on film aesthetics and theory published during the decade.[7] They unanimously hailed a new art, which they assumed to have almost magical possibilities. With singular optimism, Elie Faure would attribute to the cinema the power to transform the traditional arts, and Bela Balazs would sketch a new vision of man which the screen was to project and communicate to the masses. Reading their books today, one becomes aware that the cinema seemed to promise at once a new aesthetic religion and social revolution, the regeneration of a tired civilization. Apart from such slightly millenial hopes, which can also be found in the writings of Delluc, Eisenstein, Arnheim, Pudovkin and Vertov, avant-garde artists such as Léger, Artaud, Dali and Cocteau were equally spellbound by the medium.

The invention of sound at the end of the 1920s dashed this euphoria once and for all. Worried by the way the cinema was more and more forcefully developing in the direction of a realist-representational medium given over to narratives of dubious merit and originality, artists in the modernist vein came to regard the cinema as aesthetically reactionary, a throwback in fact to the nineteenth century. Film criticism throughout the 1930s did not recover from the blow, and the decade which witnessed an unprecedented economic expansion of the film-industries in Europe and America also saw critics only too willing to conclude that popularity automatically spelled aesthetic nullity. The new art of the talking picture came to be written off as irredeemably 'commercial', peddling to nothing but escapist entertainment, or worse still, pernicious demagogy.[8]

Because it displayed commercialism and bad taste with gusto and little sense of shame or self-consciousness, Hollywood had to bear the brunt of the disappointed expectations which quickly relegated the cinema from a potentially major artistic force to a conveyor-belt dream factory. This did not prevent some of the most well-known directors in Europe from emigrating to California, and although most of them left for good political reasons, especially from Germany, not all felt themselves to be heading for dire exile: Ernst Lubitsch, Murnau, Fritz Lang, Max Ophuls, Otto Preminger, Douglas Sirk, Robert Siodmak, Billy Wilder became established as successful Hollywood directors; René Clair and Jean Renoir made important films in America, and so did Alfred Hitchcock. The case of Hitchcock is particularly instructive, since he left England under no political pressure and at the height of his fame at home.

Faced with this massive exodus from Europe, critics rarely if ever used the opportunity to reassess their idea of Hollywood and their judgement of the films it produced. More apparent was the way they gave vent to disillusionment and ill-temper which made the émigrés seem deserters to the cause and hucksters of their talents. The reception of Hitchcock's American films in Britain can stand for many similar attitudes: '*Spellbound* and *Notorious* (are) classic examples of brilliance run to seed, . . . heartless and soulless ingenuity';[9] or about *The Man Who Knew Too Much*: 'a vulgar and debilitated remake by Hitchcock of his splendid old Gaumont-British melodrama, demonstrating once again the pernicious effect of the Hollywood system on a once brilliant entertainer.'[10] Even *Vertigo*, a film of rare subtlety and as hauntingly intense as any romantic masterpiece, was the object of a scurrilous and misinformed attack by the leading film journal of the day.[11]

Among the chorus of nostalgic voices bitterly bemoaning better days and pouring scorn on Hollywood, a few French critics, notably Roger Leenhardt and subsequently André Bazin, stand out by their lucid seriousness and moderation. Bazin, in an article he first published in 1945 and later gave the imposing title 'Ontologie de l'Image Cinématographique'[12] translated this difference of tone and emphasis into a critical position with a theoretical basis. His ambition was nothing less than to rethink the dichotomy between silent film and sound film, European cinema and Hollywood. The first had paralyzed film theory since the 1920s, and the second had made film criticism a stagnant backwater of highbrow prejudice, condescending occasionally to being amused by 'entertainers'. Bazin's system, as far as one can constitute it from his journalism and the numerous pieces of more sustained criticism,[13] based itself on an altogether different distinction, that between directors who 'believe in the image and those who believe in reality'.[14] Directors who believe in the image, according to Bazin, believe in it as a representation of some concept or idea, and their method consists in using the representational nature of the moving image to construct a synthetic reality of the intellect, in short a rhetoric or iconography, to serve an analytically conceived purpose or message. By contrast, those who believe in reality treat the image as a means to 'illuminate', 'explore' etc. the thing represented; they are committed to the aesthetics of *Anschauung*. Instead of montage techniques, superimposition and collage effects, their main aesthetic resources are depth of field (i.e. compositional tensions within the frame), camera movements (tracks, pans, lateral travellings which produce levels of ambiguity and multiple points of view), and finally long takes which allow an action to develop its own dramatic momentum while accumulating the kind of energy inherent in duration itself — as opposed to 'cutting up' a scene into snippets of action and reassembling them in the editing.

However impartial Bazin's system might have appeared, in practice it implied a strong value judgement in favour of what he himself called the 'phenomenological' approach to filmed reality. Applied polemically, his crucial argument was intended to separate those film-makers who, like Eisenstein, Pudovkin and Vertov, 'tampered' with reality because of their didactic intentions, from those who 'respected' the continuity of action as it appears in 'real life' and who deployed the temporal-narrative dimension of the cinema instead of searching out and experimenting with its conceptual-analytical possibilities. In Bazin's mind the 'phenomenological' tendency, evidently the one he preferred, was associated with the work of Stroheim, Dreyer, Murnau, Flaherty and Renoir during the silent period and Wyler, Welles, Bresson, Rossellini and again Renoir since the 1930s and the advent of sound.

One can see that Bazin was at least as anxious to dissolve the European/American dichotomy as he was to posit a continuity and tradition of aesthetic conception, bridging the supposed gulf between silent and sound era. In effect, he was able to acknowledge theoretically, and consequently to validate the historical development which had pushed the cinema towards becoming a predominantly narrative medium (the very development which had disaffected the intellectuals), but only at the price of virtually 'outlawing' the modernist strain and formulating for the sake of clarity and sharpness of definition an 'either/or' position which in its turn distorted a good deal of the evidence at hand.

What deserves to be remembered is that Bazin's efforts were directed to 'naturalizing' the compositional techniques of the feature film, which implied playing down the artificiality and manipulative nature of all filmed reality. In this he went against modernist and post-modernist suspicion about the status of fiction and fictions. Bazin's line of argument, conservative though it may seem in a literary context, could however claim to be empirical, in that it made sense (even if limited) of the predominant historical development in the cinema, without having to retreat to a sterile rejection of the narrative film or indulge in fashionable pessimism about the evils of commercial mass-culture. Implicitly, it came near to giving a negative definition of 'popular' cinema, rejecting the kind of self-consciousness about medium and means of expression that constitutes the level of truth and authenticity in much twentieth century art. The material basis of popular art is different: stereotypes, formulaic plots, clichés, melodramatic emotions and situations ensure a high degree of recognition, and the unabated popularity of gangster movies, Western thrillers, comedies and musicals confirms the expediency if not the value of this basis.[15] On the other hand, in order to show that the end-product was different from the ingredients, Bazin had to resort to a very intellectualised, philosophically demanding hypothesis about the nature and origin of the cinema, which makes a case for Hollywood only by subsuming it under that rather rarified category of 'phenomenological realism', and thus a perfectly legitimate species of traditional (i.e. highbrow) art. The American cinema found itself culturally upgraded, and rather than presenting it as a specifically popular art with a corresponding analysis of popular aesthetics, Bazin in fact explained and interpreted it by a recourse to Husserl, Sartre, Merleau-Ponty and French Catholicism.

It is altogether characteristic of Bazin's position and the influence he exerted not only on French film critics, that in some important respects he by-passed very smartly the debate about art and entertainment, popular and avant-garde, to which the options usually boil down. He did this by focussing on a director such as Renoir (who was as familiar with Marivaux or Flaubert and Zola as he was with modern painting, the novels of Georges Simenon and the midinette music-hall ambiance of Montparnasse), and on the American side, putting heavy emphasis on Wyler (born in Germany) or Welles, the most avowedly intellectual director to have come out of the Hollywood studio system. For Bazin, Welles was an innovator (along very European lines) and to be preferred to a more genuinely 'representative' director like John Ford, the very epitome of the seasoned practitioner and virtuoso professional in the popular movie idiom.

Although these correctives and the balancing of emphasis within the appraisal of Hollywood were subsequently supplied by Bazin's disciples on *Cahiers du Cinéma* (the 'Hitchcoco-Hawksiens' as they were called), the tendency towards validating the 'genre'-oriented narrative cinema in terms of high art became, if anything, even stronger in the magazine, with, as I shall hope to show, consequences that revealed significant contradictions. Bazin, because of his philosophical vocabulary, his Christian existentialism, his abstention from any kind of political controversy, helped in the main to soften up the prejudices of the educated middle-class viewer towards the American cinema by making him aware of the beauties in a Boetticher Western or a Hitchcock thriller, and ranging their films as equals alongside those by Mizoguchi, Fellini, Renoir or Bergman. Despite his strictures against Eisenstein and the Russians, it was Bazin's catholicity of cinematic tastes and his 'textual' approach to individual films that made his criticism enduring and which compensated for the equivocations that surrounded his notion of what defines artistic achievement of a specifically popular kind.

The problem will perhaps be clearer if we look at Welles, whose early Hollywood films (*Citizen Kane, The Magnificent Ambersons*) created a sensation in Europe, as indeed in the United States, though there for somewhat different reasons. As I have already hinted, in Europe he tended to be hailed as an innovator, the man who was finally giving some artistic stature to the American talkie, who had invented the aesthetics of the deep-focus shot, revitalised flashback techniques and dramatic montage, pioneered narrative ellipsis and the use of Freudian imagery to give his characters psychological depth. But Welles' case furnished arguments both for and against Hollywood: married as he then was to the pin-up idol of American G.I.s, Rita Hayworth, and making 'genre' films like *Lady From Shanghai* and *The Stranger*, he nevertheless played very convincingly the part of a persecuted genius, misunderstood and thwarted by the Hollywood system. To any dispassionate observer he appeared to be facing Hollywood, as it were, with one cheek flushed by boyish excitement ('the biggest and most expensive electric train set that anyone was ever given to play with'), and a half ironic, half sardonic smile on the other. His films breathe a sarcasm that was confusingly directed against himself as well as the people he was working for — just the kind of attitude that recommended him to interested but sceptical (about Hollywood, that is) European intellectuals, but not at all to a popular audience.

Welles' later career bears out just how a-typical and in many ways deeply antagonistic he was — not only to the working conditions imposed by even so flamboyantly nonchalant a studio boss as Howard Hughes at RKO, but to the whole Hollywood way of thinking about movie making and popular entertainment. Welles was, and remained, indifferent if not hostile particularly to the missionary idealism paired with a sound business sense which runs through the generation of producer-studio heads who had shaped the Hollywood of the 1930s and 40s. Like Cecil B. de Mille, Irving Thalberg and Samuel Goldwyn before them, Meyer, Selznick and even Zanuck possessed a curiously explicit 'ideological' outlook on their work, and a by no means crude understanding of the media and their audiences made them self-appointed apostles of their country's often contradictory aspirations and ideals. In the films they commissioned and approved from their directors and scriptwriters they were as concerned with reinforcing specifically American socialization processes and synthesizing the overall patterns of American history (always seen, to be sure, from the point of view of the economically and socially most dynamic groups) as a Henry James or Edmund Wilson was concerned with finding out what constituted American identity and American culture.

The conflict of East and West Coast, industrialisation and agriculture, the Frontier, the Civil War, urbanisation, the immigrant experience, the Depression have all been reflected, and often in a highly critical manner by Hollywood films, as indeed have social evils — from prison conditions and corruption in local and state government to racism, right-wing republicanism or such old favourites as extortion and protection rackets in boxing or baseball. That the dramatic pattern inevitably engineered a 'personalised' solution to social problems and that they distinguished only with difficulty the dividing line between the moral and the political is a matter that affects a lot of social thinking in America. The fact remains that the standard genres from Western to psychological thriller and soap opera melodrama have evolved on close analogy to underlying psychological and social tendencies, and the far from innocuous comedies of Tashlin or Billy Wilder have consistently dramatised the internal contradictions of representative American social experiences.[16] Not only is Hollywood ideologically transparent in the way films aim at internalising and psychologizing the public and social issues of American history, but their aesthetic and stylistic devices are geared towards locating the value and purpose of that experience in recognisably commonplace situations and everyday contexts, mainly by means of a visual-dramatic rhetoric, a strategy of persuasion as 'classical' and subtly adaptable as any which past civilisation have produced in periods of hegemony. During the apogee of Hollywood, even the most outlandish adventure story or musical extravaganza had to build its dramatic structure and narrative development on a familiar, easily identifiable subsoil of emotional reactions, drawn from the basic psychological dilemmas of the age. It is this emotional proximity to the viewer maintained across an immense variety of subjects, situations and filmic genres that one has to reckon with in any argument about the nature of popular culture in the cinema. And Welles, although his first four films or so (before he became sidetracked into the avatars of Shakespearomania) were squarely within the national quest for the American psyche, was nonetheless in his stylistic approach far too idiosyncratic and 'expressionist' ever to achieve or probably ever to aspire to the powerfully emotional realism of the commonplace, for the sake of which Hollywood directors, producers and script-writers fashioned iconographic stereotypes, infinitely recycling plots, psychologically one-dimensional characters, and a completely codified, carefully sifted image of the American (moral, social and geographic) landscape. By sheer force of repetition it imposed itself successfully as a symbolic system of notation within which very differentiated statements could be articulated, and it also constituted a dramatically acceptable, and for a long time ideologically accepted set of conventions by which to picture the dynamic interplay of reality and fantasy that Europeans find so characteristic of *'l'homme américain moyen sensuel'*.

These aspects of Hollywood and the resolutely 'popular' aesthetics underpinning them were not on the whole given much attention in the heyday of *Cahiers* criticism. Support of a different kind for the American cinema came at about the same time from surrealist groups, who let their love and admiration for American 'pop' — the comic-strip, science fiction, pin-up eroticism, pulp fiction — generously embrace Hollywood movies, first somewhat ambiguously ransacking them, especially the B productions of the smaller studios, for conscious or involuntary sublimities in the way of visual or emotional shocks and for that elusive quality of the 'insolite' by which imaginative authenticity could be gauged. Several 'genres' received their special attention, thus the horror movie and exotic adventure film ('le merveilleux et le fantastique' — both terms were and still are used as descriptive categories), gangster movies and thrillers with a strong romantic flavour ('le film noir'), musicals and 'low-brow' comedies (e.g. Jerry Lewis). In all cases, what was stressed was the subversive element in 'pop', where Hollywood could provide additional fire-power in the revolt against bourgeois notions of appeasement, sobriety and taste in art.

It is obviously essential to keep the middle-class, consciously intellectual approach to the American cinema via Welles, Wyler and the catholic left around Bazin, distinct from the militant anti-bourgeois, anti-academic enthusiasm of the surrealists. However, since their differences had the good fortune to be brought out into the open and ripen with the years into sharp antagonisms, the invaluable effect was to generate committed and partisan debates, thus putting pressure on the trenchancy of the arguments: the Hollywood cinema during the mid-1950s in France decidedly prospered on the crest of waves agitated by highly polemical clashes of opinion in the Paris magazines, carried into the country on the groundswell of the ciné-club movement which had already made France the most cinematically literate country in Europe. Another factor that can scarcely be overestimated was Henri Langlois' Cinémathèque, begun during the war in association with Georges Franju and Jean Mitry, but which only after the war became the unique film archive that it is today, unique mainly because from the start Langlois did not operate any form of pre-selection, least of all one dividing cinematic 'art' from 'entertainment'. He tried to preserve all the celluloid he could lay his hands on, and presented in the rue d'Ulm, as at the Palais de Chaillot, a collection from which each fraction could draw and build its own tradition and genealogy of cinematic art. Given the transitory nature of film-viewing, Langlois played a crucial role as a democratising and stimulating force, since it was only because the films were around and could be seen and re-seen that critical engagement was possible and disagreement worthwhile.

If this had been all, the vogue for Hollywood movies might not have amounted to more than a passing intellectual fad. What can't be ignored, however, is the special relation which French literary culture entertained with American writing, and the attitude of official France towards America in the first decade after the Second World War. The years of German occupation and the Vichy Régime had given the Americans the halo and aura of liberators. They had rescued Europe from fascism, they had handed France back to the good French, and even left-wing circles for a time looked upon the United States, its political system, its democratic institutions, its productivity and prosperity with something resembling respect. Jean Paul Sartre visited America on several occasions and published long, guardedly appreciative or occasionally enthusiastic pieces in *Les Temps Modernes* and elsewhere.[17] Since the 1930s French intellectuals had taken pride in having 'discovered' modern American literature, as Baudelaire had 'discovered' Poe: not just for France, but for the rest of the world and especially for Americans themselves. Malraux wrote with real knowledge and insight about Faulkner at a time when Faulkner had barely left the tutelage of Sherwood Anderson, and in his famous preface to the French edition of *Sanctuary* he spoke of it as 'the incursion of Greek tragedy into the detective story'.[18] Sartre's articles on *The Sound and the Fury* were long regarded as definitive statements on Faulkner the 'modern' novelist,[19] while Gide waxed enthusiastic over Dashiell Hammett's *Red Harvest*. Dos Passos, Dreiser, Steinbeck, Lardner, Caldwell, O'Hara were as seriously discussed and as widely read as Scott Fitzgerald, West and Hemingway. Last but not least, the mainstay of every station bookstore and newsagent in the country was American thrillers in translation: a good deal of the famous '*série noire*' publications were American or modelled on American novels, and they popularised an image of America — violent, individualist, bitter with the cynical cool of idealism gone sour, though energetic and vibrant; a fabrication compelling enough to do without a philosophical commentary and still register as the concrete embodiment of existential alienation, 'Angst' and the nihilistic 'acte gratuit', seemingly lived on the scale of an entire nation. At this level of projection, and drawing on similar inspiration, the American novel and the cinema naturally reinforced each other to produce an image in which America figured largely as a state of the imagination, a frame of mind, much in the way it had served an earlier generation of European intellectuals — those in Germany during the 1920s, for instance, of whom Brecht is probably the best-known exponent.

But the kind of revolution in aesthetic standards and attitudes to popular culture that was under way in France by the end of the 1940s is equally well illustrated by the book of a literary critic and

scholar published in 1948, and which for the first time attempted to
fuse the literary and philosophical interest in American fiction and
culture with the grass-root popularity of the movies: Claude-
Edmonde Magny's *L'Age du Roman Américain*, extremely original
in its conception, was able to catch in argument and example the
climate of informed opinion as well as the general pro-American bias
accurately and eloquently enough to become an instant classic. What
is interesting is the glimpse it gives of the evaluative criteria that
made a study of the cinema a worthwhile intellectual activity. Her
thesis is briefly this: The modern American novel — and here she
means mainly Dos Passos, Steinbeck, Hemingway and Faulkner — is
exemplary in two ways. It has managed to break through the
distinction between highbrow and low-brow fiction, and it has at the
same time assimilated into narrative forms some of the important
aesthetic achievements of imagism and symbolism, such as objectivity, neutrality of tone, a reliance on description, a deceptively
non-introspective use of language and speech or syntax that
possessed the muscularity of action. Yet this was not the result of
studying the symbolists or Flaubert, Joyce, Gide or Proust, but
because American novelists had willingly entered into a reciprocal
relation with the movies and filmic techniques, learning from them
what they could. Considerable space is devoted to Dashiell Hammett,
whose methods of description and characterisation Magny analyses in
some detail. This she uses to argue against the middle class bias in
French fiction, and she proceeds to sketch an alternative history of
the modern novel, approached through a terminology borrowed from
the cinema: there are chapters on montage and cutting in film and
novel, on ellipsis and narrative structure, on scenic presentation of
character and spatial form. The summing up of the first part of her
argument is particularly instructive:

'We are here concerned with a new convergence of the same kind
as that which has already been discussed — a convergence between
the results of psychoanalysis, behaviourism, and sociology and the
new vision of the world that the movies and the novel communicate to us almost unconsciously, by virtue of their technique
alone. It is no longer a question of a kinship between two forms
[. . .] but of one between the abstract themes that haunt
contemporary thought and the conclusions that are suggested by
the evolution toward an epoch of purely aesthetic techniques
belonging to the domain of the emotions rather than of the
intellect. [. . .] But this is not the only reason for its [i.e. the
American novel's] success: it also gives us a more simple and
direct, and therefore more universal vision of man than that

proposed by our traditional literature. Through its masterpieces
we glimpse the promise of a new humanism. If its major
importance is its content, however, why is it its technique that is
most imitated? To use Sartre's apt phrase, it is because the
technique is pregnant with a whole metaphysics.'[20]

One has to read this passage in its historical context: the reference to
Sartre, to a new humanism, to an immediate, because emotional
truth are not fortuitous. Magny lends her voice to the same guarded
social optimism which during the post-war period led Sartre to
modify his philosophy in the direction of dialectical materialism, but
one can also see how a more 'theological' existentialism might be
attracted to American literature and the movies — that of André
Bazin for instance, and reflected in the tenor of the early period of
Cahiers du Cinéma. What French intellectuals expected from things
American were works of fiction that could serve as creative models,
representative of their own situation and embodying specifically
modern tensions — between intellect and emotion, action and reflection, consciousness and instinct, choice and spontaneity. It is
remarkable for example how many of the film critics who rallied
behind the Bazin-*Cahiers* line did in fact go on to make films
themselves, using their knowledge of the Hollywood cinema as a
constant reference point in elaborating their aesthetics. The names
are too well-known to need much comment: Chabrol, Godard,
Truffaut, Rohmer, Rivette, Melville, Doniol-Valcroze and others.

Magny's book, with its copious references to films, also brings
striking confirmation that the French were ready and able to draw
on a cinematic literacy in a general debate about aesthetics which
would have been unthinkable anywhere else in the world. She is not
at all self-conscious or apologetic about mentioning movies like
Curtiz's *Angels with Dirty Faces* in the same breath as Faulkner's
Light in August to illustrate a point about narrative ellipsis and
indirection, or to compare favourably techniques of anti-psycho-
logical characterisation in Hawks's *Bringing Up Baby* with those to
be found in Camus's *L'Etranger* or a novel by Aragon. In her book
the cinema exists, and not just as the potentially vital art form of the
future (in the way it had done for so many theorists of the 1920s),
but by virtue of actual and contemporary films that were deemed to
hold their own in a comparison with writing and literature.

Consequently, what gave *Cahiers du Cinéma* its impact and made
it known abroad was the dedication with which its contributors put
the prestige of French highbrow culture behind their enthusiasm for
Hollywood. With benign self-confidence they made the cinema
appear in almost every respect on an equal, if not a superior footing

with contemporary literature, and often enough with the great art of the past. 'Griffith is to the cinema what Bach is to music';[21] 'Fuller is to Welles what Marlowe is to Shakespeare'[22]: these were the kind of opening gambits that made anglo saxon critics very nearly choke with indignation. But the recklessness of such claims was not simply '*pour épater*' those who preferred to keep their art clean or resented cultural trespassers. It was part of an effort to analyse film history and thereby consolidate critical standards appropriate to the medium: 'Stendhal is superior to Losey up to the point where the subject of his description passes from intention and mental rumination to its incarnation in a universe of bodies and forms. At this precise instant, Losey becomes incommensurably superior to Stendhal.'[23] The references across the arts were ultimately only a means of establishing priorities and a scale of evaluation within the cinema itself. This becomes clearest where *Cahiers* criticised films that didn't come up to what one could expect from the director or the genre he was working in: George Stevens's *Giant*, a hugely successful epic of the 1950s and James Dean's last film, is found wanting because 'its eclectic morality leaves no room for that spirit of satire, of severity too, nor for the sense of the grandiose, the tragic, the perilous which comes so naturally to countless American films. No comparison between the complaisance with which the characters here cultivate their clear conscience and the beautiful generosity of Nicholas Ray's heroes.'[24] However partially *Cahiers* critics judged films, their great merit was to judge them by criteria derived from other, comparable films and not from idealist notions of what 'art' or the cinema ought to be like. Yet since they were committed to the idea of the director as the creative centre, they had to retreat by necessity to a relatively tiny area of cinematic specificity, fortify it intellectually and proceed from there to conquer the whole territory of interpretation and evaluation. Given the fact that in Hollywood the director often had no more than token control over choice of subject, the cast, the quality of the dialogue, all the weight of creativity, all the evidence of personal expression and statement had to be found in the mise-en-scène, the visual orchestration of the story, the rhythm of the action, the plasticity and dynamism of the image, the pace and causality introduced through the editing. This is why the mise-en-scène could transform even the most apparently conventional Western into a profound and nuanced statement about personal guilt, redemption, existential choice, divided loyalties and moral growth (as in Anthony Mann's work), or a multi-million epic could explore the dialectics of personal commitment and moral distance, passionate spontaneity and short-sighted rashness (e.g. Otto Preminger's *Exodus*).[25]

Both concepts, however, that of the 'auteur' and 'mise-en-scène' on which was founded the *Cahiers*'s revaluation of Hollywood popular art, operated not only as aesthetic value judgements and hermeneutic principles of exegesis; but they also had in the historical context a polemical edge: the notion of the 'auteur', the temerity of assuming his very existence at the heart of the vast Hollywood machinery was intended to counter the dismissal of American films as impersonal, standardised consumer products and to militate for the attitude where every film is to be viewed on its own merits according to criteria evolved historically and empirically from actual films and the conditions under which they were made.

Nonetheless, the *Cahiers* position on Hollywood and its directors was, for all the virulence and conviction with which it was argued, a fragile one. The polemical edge cut both ways, and the contradictions that resulted from constantly trying to play both ends against the middle became in time more and more noticeable. By the early 1960s it had become all but untenable: *Cahiers* defended Hollywood and the studio system, but made a cult of the individual artist that was suspiciously intellectual and European; they recognized the uses of genre formulations and conventions in a medium with universal appeal, but they praised in preference those films that managed to subvert the conventions and transcend the limits of the genre; they approved of the aura conferred by a star (*'Charlton Heston est un axiome. Il constitue à lui seul une tragédie'*)[26], and they made great play of the fact that films appeal to the emotions and the senses rather than the intellect, but their own system of interpretation required a highly sophisticated, aesthetically conscious sensibility; they were fond of underlining the cultural significance of Hollywood films, but their main critical plank, the idea of mise-en-scène, meant at the crudest level 'form' to the exclusion of 'content', and in the hands of more skilled critics, an inordinately high regard for the strategies of aesthetic distance by which a director could transform overt content into a coded message accessible to the initiated.

For a time these contradictions were fruitful, especially where they produced the kind of friction which made the stylistic differences between Wyler and Ford, Fuller and Losey, Hawks and Anthony Mann live issues which sparked off debates about fundamentals. The *Cahiers* line remained creative as long as these tensions were felt to be intellectually challenging and a useful weapon in another struggle closer to home: that against academicism in film-making and literary-mindedness in criticism. To militate for a 'pure cinema' of mise-en-scène was to fight against the stodgily theatrical cinema of Delannoy and Cayatte, and enthusiasm for American mass-culture was meant to defy the growing embourgeoisement of popular entertainment in France and Europe. That *Cahiers*'s criteria were 'only' aesthetic and their mode of appreciation élitist highlights sharply the conflict of the intellectual when trying to articulate the values inherent in non-intellectual art, or indeed any art that grows from different cultural and social preconditions: doomed to resort to his own language, he necessarily distorts his own intuition and transforms the object of his study into a metaphor. France's relations with American culture are very much a case in point. If it took existentialism to make American fiction intellectually respectable, and if it took the histrionics of Orson Welles to give artistic lustre to Hollywood, it is scarcely surprising that a literary critic like Magny feels the need to appeal to the 'universally human' as the proper antidote to the exclusively middle-class orientation of the modern French novel, and that film critics are tempted to vindicate their interest in the action movie or the melodrama by an occasional recourse to Jansenism,[27] phenomenological vocabulary and a theory of concrete universals. The dilemma of finding a non-metaphorical critical discourse is endemic to all contemporary intellectual inquiry, even where this is Marxist or structuralist in inspiration.

Historically, *Cahiers* suffered from its internal contradictions as soon as its position began to harden into a dogma, and when the struggle on the home front brought victory in the shape of the 'nouvelle vague' and the journalistic ballyhoo created around it. By entrenching themselves in the all-importance of the mise-en-scène, they were continually forced to soft-pedal the more political implications of their preference for such 'ultra' directors as Hawks or Ford, and they were unable to bring out such significant American attitudes as the conservative radicalism of, say, Walsh or Fuller. And this is where their sharpest opponents, the critics around the magazine *Positif* and inheritors of left-wing surrealism scored most of their points. In two famous articles,[28] the Bazin-*Cahiers* aesthetics of an optimum of continuous time and space, of integrated narrative and action, directorial indirection rather than expression, drama through depth of field rather than montage etc., was mercilessly dismantled and declared to be an ideological smoke-screen disguising political timidity and impotence. At the height of the Algerian war, Bazin's 'liberal' aesthetics of ambiguity was denounced in no uncertain terms as a sitting on the fence, as the cunning tergiversations of conservatism, as the reactionary deviousness of Catholic obscurantism: '... *cette méchante église de campagne qu'est le système de Bazin*'.[29]

In many ways this attack was grossly overstating a valid enough case. It was unfair if one looks at the ideological complexion of the two or three directors whom Bazin praised most warmly: for instance Renoir and Rossellini. The latter was closely associated with neo-realism which of course at the time was considered very much as an artistic movement of the Left, and Renoir, a prominent member of the Popular Front, could by no stretch of the imagination be called a dyed-in-the-wool conservative. In this context, the Hollywood films that Bazin liked were absorbed into that floating populism — generous, emotional but also rather nebulous — which many French intellectuals, and especially those of the Catholic Left, had taken away from the days of the Résistance.

What was suspect was Bazin's pseudo-philosophical terminology and the failure of his disciples to bring their political options explicitly to bear on their critical system. The ambiguously metaphoric status of *Cahiers*'s commitment to Hollywood made their search for a cinematic tradition at the same time creatively productive and intellectually confusing, and once the critics had become film-makers in their own right, Hollywood lost much of its use as a club to swing at the establishment, thus giving some substance to the charge made by *Positif* that it was all a rather sorry spectacle of bad faith and rationalisation.[30] For *Positif*, though equally accepting the importance of Hollywood, argued from quite different premises: by and large they too subscribed to the notion of a 'director's cinema' and to a similarly textual approach, but their pantheon of directors was determined by an overall interpretation of American culture and society. Coming from an explicitly Marxist left their inclination was to look for a comparable equivalent to European left-wing thinking, and they believed they found it in the predominantly liberal or ex-Marxist left, present in Hollywood through directors such as Huston, Losey, Kazan, Mankiewicz, Rossen and some of the directors around the producer Mark Hellinger. *Positif*'s interest in Hollywood during the 1950s might be said to have coincided with that shown by McCarthy and the House of UnAmerican Activities Committee's special investigation. . . .

Positif maintained that the American cinema became an ideologically significant index of the 'state of the union' precisely because of the dialectical interplay between the directors' quest for specific statements in a cinematic language designed to level off personal expression in the interest of communicability, and the economic pressures to market a product that fulfills as nearly as can be the already existing expectations of the greatest possible number. More historically-minded than *Cahiers*, *Positif*'s staff were interested in the American cinema because they were interested in America, and not the other way round. Hollywood being a means rather than an end, they were able to keep 'faithful' to it when the tide began to turn in the middle sixties.

The same cannot be said of *Cahiers* whose line was not only internally unstable, but externally vulnerable to the historical developments at large. The cinema on whose chosen masterpieces they had lavished such eloquent praise became during the same time embarrassingly powerful and economically dominant, so much so that many of the *Cahiers* critics turned film-makers were suddenly confronted with the more materialist side of their aesthetics, namely the stranglehold which American production companies and distributors had on the European scene and on finance: the late 1950s and the 1960s were marked by the successive stages of an extremely successful move to corner markets, buy out competitors and invest capital and thus build up control in the national film industries in Britain and on the Continent.

Cahiers found it difficult to cope with this evidence, to which must be added the growing malaise among European and especially French intellectuals about American influence in world affairs — military, economic, social and cultural. Their response was to assume a heavily nostalgic tone, the films that came out of Hollywood didn't please as well as they had done, and even though it was obvious that the American film industry was undergoing a decisive internal evolution, their critical system proved inflexible and unresponsive. It had to be maintained intact, or broken. And when the rise of television began to starve the cinemas of their mass-audiences, and Hollywood production companies dissolved their studios at home and moved to Pinewood, Cinecittà or some village in Spain or Yugoslavia, *Cahiers* thought they could detect an altogether different product, with which they were impatient and bored, and they felt justified in speaking of the Hollywood cinema in the past tense.

The more, therefore, historical events threw into prominence the interventionist role of the United States in world politics, whether by force of arms, monopolising markets or cultural exports (which the film industry spearheaded long before the rock/pop/beat scene created a quite different European-American interdependence with its own vast commodity market), the more evident it became that praise of Hollywood could and did lend indirect but influential support to American ideology abroad. The events of May 1968 made the *de facto* break with the American cinema which began in 1963 de rigueur for the *Cahiers* contributors, and the magazine holds today an extreme left position of Marxist-Leninist persuasion, thus severing itself from its own past as radically as from Hollywood itself. Godard's press-release for his film *La Chinoise* (1967) rang the changes for everybody to hear:

'Fifty years after the October Revolution, the American industry rules cinema the world over. There is nothing much to add to this statement of fact. Except that on our own modest level we too should provoke two or three Vietnams in the bosom of the vast Hollywood-Cinecittà-Mosfilm-Pinewood-etc. empire, and, both economically and aesthetically, struggling on two fronts as it were, create cinemas which are national, free, brotherly, comradely and bonded in friendship.'[31]

If the decline of Hollywood in critical esteem among a certain section of European intellectuals can be seen to have such an explicitly political side to it, responding with considerable swiftness to the increase of anti-American feeling in social and political thinking, one is tempted to conclude two things: one, that the rise of Hollywood was equally affected by a specific ideological situation, which I have briefly sketched, but which the first line of *Cahiers* critics managed to displace onto the purely aesthetic level. The second point is that the episode of Hollywood in another country contains the lesson that any critical system or aesthetic discourse which is unable to refer to and reflect upon the social and economic conditions under which the medium or the art in question produce and maintain themselves is liable not only to be incoherent and distorted, but to remain ignorant about the nature of its own activity. The cinema, with its curious status, halfway between an art form of self-expression and a capital-intensive industry of international importance, may put this into particular relief, but it is a sobering thought that it might be equally true of less 'popular' manifestations of modern culture. The French intellectuals who championed Hollywood by raising it to the level of high art in order to snatch it from the clutches of the sociologists had to discover to their cost that they were themselves the victims of the ideology they had affected to transcend.

Notes

Preface

1. Karl Grun, 'The Stuff Marketing Dreams are Made of' in *Europa*, vi, March 1974.

C.W.E. Bigsby: *Europe, America and the Cultural Debate*

1. F. Scott Fitzgerald, *Tender is the Night* (New York) 1934, p.55.
2. Eldridge Cleaver, *Soul on Ice* (London) 1969, p.114.
3. Richard B. Morris, ed. *Encyclopaedia of American History* (New York) 1965, p.471.
4. The European figure appears in *Statistical Abstracts of the United States, 1971*, p.205, published by the United States Department of Commerce, Bureau of the Census. The UK figure appears in the *Digest of Tourist Statistics* No.2, p.52, published by the British Tourist Authority.
5. Jean-Jacques Servan-Schreiber, *The American Challenge*, trans. Ronald Steel (New York) 1968, pp. 191-2.
6. Matthew Arnold, *Culture and Anarchy* (Cambridge) 1971, p.19.
7. *Ibid.*, p.18.

8. Oswald Spengler, *The Decline of the West*, Vol. II, trans. Charles Francis Atkinson (New York) 1945, p.460.
9. *Ibid.*, p.98.
10. *Ibid.*, p.100.
11. *Ibid.*, p.103.
12. Vol 1, pp. 32-3.
13. *Ibid.*, pp. 33-4.
14. Quoted in Dover Wilson, 'Editor's Introduction', *Culture and Anarchy* (Cambridge) 1971, p. xviii.
15. F.R. Leavis, *Mass Civilisation and Minority Culture* (Cambridge) 1930, p.26.
16. *Ibid.*, pp. 7-8.
17. F.R. Leavis, *Nor Shall My Sword* (London) 1972, p.206.
18. *Ibid.*, p.60.
19. Karl Jaspers, *Man in the Modern Age*, trans. Eden and Cedar Paul (London) 1951, p.117.
20. *Ibid.*, p.81.
21. Quoted in Reyner Banham, *Theory and Design in the First Machine Age* (London) 1960, p.103.
22. *Ibid.*, p.159.
23. Ortega y Gasset, *The Revolt of the Masses* (London) 1961, p.14.
24. Hannah Arendt, *Between Past and Future* (London) 1961, p.7.
25. Herbert Marcuse, *One-Dimen-*

sional Man (London) 1964, p.8.

26. Walter Benjamin, *Illuminations*, trans. Harry Zohn (London) 1970, p.243.

27. Marcuse, *One-Dimensional Man*, p.58.

28. George Steiner, *Language and Silence* (London) 1967, p.420.

29. Marcuse, pp. 56-7.

30. Robert Warshow, *The Immediate Experience* (New York) 1964, pp. 7-8.

31. John A. Kouwenhoven, *Made in America* (Newton Centre) 1948, p.137.

32. Leo Lowenthall, *Literature, Popular Culture and Society* (Palo Alto) 1961, p.36.

33. Susan Sontag, *Against Interpretation* (New York) 1966, p.13.

34. *Ibid.*, p.14.

35. *Ibid.*, p.302.

36. Roland Barthes, *Writing Degree Zero*, trans. Annette Lavers and Colin Smith (London) 1967, p.22.

37. *Ibid.*, p.92.

38. Dwight Macdonald, 'A Theory of Mass Culture', in Bernard Rosenberg and David White, *Mass Culture: the Popular Arts in America* (London) 1964, p.69.

39. *Websters Third New International Dictionary*, p.1430.

40. Ian Watt, 'Literature and Society', in *The Arts in Society* (Englewood Cliffs) 1964, ed. Robert Wilson, p.313.

41. Reyner Banham, *The Architecture of the Well-Tempered Environment* (London) 1969, p.269.

42. Denis Brogan, *The American Character* (New York) 1956, p.216.

Marshall McLuhan: *The Implications of Cultural Uniformity*

1. Edward Dahlberg, *Bottom Dogs* (London) 1930, pp. ix-x.

2. W.H. Auden, *The Dyer's Hand* (New York) 1948, pp. 103-4.

3. A.T.W. Simeons, *Man's Presumptuous Brain* (New York) 1962, p.43.

4. *Ibid.*, p.43.

5. William Empson, *Collected Poems* (London) 1935, p.21.

6. T.S. Eliot, *To Criticize the Critic* (New York) 1965, p.54.

7. T.S. Eliot, 'Ulysses, Order and Myth', *James Joyce: Two Decades of Criticism* p.201.

8. W.B. Yeats, 'The Emotion of Multitude', *Essays and Introductions* (London) 1961, pp. 215-16.

9. Ward Cannel and June Macklin, *The Human Nature Industry* (New York) 1973.

10. Richard Kostelanetz, *Master Minds, Take Today*, p.87.

11. John Knowler, *Trust an Englishman* (New York) 1972.

12. T.S. Eliot, *The Auditory Imagination.*

David Crystal: *American English in Europe*

1. Etiemble, *Parlez-vous franglais?* (Paris) 1964.

2. H.L. Mencken, *The American Language* (London) revised and abridged 1963.

3. A.H. Marckwardt and R. Quirk, *A common language: British and American English* (BBC and Voice of America) 1964.

4. An article in *Morgenbladet* (26th October 1960) summarised the situation: 'The problem under discussion here may seem small and insignificant, but it is nonetheless important. If one asks why the Norwegian press use so many English expressions, the usual answer is "We have not got a Norwegian word which quite covers the concept". Quite possible, but one must then either make one or write it in another way. By adopting the English word nonchalantly instead of trying to use the tools at one's disposal in the mother tongue, one finds that the tools are gradually blunted through lack of use. Such a manifesta-

tion of mental laziness leads insidiously from linguistic poverty to cultural barrenness.'

5. N. Eliason, 'American English in Europe', *American Speech*, 32 (1957), 163-9.

6. N. Eliason. As on p.164 of his paper, for example: 'But however critical they (*sc* Europeans) may be, they envy us. Of this there can be no doubt, nor can there be any doubt either that it is an envy born of admiration rather than resentment. While essentially complimentary, this is somewhat awkward, for we Americans are not yet accustomed to compliments from others or adept at gracefully accepting compliments obliquely bestowed'.

7. See, for example, the many items of this kind (such as *ombudsman and its derivatives*) listed in the C.L. Barnhart, S. Steinmetz & R.K. Barnhart, *A dictionary of new English* (London) 1973.

Bibliography

Works on English:
Foster, B., 1970. *The Changing English Language* (London), Chapter 1.
Strevens, P.D., 1972. *British and American English* (London).

On French:
Adrienne, 1972. *The gimmick; spoken American and English* (Paris).
Deak, E., 1956 *Dictionnaire d'Americanismes* (Paris).
George, K., 1970. 'Characteristics of modern French journalese', *Modern Languages*, 51, pp.67-70.
Giraud, J., P. Pamart and J. Riverain, 1971. *Les mots dans le vent* (Paris).

On Italian:
Klajn, I., 1972. *Influssi Inglesi nella lingua Italiana* (Florence).
Rando, G., 1970. 'The assimilation of English loan-words in Italian', *Italica*, 47, pp.129-42. 'Anglicismi

nel "Dizionario Moderno" dalla quarta alla decima edizione', 1969 *Lingua Nostra*, 30, pp.107-12. 'The semantic influence of English on Italian', 1971. *Italica* 48, pp.246-51.
Rothenburg, J.G., 1969. ' "Un hobby per i cocktails"; an examination of Anglicisms in Italian', *Italica*, 46, pp. 149-66.

On Spanish:
Alfaro, R.J., 1948. *El anglicismo en el español contemporáneo* (Bogatá); *Diccionario de anglicismos* — introduction.
Gooch, A., 1971. 'Spanish and the onslaught of the Anglicism', *New Vida Hispánica*, 19, pp. 17-21.
Lang, M.F., 1969. 'The terminology of Spanish football', *New Vida Hispánica*, 17, pp. 21-6.
Lorenzo, E., 1954. 'El anglicismo en la españa de hoy', repr. in *El español de hoy: lengua en ebullicion* (Madrid) 1966, pp. 62-83.
Marcos Peréz, P.J., 1971. *Los anglicismos en el ámbito periodístico* (Valladolid).

On German:
Carstensen, B., 1965. 'Englische Einflüsse auf die Deutsche Sprache nach 1945', *Beihefte zum Jahrbuch für Amerikastudien*, 13.
Galinsky, H., 1967. *Amerikanismen der deutschen Gegenwartssprache* (Heidelberg).
Krauss, P.G., 1963. 'The Anglo-American influence on German', *American* Speech, 38, pp. 256-69, and further in Vol. 41 (1966), pp. 28-38.

On Norwegian:
Standwell, G., 1962. *A critical study of contemporary linguistic borrowings by Norwegian from American and English*, Univ. of Durham M. Litt. thesis.
Stene, A., 1945. *English loan-words in modern Norwegian* (London and Oslo).

On Dutch:
Zandvoort, R.W., 1964. *English in the Netherlands* (Groningen).

On Flemish:
Blancquaert, E., 1964. 'English words in spoken Flemish', in D. Abercrombie et al (eds.), *In honour of Daniel Jones* (London) pp. 299-305.

On Serbo-Croat:
Filipovic, R., 1961. 'L'adaptation morphologique des mots anglais empruntés par le serbo-croat', *Studia romanica et anglica Zagrabiensia.*

On Yiddish:
Feinsilver, L.M., 1970. *The Taste of Yiddish* (Cranbury, New Jersey and London).

General articles:
Filipovic, R., 1972. 'Studying the English elements in the main European languages', *Studia Anglica Posnaniensia*, 4, pp. 141-58.
Zandvoort, R.W., 1967. 'English linguistic infiltration in Europe', *Revue des Langues Vivantes*, 33, pp. 339-46.

Reyner Banham: *Mediated Environments*

1. Leonard Eaton, *American Architecture Comes of Age* (London and Cambridge) 1972.
2. The 'West End' cinema; facade outlined in Moore discharge tubes (reported in *Electrical Review*, 11 July 1914).
3. *cf.* Muntz and Kunstler, Adolf Loos (London) 1966, pp. 54-8.
4. *cf. Moholy Nagy: experiment in totality* (New York) 1950, for a documented account of the transmission of the Manhattan image to one Hungarian modernist *via* the magazine *Over Land and Sea* before 1905.

5. see, for example, drawings by Sant'Elia reproduced in the catalogue of the exhibition *Futurismo 1909-1919* (Edinburgh and London) 1972.
6. *Architectural Review* (London) July 1958, vol 124, p.8.
7. Tom Wolfe, *The Kandy-Kolored Tangerine-Flake Streamline Baby* (New York) 1965 (and numerous subsequent paper-back editions).
8. *ibid.*, pp. xv-xvii.
9. *Architectural Review* (London) May 1967, vol 132, pp. 331-5.
10. 'Non-Plan, an Experiment in Freedom' in *New Society* (London) 20 March 1969.
11. 'Learning from Las Vegas' in *Architectural Forum* (New York) March 1968, vol 128, pp. 37-42 and continued. This is preferable to the later *edition de luxe* under the same title issued by MIT Press (London and Cambridge, 1972) which does include some examples of decorated sheds of Venturi's own design, but all set in 'fine art' typography alien to the subject matter and very difficult to read.
12. *cf.* Tomas Maldonado, *La Speranza Progettuale* (Turin) 1970. English language edition as: *Design Nature and Revolution* (New York) 1972, in which the relevant argument is on pp. 60-5.
13. *Architects' Journal* (London) 22 September 1971, vol 154, pp. 638-48, and especially p.648.

Magnus Pyke: *The Influence of American Foods and Food Technology in Europe*

1. W.H. Bruford, *Germany in the Eighteenth Century* (Cambridge) 1935.
2. R. Salaman, *The History and Social Influence of the Potato* (Cambridge) 1949.
3. M. Pyke, *Chemistry and Industry* (London) 1949, p.738.

4. R.D. Buzzell and R.E.R. Nourse, *Product Innovation in Food Processing 1954-65* (Boston) 1967.

5. G. Carson, *The Cornflake Crusade* (London) 1959.

6. A. Waugh, *The Lipton Story* (London) 1951.

7. N.L.S. Carnot, *Réflexions sur la puissance motrice du feu et sur les machines propres à développer cette motrice*, 1824.

8. E.W. Williams, *Quick Frozen Foods*, Vol. 31, p.119, 1968.

9. W.G. McClelland, *Studies in Retailing* (Oxford) 1963.

10. J.H. van Stuyvenberg, *Margarine: an economic, social and scientific history 1869-1969* (Liverpool) 1969.

11. *Nutrition Reviews* Food and Nutrition Board and American Medical Association, Vol. 30, p.223.

12. C.F. Kelly, *Scientific American*, Vol 216, p.50, August 1967.

13. J. van Vierde *Current Agricultural Proposals for Europe* (London) 1970.

Bryan Wilson: *American Religious Sects in Europe*

1. For excellent recent accounts of some of these movements, see Karl J. R. Arndt, *Georg Rapp's Harmony Society 1785-1847*, Philadelphia: University of Pennsylvania Press, 1965; J.A. Hostetler, *Amish Society*, Baltimore: John Hopkins Press, 1963; John W. Bennett, *Hutterian Brethren*, Stanford: Stanford University Press, 1967; Gillian L. Gollin, *Moravians in Two Worlds* (New York) 1967.

2. A detailed discussion is provided in J. Wesley White, *The Influence of North American Evangelism in Great Britain between 1830 and 1914 on the origin and development of the Ecumenical Movement*, Unpublished D.Phil. thesis, University of Oxford, 1963. For a brief account, see Bryan Wilson, 'American Religion: Its Impact on Britain' in A.N.J. den Hollander

(Editor) *Contagious Conflict: The Impact of American Dissent on European Life* (Leiden) 1973, pp. 233-63.

3. For a discussion of this term, see Bryan Wilson, *Religious Sects* (London) 1971.

4. This point is developed in Bryan R. Wilson, 'Religion and the Churches in Contemporary America', in William G. McLoughlin and Robert N. Bellah, (eds.) *Religion in America* (Boston) 1968, pp. 73-110.

5. There is an extensive literature on some of these groups, of course, particularly the Mormons. For an excellent general over-view, see Thomas O'Dea, *The Mormons* (Chicago) 1957. On Jehovah's Witnesses, see Timothy White, *A People For His Name* (New York) 1967; and Alan Rogerson, *Millions Now Living Will Never Die*, (London) 1969. No one study of Christian Science is wholly satisfactory, but see Hugh A. Studdert-Kennedy, *Mrs. Eddy: Her Life, Her Work, Her Place in History* (San Francisco) 1947; and Charles S. Braden, *Christian Science Today* (Dallas) 1958. For a sociological account of Christian Science in Britain, see Bryan R. Wilson, *Sects and Society* (London) 1961. There is no adequate single study of the Seventh-day Adventists.

6. For a general history of Pentecostalism, see Nils Bloch-Hoell, *The Pentecostal Movement* (London) 1964; see also, for Pentecostalism in various countries, Walter J. Hollenweger, *The Pentecostals*, (London) 1972.

7. On New Thought, see Charles S. Braden, *Spirits in Rebellion* (Dallas) 1963. For concern with secular success in American religion, see Louis Schneider and Sanford M. Dornbusch, *Popular Religion: Inspirational Books in America* (Chicago) 1958.

8. We lack a complete study of Scientology as a social movement. For a short account, see Roy Wallis, 'The Sectarianism of Scientology', *Socio-*

logical Yearbook of Religion in Britain, 6, 1973, pp. 136-55. For a wider-ranging but journalistic treatment, see George Malko, *Scientology: The New Religion* (New York) 1970.

9. On Mormon migration, see Walter Mulder, *Homeward to Zion: the Mormon Migration from Scandinavia* (Minneapolis) 1957; for Britain, P.A.M. Taylor, *Expectations Westward* (London) 1965. See also Gilbert W. Scharffs, *Mormonism in Germany*, (Salt Lake City) 1970.

Jens Peter Becker: *The Mean Streets of Europe.*

1. Robert Graves and Alan Hodge, *The Long Week-end* (Penguin) 1971, p.297. Originally a witty sentence in Michael Innes's *Lament for a Maker* (London) 1971, p.159.

2. D. E. S. Maxwell in *American Fiction: The Intellectual Background* (New York) 1963, p.275 takes the same view.

3. Raymond Chandler, 'The simple art of murder', in *Pearls are a Nuisance* (Harmondsworth) 1964, p.193.

4. Leslie A. Fiedler, *Love and Death in the American Novel* (New York) 1960, p. xviii.

5. W. H. Auden, 'The Guilty Vicarage: Notes on the Detective Story, by an Addict', *Harper's Magazine* 196, May 1948, p.408.

6. cf. Robert Warshow, 'The Gangster as Tragic Hero', in *The Immediate Experience* (New York) 1970 and Stephen L. Karpf, 'The Gangster Film: Emergence, Variation and Decay of a Genre, 1930-1940', Unpubl. Doct. Dissertation, Northwestern University, 1970.

7. See for example: Brander Matthews, 'Poe and the Detective Story', *Scribner's Magazine* 42, 1907; Alma E. Murch, *The Development of the Detective Novel* (London) 1968, Paul G. Buchloh and Jens P. Becker, *Der Detektivroman.*

8. George Orwell, 'Raffles and Miss Blandish', in *The Collected Essays, Journalism and Letters of George Orwell* (Harmondsworth) 1970, p.254

9. *ibid.* p.254-5.

10. *ibid.*, p.255.

11. *ibid.*, p.260.

12. Quoted in: Klaus Kunkel, 'Ein artiger James Bond: Jerry Cotton und der Bastei-Verlag', in Jochen Vogt (ed.), *Der Kriminalroman* (Munich) 1971, p.564.

13. cf. Jens P. Becker, *Der englische Spionageroman* (Munich) 1973, pp. 132-64.

14. Raymond A. Sokolov, 'The Art of Murder', *Newsweek*, 22 March 1971, p.54.

15. *ibid.* p.58.

16. Nina Grunenberg, 'Der Hinterhof lässt grüssen: Krimis zeigen, wie das Leben spielt', in *Die Zeit*, 21 September 1973.

17. In his fragment 'Tulip'. cf. *The Big Knockover and other Stories* (Penguin) 1969, p.316.

18. cf. John A. Williams, 'My Man Himes: An Interview With Chester Himes', *Amistad 1*, 25-93 and Philip Oakes, 'The Man who goes too fast', *Sunday Times Magazine*, 9 November 1969, especially p.71.

Gérard Cordesse: *The Impact of American Science Fiction on Europe*

1. Pierre Versins, *Encyclopédie de L'Utopie et de la Science Fiction* (Lausanne) 1972.

2. Even in European comics, science fiction was not organised into an autonomous sub-genre; coexistence prevailed. When the space operas *Buck Rogers* and *Flash Gordon* reached France before the Second World War, their epic tone contrasted with the humorous angle of most French comics (*Zig et Puce au vingt-et-unième siècle*).

3. cf. H. Bruce Franklin, *Future Perfect, American Science Fiction of*

the Nineteenth Century (New York) 1966.

4. H. Gernsback, *Ralph 124C41+* (New York) 1958, p.58.

5. *Ibid.*, p.1.

6. L. S. Sprague de Camp, *A.S.F. Handbook* (New York) 1953, p.221.

7. *Ibid.*, p.171.

8. John Carnell ed., *The Best From 'New Worlds Science Fiction'* (London) 1955.

9. *Ibid.*, pp. 7-8.

10. *Ibid.*, p.13.

11. *Ibid.*, p.13.

12. *Sometime, Never: Three Tales of Imagination* (New York) 1957.

13. J. G. Ballard, *The Drowned World*, (New York) 1962.

14. J. G. Ballard, *The Voices of Time* (New York) 1962.

15. J. G. Ballard, *Terminal Beach* (New York) 1964.

16. Michael Moorcock, Preface to *The New SF* (London) 1969, p.8.

17. J. G. Ballard, in *Ambit* 29 (London) 1967.

18. The ideology of the post-1950 production was made 'more acceptable' to European sceptics with the rise of dystopia, however qualified and challenged by orthodox American writers.

19. Damon Knight, the only American writer to have crossed the language barrier, points this out in *13 French Science Fiction Stories* (New York) 1965: 'At first there were few acceptable submissions; lately there have been so many that the magazine has bought up material for years ahead' and judges French writers thus: 'at least a dozen can stand comparison with the best Anglo-Saxon writers of science fiction', which sounds over-enthusiastic.

20. Eric Losfeld, *Barbarella* (Paris) 1962.

21. Jean Ricardou, *La Prise De Constantinople* (Paris) 1965.

22. T. D. Clareson, ed., 'Robots in Science-Fiction', *in S.F.: The Other Side of Realism* (Ohio) 1971.

23. Thomas M. Disch, a message to an American SF conference, the Spring of 1967; reproduced in *England Swings SF*, Judith Merril, ed., (New York) 1968.

Roger Lewis: *Captain America Meets the Bash Street Kids*

1. Reitberger and Fuchs, *Comics, Anatomy of a Mass Medium* (London) 1972.

2. Robert Crumb, *Zap* comics.

3. George Orwell, 'Boys' Weeklies', *Inside the Whale and Other Essays* (Harmondsworth) 1962.

4. Stan Lee in *Rolling Stone*, 16 September 1971.

5. Frederic Wertham, *Seduction of the Innocent*, (New York) 1954.

6. *Captain America*, 122.

7. *New York Times Magazine*, 1 October 1972.

8. *Slow Death*, 2. Last Gasp Eco Comics.

9. *Rolling Stone*, 16 September 1971.

Martin Esslin: *The Television Series as Folk Epic*

1. Kracauer, *From Caligari to Hitler* (Princeton and Oxford) 1968.

Thomas Elsasser: *Two Decades in Another Country*

1. The term 'nouvelle vague' started its life as a journalists' tag at the Cannes Film Festival of 1959, when a dozen or so new French films by unknown, though not always particularly young directors got rave reviews from the international press. Among the films were works by Chabrol, Godard, Truffaut (who won the Festival Prize for *Les Quatre Cent Coups*). See on this an important but highly critical study: R. Borde, F.

Buache, J. Curtelin, *Nouvelle Vague* (Paris) 1962.

2. Recent writing on the cinema tends again to follow the French lead and seems to concentrate on 'the processes of signification' and the linguistic-semantic status of the image as sign. See C. Metz, *Langage et Cinéma* (Paris) 1971. In English, some of the main issues are set out in P. Wollen, *Signs and Meaning in the Cinema* (London) 1969, which also contains a chapter on the 'Auteur Theory'.

3. The man who has done most to popularise the French view of the American cinema in the United States is Andrew Sarris. Under his editorship *Film Culture* devoted a special issue to Hollywood (no.28, Spring 1963). In January 1966 Sarris brought out the first issue of an ambitious though short-lived publishing venture, *Cahiers du Cinéma in English*. The controversy over Sarris's appraisal of Hollywood directors can be studied in two numbers of *Film Quarterly*: Pauline Kael's 'Circle and Squares' (Spring 1963) and Sarris's reply 'The Auteur Theory and the Perils of Pauline' (Summer 1963). See also the Introduction to Andrew Sarris, *The American Cinema*; Directors and Directions 1929-68 (New York) 1968.

4. The American Film Institute was inaugurated in June 1967.

5. *Movie Magazine*, whose first issue appeared in 1962.

6. *Cahiers du Cinéma* was founded in 1951, as the successor to *La Revue du Cinéma* (first issue in 1946). Its editors were André Bazin, Jacques Doniol-Valcroze and Eric Rohmer.

7. See for instance: Ricciotto Canudo, *L'Usine Aux Images* (Paris) 1927; Louis Delluc, *Cinéma et Cie* (Paris) 1929; Germaine Dulac, *L'Art Cinématographique* (Paris) 1927; Elie Faure, *L'Arbre d'Eden* (Paris) 1922; Bela Balazs, *Der Sichtbare Mensch* (Vienna) 1924; V. Poudovkin and L. Kouleshov, *Film Regie and Film*

Manuscript (London) 1928; Sergei M. Eisenstein, *Film Form* (London) 1949 and *The Film Sense* (London) 1948; Rudolf Arnheim, *Film als Kunst*, 1932; Raymond Spottiswoode, *A Grammar of Film* (London) 1935.

8. The best-known example of this school is of course S. Kracauer, *From Caligari to Hitler* (New York) 1947.

9. *Sequence*, Winter 1947.

10. *Sight and Sound*, Summer 1956.

11. *Sight and Sound*, Autumn 1958.

12. originally entitled 'Problèmes de la Peinture', in *Esprit*, 1945.

13. André Bazin, *Qu'est-ce que le Cinéma*, 3 vols, Paris 1958-61.

14. 'L'Evolution du Langage Cinématographique' op.cit. vol 1, p.132.

15. 'De 1930 à 1940, c'est le triomphe à Hollywood de cinq ou six grands genres qui assurent alors son (i.e. the American cinema's) écrasante supériorité.' op.cit. vol 1, p.136.

16. see Jeffrey Richards, *Visions of Yesterday*, London 1973, especially the chapter on Frank Capra and Populism; also Raymond Durgnat, *The Crazy Mirror* (London) 1970.

17. see J. P. Sartre, *Situations III* (Paris) 1949.

18. see A. Malraux, 'Une Préface pour Sanctuary', *Nouvelle Revue Française*, November 1933.

19. see J. P. Sartre, *Situations I* (Paris) 1947.

20. C. E. Magny, *The Age of the American Novel* (New York) 1972, pp. 100-1.

21. *Cahiers du Cinéma* no.70, April 1957, p.43.

22. quoted in R. Roud, 'The French Line', *Sight and Sound*, Autumn 1960, p. 167.

23. *Cahiers du Cinéma* no.107, May 1960, p.24.

24. *Cahiers du Cinéma* no.70, April 1957, p.44.

25. For a comparable approach in English, see R. Wood, 'Exodus', in *Movie* no.2, 1963, and T. Elsasser,

'Exodus', in *Brighton Film Review* vol.2, no.5, 1969.

26. *Cahiers du Cinéma* no.107, May 1960, p.24.

27. e.g. 'William Wyler ou le Janséniste de la Mise-en-Scène' in Qu'est-ce que le Cinéma, vol 1, p.149.

28. *Positif*, nos. 46, 47 (June, July 1962).

29. *Positif*, no.46, p.59.

30. see *Positif* no.122, December 1970, R. Benayoun, 'Les Enfants du Paradigme', pp. 7-26.

31. quoted in Jean Narboni and Tom Milne (eds), *Godard on Godard* (London) 1972, p.243.